29-46

Power, Racism, and Privilege

Power, Racism, and Privilege

Race Relations in Theoretical and Sociohistorical Perspectives

WILLIAM J. WILSON
The University of Chicago

THE FREE PRESS
A Division of Macmillan Publishing Co., Inc.
NEW YORK

Collier Macmillan Publishers
LONDON

The Free Press
A Division of Macmillan Publishing Co., Inc.
866 Third Avenue, New York, N.Y. 10022

Collier Macmillan Canada, Ltd.

First Free Press Paperback Edition 1976

Library of Congress Catalog Card Number: 72-87160

Printed in the United States of America

printing number

7   8   9   10

To my mother and Aunt Janice

PREFACE

THIS book reflects my growing interest in comparative and historical race relations. For the last few years I have been working on a theoretical framework that is not bound to contemporary issues and not restricted to the United States. As is the case in the development of most theoretical frameworks, however, I am heavily indebted to many of the path-breaking ideas contained in several excellent published works, and I have attempted to document these sources throughout the volume. The theoretical discussion presented in Part One of this study represents a synthesis of existing theories of race with my own propositions and distinctions.

Chapters Five through Eight of Part Two present an interpretation and analysis of race relations in the United States (Chapters Five, Six, and Seven) and the Republic of South Africa (Chapter Eight). Although these chapters are intended to be analytical, much of the material presented is descriptive, thereby enabling the reader to grasp the largely theoretical account of race relations in the United States and South Africa advanced in Chapter Nine. This final chapter not only summarizes the major theoretical arguments of Part One but also uses them as a framework for contrasting, interpreting, and explaining racial stratification in these two societies.

The decision to discuss race relations only in the United States and the Republic of South Africa issued largely from my desire to write a relatively short, succinct book rather than the much more lengthy volume that would result from including numerous countries. I was also influenced by the fact that although South Africa and the United States continue to dominate the worldwide attention given racial conflict, very few studies have systematically attempted to draw contrasts and parallels between the racial dynamics in these two societies. Thus I decided to select race relations in the United States for fairly extensive treatment and to use South African race relations primarily as a basis for comparison. Moreover, for the sake of brevity, I have focused on black–white relations, although occasional reference is made to other groups in these two multiracial societies.

In the preparation of this volume I am particularly indebted to the department of sociology at The University of Chicago, which, through its Ford Foundation grant in urban studies, allowed me to reduce my teaching load during the academic year 1971–1972 to complete this study and provided the funds necessary for the typing of the manuscript.

I would also like to express my appreciation to the students in my race relations classes at the University of Massachusetts, Amherst, and at The University of Chicago for their penetrating and helpful comments on many of the ideas I developed for this book. It is difficult to identify all of those who contributed, but I would like to single out for special thanks Margaret Anderson, Murray Manus, Carmen Owens, Barry Skura, Marion Sleet, and Holly Jo Wicker.

If the book contains any strengths, they are in no small measure due to the immense contributions of the many scholars who read various drafts of the manuscript. Professors Robert Blauner, Jan E. Dizard, Lewis M. Killian, Morris Janowitz, Donald N. Levine, Gary T. Marx, Donald L. Noel, Peter I. Rose, William K. Tabb, and Pierre L. van den Berghe provided detailed and helpful suggestions and criticisms that led to revisions of both my theoretical framework and my discussions of race relations in the United States and South Africa. Needless to say, I alone am responsible for any shortcomings in this volume.

Finally, appreciation is expressed to my wife, Beverly, not only for her careful editing of the manuscript but also for her patience and encouragement during my fits of depression when the writing was not progressing well. Her understanding made my task less difficult and, at times, even enjoyable.

WILLIAM J. WILSON

Chicago, Illinois
July 1972

CONTENTS

PART ONE
Race Relations in Theoretical Perspective

1 Introduction   3

2 Race, Power, and the Development of Racial
Stratification   15

3 Race and Racism   29

4 Power, Racism, and the Theoretical Basis
of Racial Conflict   47

PART TWO
*Theoretical and Sociohistorical Analyses of Race
Relations in the United States and South Africa*

5 Slavery in the United States as a Power
Relationship   71

6 Jim Crow Segregation and the Growth
of Biological Racism   93

7 Competitive Race Relations and the Proliferation
of Racial Protests: 1940–1970   121

8 Power, Racism, and Privilege in South Africa   161

9 Conclusion: A Theoretical Contrast of United
States and South African Race Relations   189

BIBLIOGRAPHY   203

INDEX   217

PART ONE
Race Relations in Theoretical Perspective

CHAPTER ONE
Introduction

FEW fields in the social sciences have received the degree of attention from both scholars and laymen as has race relations. Writings on the subject range from those essentially polemical in nature to those that provide systematic empirical propositions designed to explain and predict racial phenomena. Some race relations analysts are criticized for being too detached and too objective, and others are denounced for their lack of objectivity and heavy value orientation. It would be difficult indeed for any scholar to be totally detached or objective when studying an emotionally laden area such as race relations. Nor is it absolutely necessary that he attempt to be so, for it is not the scientist's orientation or degree of detachment toward a subject matter that is important for the advancement of knowledge but the extent to which his arguments can withstand the test of validity, i.e., the standards imposed by the scientific community to accept or reject hypotheses or theories.[1] (Supra numbers refer to notes at the end of each chapter.) In this sense, then, the field of race relations, despite the polemics, is not unique. In addition to the proliferation of recent empirical studies, the gradual expansion of theoretical works has added impetus to a critical re-examination of many existing approaches to race relations and of many once widely accepted hypotheses.

APPROACHES TO THE STUDY OF RACE RELATIONS

Much of the behavior usually defined as "race relations" could be treated as subject matter in other recognized areas of sociology, e.g., social stratification, social movements, and urban sociology. In fact, one author has maintained that the field of race has "little claim for autonomous theoretical status."[2] Certainly, when one considers that interpersonal relations between dominant and subordinate members can often be explained by theories of social psychology,[3] that minority liberation and nationalistic movements are forms of collective behavior, and that racial caste systems are instances of social stratification, it is not unreasonable to conclude that theories of race that fail to incorporate the accumulated knowledge of other relevant substantive fields tend to be too restrictive in their application and overly selective in their focus. It is because of their lack of scope that many of the traditional models of race relations are under attack by students of race. Race relations analysts were shackled for several decades by the narrow perspectives of assimilation models and by the heavy preoccupation with theories of prejudice, and therefore found themselves unprepared to predict or explain the violent confrontation of ghetto revolts, the emergence and growth of the Black Power Movement, and the rapid rise of cultural nationalism within the black community.[4]

As early as 1962, Harold Cruse discussed in prophetic words the limited perspective of earlier sociological approaches to race relations:

> Integration vs. separation has become polarized around two main wings of racial ideology, with fateful implications for the Negro movement and the country at large. Yet we are faced with a problem in racial ideology without any means of properly understanding how to deal with it. The dilemma arises from a lack of comprehension of the historical origins of the conflict.
>
> The problem is complicated by a lack of recognition that the conflict even exists. The fundamental economic and cultural issues at stake in this conflict cannot be dealt with by American sociologists for the simple reason that sociologists never admit that such issues should exist at all in American society. They talk of "Americanizing" all the varied racial elements in the United States: but, when it is clear that certain racial elements are not being "Americanized," socially, economically, or culturally, the sociologists proffer nothing but total evasion or more studies on "the nature of preju-

dice." Hence the problems remain with us in a neglected
state of suspension until they break out in what are considered to be "negative," "antisocial," "antidemocratic" reactions.[5]

Although race relations specialists earlier tended to confine
their studies to the United States and to concentrate heavily
on synchronic studies of prejudice,[6] at present more attention
is being directed to historical and cross-cultural studies. A
number of recent studies have attempted to use historical and
comparative data to develop general theoretical propositions of
race and ethnic relations.[7] The form of these propositions has
varied, ranging from those explicitly formulated and advanced
as hypotheses requiring further testing to those implicitly
stated in typological schemes.[8]

This book develops a theoretical framework with a historical
and comparative focus and then applies it to race relations in
the United States and South Africa. Although I have approached this study with the belief that many aspects of race
relations in these two societies are not unique and hence can
be explained by general theoretical propositions, it is true that
some theoretical constructs may be more relevant to some societies. Recognizing this fact and considering the nature of
both United States and South African race relations, I have
given concepts of "racism" and "power" special attention in
this study. In fact, the central arguments of this volume are (1)
that a comprehensive account of the nature of race relations in
these two societies must deal with the dimensions of power
and their relation to dominant- and minority-group contact
and (2) that the dimensions of power cannot be completely
understood if treated independently of the phenomenon of racism.

Both power and racism have received an increasing amount
of attention in the field of race relations during the past few
years,[9] although there is still some disagreement about what
sorts of human experiences these concepts actually represent.
In some studies, discussion of power is limited to cases of overt
conflict between racial groups and racism is treated as a syn-

onym for individual prejudices. However, the analyses involving racism and power in the following chapters are guided by the belief that a dynamic interrelationship exists between the two concepts, that the nature of this association must be understood in order to explain adequately the basis of United States and South African race relations, and that neither can a power analysis of racial groups in interaction be restricted to overt conflict nor can racism be explained solely in terms of individual prejudices.

RACE AND ETHNICITY

The ensuing arguments, although relevant to the experiences of ethnic groups in many cases, are strictly applied to racial groups in interaction. Whereas racial groups are distinguished by socially selected physical traits, ethnic groups are distinguished by socially selected cultural traits. Designations such as ethnic group and racial group therefore have little or no meaning if members of society neither recognize nor acknowledge the traits said to distinguish groups. The classification of a particular group as either racial or ethnic is dependent on the perceptions and definitions of members of the larger society. Whereas Jews, Italians, Poles, and Irishmen are all distinguished as ethnic groups in the United States, they are not differentiated as distinct racial minorities. As members of the dominant racial group in American society, neither do they regard themselves as racial minorities nor are they so regarded by other groups in society. We classify such groups therefore as "nonracial ethnics."

However, certain racial minorities are also classified as ethnic groups, and some writers, in fact, have subsumed the concept of racial group under the general category of ethnic group (racially defined ethnic groups).[10] If a given racial group is ethnically distinct, i.e., viewed as having a distinct subculture and as being bound by similar cultural ties, such a designation is valid. It is only when social and cultural attributes are associated with physical features that the concept "racial" and hence that of racial groups takes on special signifi-

6

cance. To be sure, many subordinate racial groups have experiences comparable to those of nonracial ethnics (e.g., being victims of discrimination and social class exploitation), but, in addition, subjugated racial minorities often suffer from forms of exploitation that are directed by racist norms or racist ideologies and that are perpetrated not only by the middle-class segments of the dominant group but also by lower-class nonracial ethnics. Thus, racial groups have some experiences often quite distinct from those of groups that can be distinguished only by their ethnicity. In this study the concept of racism will be used to help identify and explain such experiences.

Power Conflict Versus Systems Integration

Although racism is strictly applied to racial groups in interaction, the concept of power can be more generally applied. In fact, power is a concept of considerable scope: it can be used to help account for group oppression per se and to explain the continued association of certain racial groups with certain class or caste positions. Class or caste membership develops from historical contact in which groups possessing a power advantage have been able to place themselves in superior positions by solidifying a social structure that features a racial stratification system.

However, social scientists have only recently paid significant attention to the role of power in determining patterns of interracial behavior. Prior to the 1960s, sociologists (with a few noteworthy exceptions such as Frazier, Cox, and Blumer[11]) tended to treat concepts such as "prejudice" and "discrimination" as if they existed in a vacuum. Only tacit recognition was given to the fact that the frequency and degree of discrimination and other manifestations of prejudice against racial minority groups reflected the power of the white majority to dominate.[12] Commenting on this point, Hubert Blalock has stated: "it is important to note that without the resources or power potential . . . prejudices cannot be translated into effective discrimination. This particular point has been repeatedly emphasized by sociologists objecting to the simple assumption

7

that theories of prejudice are sufficient to understand discrimination."[13]

Whereas some sociologists have objected to the lack of attention given to the relationship between power and race, Richard Schermerhorn has warned that the exclusive use of a power model may prove to be unnecessarily restrictive, especially when comparative studies of race and ethnic relations are made.[14] Specifically, he maintains that patterns of integration, not defined in the traditional sense as an end state of interracial cooperation and reciprocal participation, but as a "*process whereby units or elements of a society are brought into an active and coordinated compliance with the ongoing activities and objectives of the dominant group in that society*,"[15] are insufficiently accounted for when a power or conflict model is used. Schermerhorn contends that "*There are times when integration can only occur in and through conflict, and conversely, other times when conflict is necessary to reach a new order of integration.*"[16]

Schermerhorn argues that the pure form of integration (completely harmonious relationship with no conflict) and the pure form of conflict (completely disruptive relationship with no integration) are rare indeed and that a dialectical relationship exists in an overwhelming number of instances involving intergroup contact characterized by compounded or overlapping processes of conflict and integration, antagonistic cooperation, peace in feud, integrative functions of conflict, and forms of accommodation. However, he carefully notes that there will very likely be widespread societal differences with regard to both the extent and the nature of overlapping in the processes of conflict and integration.

I agree with Schermerhorn that a power-conflict model that does not account for the dialectical relationship between the processes of integration and conflict has limited application. However, some of the recent power formulations applied to the subject of race do, in fact, address this issue. For instance, in his theory of power and discrimination, Blalock argues that race relations can be thought of as intergroup "power contests." Commenting on the significance of this distinction, he states:

The term "power contests" is used in preference to one such as "power struggle" in order to emphasize that there need be no overt conflict. I specifically wish to avoid a Marxian type of interpretation, namely, that discrimination results from a conscious, rational attempt on the part of elites to subordinate the minority to their own interests. The processes involved are certainly more complex than this, and usually much more subtle.[17]

The subtle dimensions of a power contest are often difficult to recognize because they are not marked by overt conflict. Yet it is reasonable to assume that a dialectical relationship exists. Antagonistic cooperation and forms of accommodation may be a direct result of the distribution and mobilization of power resources by both the dominant and the minority groups. Minority-group members may feel compelled to comply with the dominant group's norms, not because they identify with or have internalized these norms, but because they lack sufficient resources to openly challenge them. If there is minority resistance in such situations, it will likely be very subtle and indirect, frequently an individual rather than a collective endeavor. For example, Raymond and Alice Bauer have argued that although many slaves in the antebellum South resigned themselves to their subordinate position and for self-protection refrained from directly challenging plantation authority, they did, on numerous occasions, engage in subtler forms of resistance such as breaking tools, destroying crops, setting barns afire, and feigning illness.[18] Black leaders in more recent times, although openly rejecting many dominant-group norms of racial subordination, have urged their followers to comply with these norms in order to prevent further suppression and bloodshed, because of the unequal distribution of power resources between blacks and whites. In juxtaposition, the black protest movement of the 1960s that produced unprecedented forms of racial conflict was a direct response to an increasing sense of power and a feeling that positive change could be effected and therefore meek submission to racial norms was no longer necessary. Thus there is no reason to assume that the use of a power model to explain interracial be-

9

havior necessarily leads one to ignore either the processes of integration or the dialectical relationship between integration and conflict.

Nonetheless, the critical observer might challenge the extent to which a power-conflict model does in fact explain the fundamental basis of normative integration, because it is conceivable that minority members comply in many instances, not because they are coerced, but because they view the norms, values, and objectives of the dominant group as legitimate. Critics of the conflict thesis insist that overstressing tension, dissension, and conflict leads one to ignore the very foundation of society—i.e., the shared values enabling a social system to persist.[19] Disagreeing with this position, M. G. Smith argues that

> The difficulties which this social theory faces are clear and important. From this viewpoint, the rejection of European rule by colonial peoples remains utterly incomprehensible; but so must any conflict which revolves around "subordinate identifications" and segmental loyalties, simply because the thesis that society rests on shared common values inevitably implies their dominance, and so minimizes the strength of "subordinate identification" within segments of the total unit. It is perfectly clear that in any social system based on intense cleavages and discontinuity between differentiated segments, the community of values or social relations between these sections will be correspondingly low.[20]

It is true, as Ernest Barth and Donald Noel have pointed out, that racial and ethnic groups in a given society must share communication symbols, but "the critical issue is the presence or absence of consensus *between* groups on other than communication symbols."[21] In traditional racial orders such as in the United States and the Republic of South Africa, despite racial consensus on fundamental issues of morality not related to race relations (e.g., support of the legal code with respect to property crime and murder) and despite the sharing of communication symbols and the interdependence in the division of labor, one must conclude that there is and has been significant dissensus between dominant and subordinate groups with respect to values and norms reinforcing racial stratification. Although some segments of the subordinate-group population in both societies have from time to time internalized dominant-group norms of racial domination and have been influenced by racist thought to the degree that they openly reject black identity and desperately strive to identify with white society,[22] to assume that this sort of consensus on race relations is or has been typical of these two societies and hence a valid explanation for periods of integration or lack of open conflict is unwarranted in the face of historical evidence.

Of course, it should be recognized that there may be discrepancies in views and opinions within the respective racial groups. Some minority members are more heavily committed to ending racial stratification and are more upset about the structural arrangements than others. Indeed, as E. Franklin Frazier attempted to show, many black professionals serving the black community have a vested interest in maintaining racial segregation because they are not thrown into competition with whites.[23] Likewise, some dominant members are more heavily committed to maintaining racial stratification than others. As we shall see in subsequent chapters, it would certainly be a mistake to treat the various racial groups as homogeneous units in analyzing all areas of racial interaction.[24] However, this should not obscure the fact that in accounting for significant black–white relations in the societies of the United States and South Africa, differential power has proved to be of greater historical importance than value consensus. Although between-group value consensus concerning race relations has had some effect on social behavior (e.g., the support given by Northern whites in the United States in the early 1960s to black demands that were consistent with, say, the Bill of Rights), the position taken in this volume is that both historical patterns of overt conflict and processes of integration in these two societies are largely explained in terms of a theoretical framework of power.

NOTES

1. For a discussion of this point, see Richard S. Rudner, *Philosophy of Science* (Englewood Cliffs, N.J.: Prentice-Hall, 1966), p. 6.

2. Pierre van den Berghe, *Race and Racism: A Comparative Perspective* (New York: Wiley, 1967) p. 6.

3. Concepts such as "dominant group," "subordinate group," and "minority group" have invited confusion in the literature of race relations because of their ambiguity. In this study, the terms "dominant group" and "majority group" are interchangeably used to refer to the racial group in a given society that has differential access to and control of power resources; conversely, the terms "subordinate group" and "minority group" are interchangeably used to refer to racial groups who relatively lack control of or access to power resources.

4. William J. Wilson, "Race Relations Models and Ghetto Behavior," in *Nation of Nations: The Ethnic Experience and the Racial Crisis*, ed. by Peter I. Rose (New York: Random House, 1972), pp. 259–275.

5. Harold Cruse, "Revolutionary Nationalism and the Afro-American," *Studies on the Left*, 2:16 (1962).

6. There were a few notable exceptions to these approaches. Pioneer race relations scholars such as E. Franklin Frazier and Oliver Cromwell Cox not only emphasized the sociohistorical approach to race relations but also placed a great deal of stress on the use of comparative data. See, for example, E. Franklin Frazier, *Race and Culture Contacts in the Modern World* (New York: Knopf, 1957), and Oliver Cromwell Cox, *Caste, Class, and Race: A Study in Social Dynamics* (Garden City, N.Y.: Doubleday, 1948). Also see Charles Wagley and Marvin Harris, *Minorities in the New World* (New York: Columbia U.P., 1958).

7. See, for example, van den Berghe, op. cit.; Richard Schermerhorn, *Comparative Ethnic Relations: A Framework for Theory and Research* (New York: Random House, 1970); Herbert Blumer, "Industrialisation and Race Relations," in *Industrialisation and Race Relations: A Symposium*, ed. by Guy Hunter (London: Oxford U.P., 1965), pp. 220–253; Stanley Lieberson, "A Societal Theory of Race and Ethnic Relations," *American Sociological Review*, 26:902–910 (Dec. 1961); Donald L. Noel, "A Theory of the Origin of Ethnic Stratification," *Social Problems*, 16:157–172 (Fall 1968).

8. There is, of course, a technical distinction between an empirical proposition and a typology. The former is designed to explain and predict behavior, whereas the latter is intended to categorize or classify behavior. However, many propositions are implied in typologies by the item arrangement and hence may become explicit when they are formulated as statements that relate the items in a manner making them amenable to direct empirical testing. For an excellent discussion of this

point, see Carl G. Hempel, *Aspects of Scientific Explanation* (New York: Free Press, 1965).

9. See, for example, Schermerhorn, op. cit.; H. M. Blalock, Jr., *Toward a Theory of Minority-Group Relations* (New York: Wiley, 1967); and Noel, op. cit., for a discussion of power and race. For a systematic discussion of racism, see Robert Blauner, "Internal Colonialism and Ghetto Revolt," *Social Problems*, 16:395–408 (Spring 1968), and "Black Culture: Myth or Reality?" in *Americans from Africa: Old Memories, New Moods*, ed. by Peter I. Rose (New York: Atherton, 1970), pp. 417–441; van den Berghe, op. cit.; Schermerhorn, op. cit.; and Donald L. Noel, "Slavery and Rise of Racism," in *The Origins of American Slavery and Racism*, ed. by Donald L. Noel (Columbus, O.: Merrill, 1972), pp. 153–174.

10. Schermerhorn, op. cit., and Tamotsu Shibutani and Kian M. Kwan, *Ethnic Stratification: A Comparative Approach* (New York: Macmillan, 1965).

11. See, for example, Herbert Blumer, "Race Prejudice as a Sense of Group Position," *Pacific Sociological Review*, 1:3–7 (Spring 1958); Cox, op. cit.; and E. Franklin Frazier, "Theoretical Structure of Sociology and Sociological Research," *British Journal of Sociology*, 4:292–311 (Dec. 1953).

12. Other sociologists have emphasized this point. See Robin M. Williams, Jr., *Strangers Next Door* (Englewood Cliffs, N.J.: Prentice-Hall, 1964); Peter I. Rose, *The Subject Is Race* (New York: Oxford U.P., 1968); Blalock, op. cit.; and Schermerhorn, op. cit.

13. Blalock, op. cit., p. 111.

14. Schermerhorn, op. cit., chap. 1.

15. Ibid., p. 14.

16. Ibid., p. 58.

17. Blalock, op. cit., p. 109.

18. Raymond and Alice Bauer, "Day to Day Resistance to Slavery," *Journal of Negro History*, 27:388–419 (Oct. 1942).

19. See, for example, Lloyd Braithwaite, "Social Stratification and Cultural Pluralism," in *Social and Cultural Pluralism in the Caribbean*, ed. by Vera Rubin, *Annals of the New York Academy of Science*, 83:816–831 (1960).

20. M. G. Smith, *The Plural Society in the British West Indies* (Berkeley: U. of California, 1965), p. xi.

21. Ernest A. T. Barth and Donald L. Noel, "Conceptual Frameworks for the Analysis of Race Relations: An Evaluation," *Social Forces*, 50:340 (Mar. 1972).

22. In some measure, this may also be ascribed to an unequal power relationship in the sense that the dominant group, through its superior power resources, is able to control and influence patterns of thought among minority members. Included here is the effective technique of

co-optation, whereby minority leaders are rewarded by the dominant group to the extent that they openly support dominant-group norms.

23. E. Franklin Frazier, *Black Bourgeoisie* (New York: Free Press, 1957).

24. For a discussion of this point, see James Blackwell and Marie R. Haug, "Black Bosses, Black Workers: Or Are Black Bosses Beautiful?" paper read at the Annual Meeting of the American Sociological Association, Denver, Colo. (Sept. 1971).

CHAPTER TWO

Race, Power, and the Development of Racial Stratification

OWER as a concept has been applied universally to all forms of human behavior—not only to explain intergroup behavior but also to explain dyadic relationships and individualistic behavior. Power has different considerations and different empirical referents depending on the level of analysis.[1] For our purposes, however, power is viewed strictly from the vantage point of intergroup behavior.

THE CONCEPTUAL DIMENSIONS OF RACIAL-GROUP POWER

From a group perspective, power may be conceptualized in terms of two dimensions—"active power" and "power ability." By active power, I mean the actual exercising of influence by Group A over Group B such that the behavior of Group B is modified in accordance with the wishes of Group A. However, it should not be inferred that "actual influence" refers only to the overt efforts of Group A to control Group B. In fact, the behavior of B can be affected by what it perceives to be A's power or power ability, and hence B is not likely to behave in a manner that will produce negative sanctions from A. To the extent that B has little regard for A's power, it can behave independently and not feel constrained to follow what it assumes to be a course of action that A will approve.

Power ability—as the name implies—refers to the ability of Group A to control or influence the behavior of Group B regardless of whether A has actually influenced B's behavior. The best way to amplify the notion of power ability is to introduce the concept of "power resources." Broadly defined, power resources have to do with the properties that determine the scope and degree of the group's ability to influence behavior.[2] These properties could include high social status, reputation for power, capability to bear arms, control of political office, control of mass media, wealth, and land ownership, to mention a few. Resources can be used to coerce a group to behave in the desired manner (e.g., B's boycotting the stores controlled by A), to induce individuals to behave in certain ways (e.g., B's promising to vote for certain political candidates of A if the latter supports certain kinds of legislation), or, finally, to persuade individuals to follow a certain course of action. Generally, inducement and persuasion resources are applied by groups that have placed themselves in a position whereby they can often influence another group without resorting to threats or penalties (i.e., constraint or pressure resources).[3] Here I am referring to group economic and political power, the possession of certain desired skills such as are acquired through formal education, and the control of certain prestige symbols. For the sake of brevity, I will often refer to inducement and persuasion resources as "competitive resources."[4]

The decision of whether a given item is relevant to the exercise of power and hence qualifies as a power resource can only be made by consideration of the objectives providing the reasons or justifications for the group's entering into and/or continuing a power confrontation with another party. In other words, objectives furnish the rationale not only for identifying an item as a power resource but also for suggesting its relative importance to the exercise of power. For example, in recent years black economic boycotts have proved to be quite an effective resource in eliminating racial discrimination in department stores, yet it is unlikely that group silent prayers by blacks would have had the same impact on white entrepreneurs.

Resources can be general in nature or highly particular;[5] that is, some resources are applicable to a number of different

16

situations whereas others are restricted to specific cases and to narrow ranges of people. Accordingly, the greater the generality of the resources a group controls, the greater is the scope of the group's power ability; the larger the number of resources a group has at its disposal, the more alternative means it has to reach its goal.

Finally, resources should be considered in terms of their liquidity, that is, the extent to which they can be deployed or mobilized to exert influence.[6] Some resources can be deployed easily and quickly because the mechanisms that facilitate their mobilization or application exist. For example, the NAACP (National Association for the Advancement of Colored People) has legal machinery that can immediately be put into operation in order to win court cases involving civil rights. When successful litigation is the goal, the NAACP has resources of high liquidity that can yield influence without having to be extensively mobilized. On the other hand, if black leaders were to call for a nationwide boycott of products produced by American organizations practicing racial discrimination, they would lack ready mechanisms to facilitate such an operation, and hence the resources needed would be of low liquidity, because a successful boycott would, under the circumstances, entail extensive mobilization or redeployment of manpower, communications network, and organizational efforts.

In the final analysis, the greater the scope and the higher the liquidity of a group's resources, the greater is the group's power ability. In the study of racial-group power, the focus of analysis shifts from power ability to active power to the extent that the group's resources become mobilized to exert influence. However, for the sake of convenience, the term power will be used in this study to connote both a group's active power and its power ability (including its power resources) unless otherwise specified.

POWER AND THE ORIGIN OF RACIAL STRATIFICATION

Racial domination and exploitation have occurred repeatedly throughout history. Usually when two distinct racial groups have established contact and have interacted for a continuous period, one group ends up dominating the other.[7] Continuous or sustained interaction between racial groups after contact is a prerequisite both for the development of racial stratification and for the establishment of equalitarian relations between racial groups.[8] In actual fact, however, there are no known cases of racial groups in advanced nation states having established equalitarian relationships. By the same token, there are no known cases in which the relationships between racial groups have been based on complete equality of power. Differential power is a marked feature of racial-group interaction in complex societies: the greater the power discrepancy is between subordinate and dominant racial groups, the greater are the extent and scope of racial domination. In most cases, the existing power relationships have their basis in the manner in which the groups first established contact. Stanley Lieberson has commented on this point:

> In short, when populations begin to occupy the same habitat but do not share a single order, each group endeavors to maintain the political and economic conditions that are at least compatible with the institutions existing before contact. These conditions for the maintenance of institutions can not only differ for the two groups in contact, but are often conflicting. European contacts with the American Indian, for example, led to the decimation of the latter's sources of sustenance and disrupted religious and tribal forms of organization. With respect to a population's efforts to maintain its social institutions, we may therefore assume that the presence of another ethnic group is an important part of the environment. Further, if groups in contact differ in their capacity to impose changes on the other group, then we may expect to find one group "superordinate" and the other population "subordinate" in maintaining or developing a suitable environment.[9]

The original contact situation involving racial groups currently concentrated in modern nation states was typically of one of three major forms—slave transfers, colonization, and voluntary migration, with each situation involving at least one racial group migrating to the region and at least one indigenous racial group. Following Lieberson's usage, the term "indigenous" is not restricted to aborigines "but rather to a population sufficiently established in an area so as to possess the institutions and demographic capacity for maintaining some minimal form of social order through generations."[10] In the case of colonization, the migrating population is the dominant racial group (or superordinate in Lieberson's terminology), whereas in slave transfers and voluntary migration, the migrating population is the subordinate racial group.[11] In each instance, the dominant racial group assumes a certain degree of control over the subordinate population, with the most rigid control and greatest power discrepancy occurring in slave transfers, followed by colonization and voluntary migration in descending order. Let us focus briefly on these three forms of contact.

Slave transfers present a situation in which the dominant racial group has supreme power over the subordinate population—involving continuous coercion from the time of the slaves' capture to their day-to-day activities after arrival. Historically, slave transfers have been associated with plantation economies having a racial caste system with a rigidly stratified occupational structure. On the plantations, slaves perform menial tasks under the close supervision of dominant-group overseers and plantation owners. Thrust into a new environment, often separated from their families, and isolated in groups on rural plantations, slaves are vulnerable to control by plantation owners. Such control is further reinforced by the marked differences in culture and history that typically distinguish the groups in contact and make it difficult for the slaves to adapt to the new situation in ways other than those dictated by the slavemasters. Specifically, slaves who are separated from their families and communities and forcibly transferred to a new and alien environment populated with strange people with strange ways find themselves of necessity in a much greater dependent relationship with the slavemaster than are indigenous racial groups forced to be slaves in their own territory or country. Because members of the latter groups are familiar with their home environment and are not completely separated from their families, groups, and communities, they are able to mount greater resistance to dominant-group exploitation. Edgar T. Thompson sums the matter up very well: "Thus the native Negro in many parts of Africa is regarded as a very unsatisfactory plantation laborer, but in early Virginia he was regarded as superior not only to the native Indian but also to the white indentured servant. With imported laborers, usually familyless, the control situation changed in favor of the planter."[12]

The second major contact situation, colonization, entails control of a given territory by a nonindigenous racial group.[13] Although the nonindigenous population attempts to gain maximum control over the indigenous population, the task is difficult and the degree of control typically found in the slave-transfer situation is never reached. The reasons for this have just been stated briefly but deserve repeating: the indigenous population is familiar with the home territory, often lives in large, organized societies, and therefore can launch reprisals against the nonindigenous population if the need arises. This was exactly the situation that the colonizers in America faced when they attempted to enslave the American Indian. Even though the colonizers had access to greater power resources and in effect virtually annihilated the Indians in numerous skirmishes, at no time were they able to force the Indians to submit to the degree of total submission that characterized black–white interaction during the slavery period.[14] Nonetheless, the initial phases of colonization involve situations in which the dominant racial group is able to seriously undermine the social, economic, and political institutions of the indigenous population and hence disrupt both their social organization and their cultural life.[15]

Of the three types of racial contact, voluntary migration represents a situation of greatest freedom of choice and movement for the migrating group; hence the degree of racial domination is not as great as in slave transfers and colonization. Because the immigrant racial group comes of its own free will, it is able to establish its separate and autonomous communities and practice its cultural forms with greater liberty and less interference from the dominant racial group. However, immigrant racial groups often experience exploitation and discrimination by the receiving dominant group, especially in racially ordered societies where the immigrant group finds itself in direct competition with certain segments of the dominant group for scarce goods and positions.[16] Moreover, even though voluntary migrants come of their own free will, their migration is often encouraged for purposes of exploitation by, say, industrialists, managers, and proprietors of the receiving society. Nonetheless, unlike the racial groups subjected to slave transfers and colonization, voluntary migrants have the option of returning to their home country if their persecution becomes unbearable.[17]

Contract labor is a major form of voluntary migration involving a situation "where the movement from one country to another follows the instigation of agents from either side."[18] However, as Schermerhorn has noted, it is the case that

> The distinction between slave labor and contract labor is not always clear empirically since the latter often involves force and compulsion. The legal or analytical differences between the two may be important, but one must recognize that contract labor runs the gamut from enforced servitude without chattel ownership to carefully stipulated intervals of work obligation terminated abruptly when contracts end.[19]

Usually, however, contract labor is voluntary, and on completion of the initial work obligation the migrants may exercise one of three options: (1) renew the old contracts or continue to work without a formal contract, (2) seek other forms of employment but continue to reside in the country, or (3) return to their homeland.[20] An exception to this general pattern was seen in the case of early black migrants to the United States. The first blacks involuntarily brought to this country were defined as indentured servants (one kind of contract laborers) and initially had the same legal status as white indentured servants. However, for blacks, indentured servitude was, within a few years, defined as unlimited servitude and hence treated synonymously with slavery.

The type of racial domination emerging from the initial contact situation often leads to the development and institutionalization of special kinds of racial stratification systems (e.g., caste systems) that persist through generations. In Chapter Four, I will examine the reasons some of these systems undergo change whereas others persist with little or no alteration. However, at this point, we must confront a basic question: why, given the existence of a power differential between racial groups, will one group typically attempt to control the other?

It is conceivable that when two racial groups come into contact they might live side by side in mutual harmony despite a power differential, but rarely has such a situation occurred. In complex nation states, attempts at racial dominance invariably occur when groups establish contact and interact for a sustained period of time.[21]

Some explanations of racial dominance may be applied to any form of intergroup contact, whereas others are more specifically relevant to interracial interaction. For our purposes, certain aspects of Gerhard Lenski's theory of power and privilege explain racial dominance in general terms, whereas more specific explanations involve matters pertaining to the complex dimensions of racism.[22] The latter will be discussed in some detail in Chapter Three, so let us now direct our attention to the former.

Implicit in any power explanation of group behavior are fundamental postulates regarding the nature of self- and group interests. In his theory, Lenski introduces and discusses these postulates. Specifically, Lenski maintains that *"man is a social being; obliged by nature to live with others as a member of society"*[23] (in other words, the cooperative activity of men is necessary to obtain maximum satisfaction of their human desires and needs), that conflict often emerges from cooperative activity because most of man's *important decisions or actions* are prompted by self-interests or partisan group interests, that most of the many objects that man strives to control or possess are in short supply ("Unlike the various plants and animals, *man has an insatiable appetite for goods and services.*" Regardless of how much he produces and consumes, man is never completely satisfied because in addition to the utilitarian value there is also a status value attached to the goods and services consumed. "The very nature of status striving makes it inevitable that the demand will exceed the supply"[24]), and that because of the foregoing points "*a struggle for rewards will be present in every human society*",[25] and the outcomes of the struggle (be it violent or nonviolent or within the framework of some established system of rules) will largely be a function of differential power resources.[26]

By applying Lenski's arguments to the interracial arena, we may argue that the efforts of a racial group to subjugate another group are, in some cases, motivated by desires to control or increase control of scarce goods. Through the process of domination, the subordinate group can be eliminated or neutralized as a competitor.

Competition can be either an interindividual or an intergroup phenomenon. In this connection, Amos Hawley insightfully suggests that

> Competition is a function of the ratio of resources to population. Its intensity rises and falls as the relative value of the denominator in the fraction increases or decreases. But where the population is subdivided into groups competition tends to shift from an individual to an intergroup basis. When this occurs the fundamental competitive issue is altered; to the problem of how much each individual competitor will be able to obtain is added the problem of how many individuals from each group will have the opportunity to enter into the competition.[27]

Hawley furthermore suggests that if only a very small number of subordinate individuals are involved, competition is likely to remain more on an interindividual than on an intergroup basis. However, as subordinate-group members tend to increase proportionately to dominant individuals, competition may be expected to become increasingly intergroup in character; accordingly, when the subordinate group looms "progressively larger as a competitive force, tensions develop, restrictions accumulate, and the minority is more and more suppressed."[28]

Racial stratification may also be used by the dominant group to exploit the labor of the minority group in order to increase or maximize rewards. For example, the use of slave labor to increase farm production cannot be explained solely by the argument that this form of domination was designed to eliminate the slave as a major competitor. In fact, it could be contended that in some situations slaves brought to Brazil and to the United States were initially indifferent to the materialistic rewards Westerners endlessly sought. On that basis alone, they would not be in competition with the dominant group. Theoretically, the competition for goods could be minimized if one group has no interest in them.[29] However, if a group attaches a status value to certain goods its members consume or produce, it is likely that regardless of the degree of competition from other groups an endless struggle for rewards will exist within the group. Accordingly, if the individual members of a dominant group feel that their control of these goods can be maximized by exploiting the labor of minority groups, they will strive to develop and maintain racial stratification.

Of crucial importance in this connection is the manner in which the ruling classes of the dominant racial group, particularly the segments controlling the government and the means of production, are able to get the masses to support and reinforce racial stratification even though the latter may not materially benefit from minority subjugation. In other words, in situations where the ruling classes have a vested interest in the development and institutionalization of a racial order while at the same time they control the agencies of communication virtually necessary to mold public opinion, a normative consensus in favor of racial stratification may develop among all segments of the dominant group. For example, the institution of slavery in the United States was directed by a handful of powerful plantation owners who not only controlled the political and economic life of the South but also had a very strong influence on patterns of social thought during the antebellum period. Indeed, by 1860 only one quarter of Southern families owned any slaves at all, yet slavery was fervently supported by the nonslaveholding masses. Although it is true that the nonslaveholders derived some psychic benefit from identifying with a "superior" caste, the motivation for the system of slavery initially came from the privileged classes, whose desire to maximize their own resources led to the permanent servitude of blacks. Without the solid backing of the Southern aristocracy, it is unlikely that slavery in America would have become such a mammoth institution and lasted as long as it did.

Although examination of the role of differential power in the struggle for scarce goods helps to account for the emergence and continued existence of racial stratification, such explanations are general enough to apply to various nonracial ethnics in contact or even to groups distinguishable in terms of social class. In fact, the previous discussion could provide the basis for a general theory of intergroup stratification in which racial stratification would merely be one special case. It is at this level that racial-group interactions have elements in common with patterns of other distinct groups in contact, and certainly any fully developed theory of racial stratification would have to take this into account. But once we move beyond this general level and begin to examine the dynamics of group behavior in the formation and institutionalization of a system of racial stratification, a general explanation of this sort leaves a great deal unexplained. Here is where the unique factors associated with racial contact, in particular the role of racism in molding group attitudes and shaping group behavior, have to be considered, and I will give this subject considerable attention in the next chapter.

NOTES

1. Mary Rogers, *The Concept of Power in Community Research*, unpublished doctoral dissertation, U. of Massachusetts, Amherst (1971).
2. Ibid.

3. William Gamson, *Power and Discontent* (Homewood, Ill.: Dorsey, 1968). Also see H. M. Blalock, Jr., *Toward a Theory of Minority-Group Relations* (New York: Wiley, 1967).

4. The term "competitive resource" is borrowed from op. cit., p. 118.

5. Rogers, op. cit.

6. Gamson, op. cit., p. 95.

7. For a discussion of this argument as it applies to both racial and ethnic groups, see Richard Schermerhorn, *Comparative Ethnic Relations: A Framework for Theory and Research* (New York: Random House, 1970), p. 68. There have been a few cases where one racial group has been culturally and physically absorbed by another group following a period of racial friction. In South Africa the early Hottentot tribes were miscegenated out of existence after struggling with the Dutch settlers for land and cattle in the seventeenth and eighteenth centuries. White colonists in Brazil miscegenated and intermarried with American Indians to form the mestizo population. Both of these "mergers" were, in part, prompted by a shortage of white women.

8. Donald L. Noel, "A Theory of the Origin of Ethnic Stratification," *Social Problems*, 16:157–172 (Fall 1968).

9. Stanley Lieberson, "A Societal Theory of Race and Ethnic Relations," *American Sociological Review*, 26:904 (Dec. 1961).

10. Ibid., p. 903.

11. The major distinction between voluntary migration and colonization is that in the former the group migrating voluntarily is in a subordinate position vis-à-vis the indigenous population, whereas in the latter the group migrating voluntarily is in a dominant position. For a more detailed discussion of slave transfers, colonization, and voluntary migration, see Schermerhorn, òp. cit., chap. 3.

12. Edgar T. Thompson, "The Plantation: The Physical Basis of Traditional Race Relations," in *Race Relations and the Race Problem*, ed. by Edgar T. Thompson (Durham, N.C.: Duke U.P., 1939), p. 185. Also see Winthrop D. Jordan, *White Over Black: American Attitudes Toward the Negro 1550–1812* (Chapel Hill: U. of North Carolina, 1968). A fuller treatment of this subject is presented in Chapter 5.

13. Schermerhorn has outlined three major types of colonization— limited settlement, substantial settlement, and massive settlement expanding to majority rule (the last type represents the history of white settlement in the United States). All types signify the relative control by the nonindigenous population of the indigenous population. Schermerhorn, op. cit., chap. 3.

14. Jordan, op. cit., chap. 2. Also see Gary B. Nash, "Red, White, and Black: The Origins of Racism in Colonial America," in *The Great Fear: Race in the Mind of America*, ed. by Gary B. Nash and Richard Weiss (New York: Holt, 1970), pp. 1–26.

15. For insightful discussions of the relations between the colonizers

and the colonized in North Africa, see Frantz Fanon, *The Wretched of the Earth* (New York: Grove Press, 1963), and Albert Memmi, *The Colonizer and the Colonized* (Boston: Beacon, 1967).

16. Herbert Blumer, "Industrialisation and Race Relations," in *Industrialisation and Race Relations: A Symposium*, ed. by Guy Hunter (London: Oxford U.P., 1965), pp. 220–253, and Peter I. Rose, "Outsiders in Britain," *Trans-Action*, 4:18–23 (March 1967).

17. Lieberson, op. cit., p. 905.

18. Schermerhorn, op. cit., p. 98.

19. Ibid., p. 110.

20. Ibid., p. 68.

21. Noel, op. cit., and Schermerhorn, op. cit.

22. Gerhard Lenski, *Power and Privilege: A Theory of Social Stratification* (New York: McGraw-Hill, 1966).

23. Ibid., p. 35.

24. Ibid., p. 31. It should be noted that Lenski does in fact consider altruistic behavior in individual and group decision making; however, he argues that altruism, unlike self-interest behavior, is largely confined to *unimportant* actions or decisions.

25. Ibid., pp. 31–32.

26. One qualification should be introduced here. Lenski states: "In our discussion of the nature of man, it was postulated that where important decisions are involved, most human action is motivated by either self-interest or by partisan group interests. This suggests that power alone governs the distribution of rewards. This cannot be the case, however, since we also postulated that most of these essentially selfish interests can be satisfied only by the establishment of cooperative relations with others. Cooperation is absolutely essential for survival and for efficient attainment of most other goals. In other words, men's selfish interests compel them to remain members of society and to share in the division of labor.

"If these two postulates are correct, then it follows that *men will share the product of their labor to the extent required to insure the survival and continued productivity of those whose actions are necessary or beneficial to themselves.*" Ibid., p. 44.

27. Amos Hawley, "Dispersion Versus Segregation: Apropos of a Solution of Race Problems," *Papers of the Michigan Academy of Science, Arts, and Letters*, 30:669 (1944).

28. Ibid., p. 670. Also see Robin Williams Jr., "The Reduction of Intergroup Tensions," *Social Science Research Council Bulletin* 57 (1947), chap. 3. Of course, this argument presupposes the existence of what Blumer calls "a sense of group position," as one racial group defines its position vis-à-vis another group. The more that minority individuals involve themselves in competition with the dominant group, the greater is the challenge to the latter's superior position. In Chapter Three, I will

discuss the sense of group position as a factor in racial stratification. See Herbert Blumer, "Race Prejudice as a Sense of Group Position," *Pacific Sociological Review*, 1:3–7 (Spring 1958).

29. For a discussion of this point, see Blalock, op. cit., chap. 4, and Noel, op. cit.

CHAPTER THREE
Race and Racism

FOLLOWING the publication of the *Report of the National Advisory Commission on Civil Disorders*, nationwide attention was focused on the concept of racism.[1] A point heavily stressed in this report was that because blacks have experienced discrimination and exploitation they have been excluded from meaningful participation in the dominant institutions of the United States. White racism—defined as white prejudiced attitudes toward blacks—was identified in the report as the major cause of this problem. Critical of this approach, a number of authors have pointed out that stressing white prejudiced attitudes led to the failure to gauge other manifestations of racism.[2] In the words of Gary Marx,

> The report would have been more persuasive if it had differentiated institutional from idiosyncratic racism, racist attitudes from racist behavior, self-conscious and intended racism from subconscious or nonreflective and unintentional behavior and attitudes that may have racist consequences, and done more to document rather than simply assert the importance of current racism.[3]

Marx's criticisms give some idea of the variety of ways racism can be approached. On the other hand, they reflect the recent tendency to expand the term "racism" to so many different categories that a precise conceptual and empirical application becomes difficult. Racism should be distinguished from "discrimination," "prejudiced attitudes," "ethnocentrism," and other locutions used to describe minority- and dominant-group interaction, and this is one of the central tasks of this chapter.

29

The Variable Meaning of Racism

In their respective analyses of racial and ethnic relations, Noel and Schermerhorn have introduced conceptions basic to an analytical and empirical discussion of racism.[4] Schermerhorn first of all distinguishes racism as "minimal racism" and "maximal racism." This differentiation represents a fundamental departure from the traditional definition and treatment of racism in the literature, and its essential uniqueness derives from Schermerhorn's conception of minimal racism:

> In its minimal form, racism defines darker people as backward or less evolved, different in degree but not in kind from their master, therefore, capable, with training and education, to rise individually from their lowly position to a status of equality with the ruling group.[5]

It is important to recognize that the concept of minimal racism is quite clearly related to the general notion of ethnocentrism, because evaluations of a particular race's cultural achievements are based, not on assumptions about that group's biological inferiority, but on factors of social and cultural origin.

Unlike minimal racism, maximal racism asserts a categorical association between biological features and cultural attributes. Schermerhorn states:

> racism takes a maximal form where the distinctions between superordinates and subordinates assume an absolute rather than a relative character, one of kind and not of degree. . . . The key notion in maximal racism becomes the inherent superiority of peoples with lighter color, together with its obverse, the inherent inferiority of the darker colored. In this view, the rule of the former over the latter is therefore inevitable, not arbitrary.[6]

Although accepting Schermerhorn's notion of maximal racism as being fairly consistent with the way racism is generally defined in systematic usage, Noel rejects the concept of minimal racism.[7] He feels that "racism" should be restricted to an ideology justifying a discriminatory social structure and "based on the conception that racial groups form a biogenetic hierarchy,"[8] that what Schermerhorn calls minimal racism is essentially nothing more than cultural ethnocentrism. Noel writes:

> Cultural ethnocentrism assumes that with opportunity and training out-group members could be acculturated and become the equals of the in-group. On the other hand, physical ethnocentrism (i.e., racism) assumes that members of the relevant out-group are biogenetically incapable of ever achieving intellectual and moral equality with members of the in-group. Where cultural ethnocentrism attributes differences in behavior and culture to historical accident, racism attributes them to differences in innate endowment[9]

I agree with Noel that Schermerhorn's concept of minimal racism should be relabeled "ethnocentrism" (or "cultural ethnocentrism"), especially in view of the way the term is usually defined in the literature. However, I disagree with his equating physical ethnocentrism with racism. Noel's position is that racism represents one form of the more general phenomenon of ethnocentrism—hence the term "physical ethnocentrism." Although he defines ethnocentrism as "preeminently a matter of in-group glorification"—i.e., the "focus is on the virtues of the in-group" even though the inevitable concomitant is generalized rejection or disparagement of the out-group[10]— he is willing to stretch the meaning of the term to incorporate an ideology *justifying racial domination in biogenetic terms.*

The position taken in this study is that there is an essential difference between ethnocentrism and racism and that it is indeed misleading to treat the latter as a special instance of the former. Let me be more specific. The fundamental distinction between these two concepts is that ethnocentrism is a principle of invidious group distinction, whereas racism is a philosophy or ideology of racial exploitation. In speaking of ethnocentrism

31

as a principle of invidious group distinction, I have in mind evaluative judgments of not only cultural criteria (i.e., cultural ethnocentrism) but also of group physical traits such as skin color and height (i.e., physical ethnocentrism). However, unlike Noel's, my concept of physical ethnocentrism does not entail an in-group ideology justifying racial domination by assumption of a biogenetic hierarchy; rather, it denotes a general disdain or contempt for out-group physical features and nothing more. For example, early connotations of the term "black" contributed significantly to the development of unfavorable English attitudes toward black-skinned Africans when the two races established contact. "As described by the Oxford English Dictionary," states Winthrop Jordan, "the meaning of *black* before the sixteenth century included, 'Deeply stained with dirt; soiled, dirty, foul. . . . Having dark or deadly purposes, malignant; pertaining to or involving death, deadly; baneful, disastrous, sinister. . . . Foul, iniquitous, atrocious, horrible, wicked. . . . Indicating disgrace, censure, liability to punishment, etc.' Black was an emotionally partisan color, the handmaid and symbol of baseness and evil, a sign of danger and repulsion."[11] Of course, juxtaposed with the concept of blackness was that of whiteness. White signified purity, virginity, virtue, beauty, and beneficence.[12] Although invidious distinctions against Africans were also based on cultural ethnocentrism, one cannot dismiss the negative evaluation based on skin color. However, this instance of physical ethnocentrism did not entail a commitment to a view positing the biogenetic hierarchy of races. As Jordon has argued, such an ideology was virtually unknown in English thought prior to the eighteenth century.[13]

Whereas ethnocentrism is viewed in this study as a principle of invidious group distinction with reference to either cultural or physical criteria, racism is defined as an *ideology of racial domination or exploitation that (1) incorporates beliefs in a particular race's cultural and/or inherent biological inferiority and (2) uses such beliefs to justify and prescribe inferior or unequal treatment for that group.*[14] The crucial distinction in this definition is that racism has two major dimensions—

biological and cultural. Biological racism is straightforward, is consistent with Noel's conception of racism and Schermerhorn's definition of maximal racism, and poses few analytical problems—in fact, a rationale or justification for racial domination is implicit in assumptions about inherent biological inferiority. A fundamental reason for a racial hierarchy is logically implied when assumptions are made concerning the minority race's inherent inferiority to the dominant race, and the more virulent the racism, the more explicit the rationale becomes. Cultural racism, however, departs significantly from racism as usually discussed. In fact, some readers may argue that I am taking liberties with the notion of racism by giving it a cultural base, that cultural racism has no biological basis and hence the connotation of race in the concept is misleading. However, the distinction is not without merit because what I am saying is that a particular *race* is judged to be culturally inferior and set aside for discriminatory treatment.[15] As discussion in subsequent chapters will show, dominant-group rationales for racial exploitation based on cultural criteria actually preceded rationales grounded in biological distinctions in both the United States and South Africa. To stretch the meaning of cultural ethnocentrism to incorporate a philosophy of racial exploitation (i.e., cultural racism) would be confusing, for we would not know when purely invidious distinctions are being invoked or when a distinct rationale is being used to justify the inferior treatment of a particular racial group.

Finally, it should be noted that, unlike in biological racism, a rationale for minority subjugation is not logically implied in beliefs of cultural inferiority, because there it is not assumed that the minority race is biologically incapable of achieving equality with the dominant group. For example, racial stratification justified in terms of cultural criteria, particularly religion (Africans were viewed as heathens and therefore were not permitted to receive equal treatment with Europeans until they converted to Christianity), in South Africa during the seventeenth century did not lead to the conclusion that Africans could never reach equality with Europeans. Therefore, the arbitrary nature of racial stratification based on cultural

33

differences is more vulnerable to attack, and, as we shall see, in certain periods of history cultural racism was supplanted by biological racism to strengthen racial stratification.

Viewing racism as a philosophy of racial exploitation prescribing inferior treatment for a particular racial group reveals it to have a normative quality. In other words, racism produces certain societal or group norms indicating the way that dominant members ought to relate to or treat minority members. In this sense, both cultural and biological racism can be analyzed on three different levels—"institutional," "collective," and "individual."

When the ideology of racial exploitation gives rise to normative prescriptions designed to prevent the subordinate racial group from equal participation in associations or procedures that are stable, organized, and systematized (e.g., the electoral process, residential patterns, and formal education), institutional racism exists. Institutional racism therefore represents the structured aspect of racist ideology. The other two levels of racism are more unstructured elements of the ideology of racial exploitation. Specifically, collective racism connotes the existence of informal societal or group norms that specifically reinforce sporadic collective acts of racial discrimination, exploitation, and suppression (e.g., demonstrations against a black who moves into a white neighborhood or more violent acts such as lynchings or programs), whereas individual racism refers to a given person's set of attitudes (that members of the minority group are culturally or biologically inferior to the dominant group and therefore should be exploited or discriminated against) "derived from" or influenced by racist norms and ideology.

Although I take the position later in this chapter that racial stratification often exists before racist norms are developed, this does not in any way negate the importance or influence of racism on human behavior. To be more specific, explicit racist norms not only reinforce already established patterns of race exploitation (e.g., increasing group or individual motivation to discriminate), but they also may give rise to new forms of exploitation (e.g., psychic exploitation, that is, the dehumanization of minority individuals, leading them to question their humanity and lose their spirit of resistance to subjugation). Equally as important, racist beliefs regarding minority inferiority provide the needed justification for race exploitation when the system of inequality is challenged or criticized.

THE EMERGENCE OF RACISM IN SOCIETY

The development of racism in society is ultimately a collective process. Although a number of writers have focused on individual psychological factors in the etiology of racism, my position in this study is that racism can only be understood as a product of collective action. However, this does not mean that individual racism is not a legitimate subject of study; rather, it implies that individual racism, like collective and institutional racism, is a product of an ongoing process of group interaction whereby the status and behavior of the minority group are defined and redefined with respect to the dominant group.

This position is based on Herbert Blumer's path-breaking analysis of "Race Prejudice as a Sense of Group position."[16] Although Blumer's analysis is devoted to explaining the nature of what he calls "race prejudice,"[17] as we shall see his arguments, with a few modifications, are useful in a conceptual framework of racism; therefore, I shall outline the central propositions of Blumer's study. He states:

> A basic understanding of race prejudice must be sought in the process by which racial groups form images of themselves and of others. This process . . . is fundamentally *a collective process*. It operates chiefly through the public media in which individuals who are accepted as spokesmen of a racial group characterize publicly another racial group. To characterize another racial group is, by opposition, to define one's own group. This is equivalent to placing the two groups in relation to each other, or defining their position vis-à-vis each other. It is the sense of social position emerging from the collective process of characterization which provides the basis of race prejudice.[18]

Blumer has outlined four basic types of feeling that constitute dominant-group "prejudice": (1) an attitude that the minority race is inferior,[19] (2) a sense that the minority race is intrinsically alien and different, (3) a feeling of prior claim to certain rights and privileges, and (4) an apprehensiveness that the minority plans to encroach on or challenge the dominant group's prerogatives. Blumer notes that even though the first two feelings engender antipathy toward the minority group and the third makes dominant-group members believe that they are entitled to either prior or exclusive rights in many important spheres of life, these feelings are not in themselves sufficient to create "race prejudice." In fact, Blumer emphasizes that these three feelings are often prevalent in caste societies and in certain types of feudalism where, because claims have become crystallized into a structure respected and accepted by all, group "prejudice" does not seem to exist. He maintains that it is the fourth feeling, the apprehensiveness that the subordinate racial group is about to challenge the dominant group's position, that is essential to "race prejudice." This fear is often reflected in the dominant group's hostile cries that the subordinate racial group is "getting out of place."

Because the minority group is considered to be inferior, alien, without prior rights or privileges, and threatening, it is easy for dominant members to develop a sense of group position vis-à-vis the subordinate members. There is, to be sure, considerable variance in the feelings of dominant members toward the subordinate group, ranging from bitter hostility and strong antipathy to mild contempt and condescension. But the common denominator is the sense of superior group position.[20] Because dominant members often feel compelled to behave in accordance with group expectations, the sense of group position actually serves as a special kind of social norm, particularly for individuals who strongly identify with or consider themselves a part of the group. Blumer comments:

> Thus, even though given individual members may have personal views and feelings different from the sense of group position, they will have to conjure with the sense of group position held by their racial group. If the sense of position is

strong, to act contrary to it is to risk a feeling of self alienation and to face the possibility of ostracism. I am trying to suggest, accordingly, that the locus of race prejudice is not in the area of individual feeling but in the definition of the respective position of the racial group.[21]

The sense of group position is a historical product often emerging from the conditions surrounding the initial contact situation, when one racial group establishes dominance over other groups. As the group in the dominant position continuously interacts with subordinate racial members, the sense of group position can either grow and become solidified, or it can never take root and become weak.

The collective image of the subordinate racial group is developed and shaped within the "public arena," which might include such media as the press, conventions, public meetings, and legislative assemblies.[22] Although most or even a significant percentage of dominant members do not directly participate in these public discussions, the views expressed are often assumed to be those of the dominant group. Individuals possessing persuasion resources, i.e., having power or prestige or believed to have considerable knowledge, are particularly influential in shaping public opinion.

Finally, Blumer stresses that the role played by powerful vested interests in shaping the sense of group position should not be ignored. For instance, individuals or groups profiteering off minority labor will often attempt to develop public opinion supporting this form of exploitation. They may openly denounce subordinates, describe them as unfit, and maintain that they pose a serious threat to the rights and privileges of dominant-group members. Because such discussions often give the appearance of having great collective significance, they are especially potent in increasing "racial prejudice." If not seriously challenged within the dominant group, negative characterizations of racial subordinates will solidify the sense of group position, help to preserve the racial order, and protect the interests of special parties benefiting from racial subordination. Blumer concludes his analysis by pointing out that

When events touching on relations are not treated as "big events" and hence do not set crucial issues in the arena of public discussion; or when the elite leaders or spokesmen do not define such big events vehemently or adversely; or where they define them in the direction of racial harmony; or when there is a paucity of strong interest groups seeking to build up a strong adverse image for special advantage— under such conditions the sense of group position recedes and race prejudice declines.[23]

In interpreting Blumer's statements, it is important to note the meaning he assigns to the term "race prejudice." Although the terms "race prejudice" and "racism" are often used interchangeably, for the purposes of this study they are distinguished on the following grounds: Whereas race prejudice, traditionally defined, connotes individual or group feelings of antipathy toward a particular racial group because of "objectionable qualities ascribed to the group,"[24] these feelings may or may not involve assumptions that the disdained group is inferior. Racism specifically incorporates the concept of a particular racial group's believing another group to be biologically or culturally inferior. Moreover, unlike racism, prejudice cannot be readily classified as an ideology of racial domination. Commenting on prejudice as an attitude, Noel states:

While it is meaningful to speak of positive attitudes, including positive prejudices, the concept of prejudice generally implies a negative orientation. This is particularly true in the interethnic context. Hence we can define prejudice as a hostile or negative attitude toward the members of a specific group solely because they are members of that group. In contrast to ethnocentrism, with its in-group focus and derivative generalized rejection of out-groups, prejudice is focused on and directed toward a specific out-group.[25]

My position is that Blumer's analysis is actually more of racism than of either race prejudice or ethnocentrism. To be more explicit, two of the basic feelings of dominant-group "prejudice" (the subordinate racial group is naturally inferior and intrinsically alien) outlined in his study are directly related to my prior discussion of racist ideology based on beliefs asserting the biological and cultural inferiority of the minority group.

There are two other major points of convergence between Blumer's analysis and my discussion of the components of racism: First, his statement that the dominant group feels that it has prior claim to certain rights and privileges is indicative of racist social norms. Indeed, Blumer acknowledges a direct association between proprietary claims of advantages and beliefs of racial superiority.[26] Second, Blumer's argument that individual "race prejudices" must be studied in conjunction with the sense of group position is consistent with my supposition that the manifestation of individual racism is, to a large extent, a function of the social norms that define racial group contact. Individual acts of racism cannot be exclusively explained by personality factors. Psychological explanations, often invoked to explain individual attitudes and acts of discrimination, prove to have little predictive value when social factors are taken into account.[27]

However, the basic difference between my formulation and Blumer's has to do with his inclusion of the fourth feeling (the apprehension that the minority group plans to encroach on the dominant group's prerogatives) as an element of "race prejudice" (or racism). Rather than considering this feeling as one of the indicators of racism, I feel that it is more appropriately viewed as one of the variables that help to predict the existence, form, and intensity of racism in society. This point is discussed more fully later.

In concluding this section, I need to explain a point about the sense of group position among subordinates. Unlike that of dominant members, their collective image is in part a result of negative factors such as lack of power resources, discriminatory treatment by dominant members, and restricted rights and privileges. Although subordinate racial members may be able to offset a negative group image by cultivating other aspects of their experience, (e.g., their cultural achievements), the more dependent they are on the dominant group for survival and the greater their desire is to share the rights and privileges of the dominant group, the less likely they will be to sustain a group ethnocentrism. Furthermore, as long as the subordinate group remains in a state of subjection and dependency, an ideology of exploitation based on claims of dominant-group cultural and/or biological inferiority is unlikely to take root. It is true, however, that in time some exploited groups attempt to overcome the effects of racial oppression through cultural revitalization and nationalistic movements, which frequently develop in conjunction with efforts to establish some degree of political and economic autonomy. And the more minority members press for their independence, the more likely racist views toward the dominant group could mature.

RACISM, POWER, AND THE EMERGENCE OF RACIAL STRATIFICATION

The sense of group position must be understood as a summation of historical experiences, often originating when racial groups first establish contact. Although racism is most certainly a *sufficient condition* for a group's sense of collective identity vis-à-vis other groups, it is not a *necessary condition* for the development of a firm sense of group position. In fact, a coherent philosophy of racism is most likely to occur after a sense of group position has been crystallized. Let me elaborate on this point.

Group differences in cultural or behavioral patterns universally provide the basis for collective identities. Ethnocentrism, a phenomenon characteristic of all racial and ethnic groups, increases awareness of these differences. In fact, regardless of how extreme the dissimilarity of cultural patterns of groups in contact, there will be *mutual* ethnocentrism if each is able to maintain its autonomy. Noel has applied this argument to the early relations between the European settlers and the American Indians:

> Indians in the Americas did not automatically surrender their ethnocentrism in the face of European technology and

scientific superiority. Indeed, if the cultural strengths (including technology) of the outgroup are not relevant to the values and goals of the ingroup they will, by the very nature of ethnocentrism, be negatively defined.[28]

On the other hand, if the ingroup finds itself in a dependent relationship with the outgroup (or vice versa), wherein both share the same social order but with differential power resources, ethnocentrism will be greater among the group in the dominant position. Ethnocentrism, having its basis in perceived cultural differences between groups, receives its strength from perceived differences in power. These two factors, ethnocentrism and differential power, shape the sense of group position among dominant- and subordinate-group members.

For distinct racial groups, perceived differences in skin color further contribute to the formation and crystallization of a sense of group position. As I have attempted to show, although invidious comparisons of a subordinate group's culture and physical features constitute ethnocentrism, they also provide the necessary, but not sufficient, condition for racism.[29]

However, the question before us is what are the factors that give rise to cultural and biological racism? Before even attempting to answer such a question, we should briefly consider the historical proposition that in societies where initial contact between particular racial groups *is not* preceded by a tradition of race exploitation, the development of racism, if indeed it emerges at all, takes place after racial stratification has been firmly established.[30] Racism is therefore not essential for racial stratification. The factor that is absolutely necessary to the emergence of racial stratification is differential power. Without an unequal power balance, group efforts to achieve racial domination will simply generate conflict until a state of symbiosis or pluralistic equilibrium is reached.[31] Although differential power provides the basis for a system of racial stratification, group desires to control or maximize scarce resources furnish the motivation for developing the system and for putting it into operation. As I noted previously, control of scarce resources may be maintained or increased either through the elimination of the subordinate racial members as competitors or through the exploitation of their labor.

Group vested interest leading to racial stratification is ultimately a product of the original sense of group position: the initial collective identity that develops because of differential racial power, skin color, and cultural differences and the subjective state of ethnocentrism that feeds on the differences. The more that dominant-group members identify with their group position, the greater is the likelihood that they will strive to perpetuate their position. It is out of this process that group interests are defined and special norms are developed in turn to protect these interests.

But dominant members may have ethnocentric feelings or contempt for minority culture and behavior patterns and still not attempt to justify their privileged position with claims of cultural or biological superiority, thereby obviating the need for a rationale to support racial exploitation. I previously mentioned caste systems and feudal societies in which claims of superiority were openly respected or accepted by all.[32] On the other hand, a rationale could be based simply on notions that it is in the dominant group's best interest to create and sustain racial stratification without any reference to minority traits or characteristics.[33]

However, when the system of racial stratification is challenged both by subordinates seeking to share the dominant group's rights and privileges and by other individuals and groups opposed to race exploitation, the need for a more explicit and forceful justification of racial domination emerges. This is when dominant-group spokesmen with vested interests begin to denounce the subordinate racial group publicly.

Available historical evidence is not sufficient to allow us to advance propositions concerning the origins of cultural and biological racism with any degree of certitude. What evidence we do have from our examination of the emergence of racism in Western societies suggests that both forms of racism tend to emerge and develop when racial stratification is under challenge and the position of the dominant group is being threatened.[34] The greater the challenge to racial stratification, the more likely it is that biological racism rather than cultural racism will be used both to justify dominant-group claims of prior rights and privileges and to reinforce already established patterns of race subordination. However, this hypothesis must be advanced cautiously, because the development of racist thought is to some extent dependent on existing societal conceptions of man and human behavior derived from a society's theology, science, philosophy, and so on, and therefore belief in biological racism may be more easily nurtured in one period of time than in another.

Unlike cultural racism, biological racism provides dominant members with an ideology convincing them of the inevitability of their rule. They can claim that they are in a superior position because they are naturally superior, that subordinate members do not possess qualities enabling them to compete on equal terms. Such beliefs solidify the sense of group position, reinforce patterns of racial subordination, and provide a powerful rebuttal to humanitarian attacks against race exploitation.

In the final analysis, regardless of the manner in which the minority group is demeaned (on the basis of either cultural traits or physical attributes) in public deliberations to preserve the racial order, if such discussions are continuous rather than intermittent, are capable of generating and sustaining collective interests, and are not neutralized or offset by arguments opposed to racial stratification, it is overwhelmingly probable that norms of racial subordination will be generated. The net effect is the development of racism on individual, collective, and institutional levels. Although all three levels of racism have harmful social and psychological effects (this is particularly true if the racist norms are based on assumptions of biological inferiority, because the humanity of minority individuals is called into question), in the long run institutional racism has the most serious consequences. As long as minority individuals are excluded by racist norms from meaningful participation in the ongoing process of institutional life, their chances of developing the power resources needed to promote or protect their interests are seriously limited. However, even institutional racism and discrimination undergo change in the face of sufficient pressures, but this is a matter to be discussed in the next chapter.

NOTES

1. *Report of the National Advisory Commission on Civil Disorders* (New York: Bantam Press, 1968).

2. See, for example, Gary T. Marx, "Two Cheers for the National Riot Commission," in *Black Americans*, ed. by J. Szwed (New York: Basic Books, 1970), pp. 78–96. William K. Tabb, "Race Relations Models and Social Change," *Social Problems*, 18:431–444 (Spring 1971).

3. Marx, op. cit., p. 83.

4. Richard Schermerhorn, *Comparative Ethnic Relations: A Framework for Theory and Research* (New York: Random House, 1970), and Donald L. Noel, "Slavery and the Rise of Racism," in *The Origins of American Slavery and Racism*, ed. by Donald L. Noel (Columbus, O.: Merrill, 1972), pp. 153–174.

5. Schermerhorn, op. cit., p. 73.

6. Ibid., p. 74.

7. Noel, op. cit., pp. 170–171.

8. Ibid., p. 156.

9. Ibid., p. 157.

10. Ibid., p. 156.

11. Winthrop D. Jordan, *White over Black: American Attitudes Toward the Negro 1550–1812* (Chapel Hill: U. of North Carolina, 1968), p. 7.

12. Ibid.

13. Ibid., p. 26. This subject is discussed more fully in Chapter Five.

14. This definition could apply to both the dominant and the subordinate racial groups. However, if both groups share the same social order, it would be more difficult for subordinate racial members to develop and sustain a racist philosophy, because they have an inferior status and lack the power resources of the dominant group (this point is further discussed in a later section of this chapter). In this study, my concern is with racism among dominant group members and the way it sustains and reinforces racial stratification.

15. The concept of cultural racism advanced in this study should not be confused with the term as used by James M. Jones in his study of prejudice and racism. Jones states: "In its broadest sense, cultural racism is very closely related to ethnocentrism. However, a significant factor which transcends simple ethnocentrism is power. This power to significantly affect the lives of people who are ethnically and/or culturally different is the factor which transforms white ethnocentrism into white, cultural racism." The problem with Jones's discussion of cultural racism is that its broad application does not allow one to distinguish sheer exploitation or discrimination without a racist base from exploitation guided by a philosophy of racial domination. See James M. Jones, *Prejudice and Racism* (Reading, Mass.: Addison-Wesley, 1972), p. 149.

16. Herbert Blumer, "Race Prejudice as a Sense of Group Position," *Pacific Sociological Review*, 1:3–7 (Spring 1958).

17. See pp. 38–39 for a distinction between racism and race prejudice.

18. Blumer, op. cit., pp. 3–4.

19. Commenting on this first feeling, Blumer states: "In race prejudice there is a self-assured feeling on the part of the dominant racial group of being naturally superior or better. This is commonly shown in a disparagement of the qualities of the subordinate racial group. Condemnatory or debasing traits, such as laziness, dishonesty, greediness, unreliability, stupidity, deceit, and immorality, are usually imputed to it." Ibid., p. 4.

20. Ibid., p. 5. For a related discussion of this point, see Roger Daniels and Harry H. L. Kitano, *American Racism: Exploration of the Nature of Prejudice* (Englewood Cliffs, N.J.: Prentice-Hall, 1970), chaps. 1 and 2, and E. Franklin Frazier, "Theoretical Structures of Sociology and Sociological Research," *British Journal of Sociology*, 4:292–311 (Dec. 1953).

21. Blumer, op. cit., p. 5.

22. Because the subordinate group is defined as an aggregate entity, this collective image tends to be abstract. "While actual encounters are with individuals," writes Blumer, "the picture formed of the racial group is necessarily a vast entity which spreads out far beyond such individuals and transcends experience with such individuals." Ibid., p. 6.

23. Ibid., p. 7.

24. Gordon W. Allport, *The Nature of Prejudice* (New York: Addison-Wesley, 1954), p. 12.

25. Noel, op. cit., pp. 158–159.

26. Blumer, op. cit., p. 4.

27. After examining sociological studies of racial attitudes, van den Berghe was led to conclude that if racism is overtly and blatantly endorsed, individuals will exhibit racist behavior regardless of personality factors. Van den Berghe also notes that psychological explanations of racist behavior have their greatest explanatory power in situations where individuals practice racial discrimination despite the fact that strong social norms exist prohibiting expression of racism. In such instances, he notes, racial bigotry fulfills a psychological need. However, such cases represent the exception rather than the rule. Pierre van den Berghe, *Race and Racism: A Comparative Perspective* (New York: Wiley, 1967), p. 20; also see Lewis M. Killian, "The Adjustment of Southern White Migrants to Urban Norms," *Social Forces*, 32:66–69 (Oct. 1953), and "The Effects of Southern White Workers on Race Relations in Northern Plants," *American Sociological Review*, 17:327–331 (June 1952); and Bruno Bettelheim and Morris Janowitz, *Social Change and Prejudice* (New York: Free Press, 1964), p. 77.

28. Noel, op. cit., p. 159.

29. It is easier to distinguish these two ideas on a conceptual basis than it is to apply them empirically. Obviously, some dominant-group behavior typically characterized as racist will at times exhibit elements of ethnocentrism, and, conversely, behavior typically defined as ethnocentric will sometimes manifest elements of racism. There will always be some overlapping when these concepts are empirically applied.

30. This is true of Western societies, where a racist ideology did not develop until after contact was made with the Africans. For further discussion of this point, see Chapter Five.

31. Noel, op. cit., p. 163.

32. Blumer, op. cit., p. 4.

33. In this regard, Thorpe has stated that, unlike in the United States, "Latin American culture accepted the institution of slavery as a necessary evil . . . there was no need to create myths and stereotypes to justify the institution." Earle E. Thorpe, "Chattel Slavery and Concentration Camps," in *Slavery and Its Aftermath*, ed. by Peter I. Rose (New York: Atherton, 1970), p. 58.

34. Some of this evidence will be examined closely in subsequent chapters by drawing on historical data from the United States and the Republic of South Africa.

CHAPTER FOUR
Power, Racism, and the Theoretical Basis of Racial Conflict

SOCIAL scientists have often remarked that rebellions against institutionalized inequality by an oppressed racial group are least likely to occur in a rigidly stratified system characterized by the dominant group's almost complete control over the lives of the subordinate group.[1] With few exceptions, the empirical evidence indicates that the major preoccupation of the subordinate racial group in such societies is with survival, the day-to-day struggle to satisfy basic physical needs. "Far from making people into revolutionaries," states James C. Davies, "enduring poverty makes for concern with one's solitary self or solitary family at best and resignation or mute despair at worst."[2] However, in some situations some members of the oppressed minority may manage to improve their position to a point where the satisfaction of their basic human needs becomes a secondary concern, and as their status improves their expectations increase and dissatisfaction with their position in society intensifies. It is only when subjugated racial members sense the possibility of change that they are likely to apply pressure to improve their situation.

Gary T. Marx has incorporated this principle in his analysis of black militancy in America:

> militancy requires at least some degree of hope, a belief in the possibility of beautiful tomorrows. Morale is needed— which, although linked with dissatisfaction, is the opposite

47

of despair. A sense of futility would seem to work against the development of the morale and hope required for a militant vision. One of the reasons that militancy is more pronounced among those in higher positions may be that this group is more likely to have the high morale needed to sustain it. No matter how dissatisfied and distraught an individual may be over his personal and group situation, unless his discontent is found together with a positive morale, it is likely to lead not to militancy but to apathy, despair, and estrangement.

This does not mean that the underprivileged are filled with love or respect for the system that oppresses them. But they are likely to lack the energy, incentive, and will to challenge it in the disciplined way of civil rights organizations. If their concern does lead to attack, it is more likely to take the form of violent outbursts.[3]

Nevertheless, in some cases the power gap between the dominant group and the minority group may be so great that the minority's desire for change is superseded by the conviction that any effort to effect change will be abortive. Accordingly, despite increased minority motivation to overcome oppressive conditions, interracial relationships may continue to exist in what Schermerhorn has called a state of "integration" —in which the various groups of society actively and coordinately comply with norms of the dominant members.[4] Race relations observers may often interpret open compliance with or accommodation to oppression as an indication of minority acceptance of racial stratification when it more nearly reflects the subordinate group's pessimism about successful resistance. I believe that a comprehensive theory of minority mobilization of power resources (i.e., "the portion of the total resources that are actually utilized or expended to achieve a given objective"[5]) must take into consideration, not only a group's desire for change, but also (1) its expectation that change can in fact be brought about and (2) its perception of the rewards and punishments associated with change.[6] If a group's desire for change is low and/or it feels unable to apply the kinds of pressure needed to effect significant change, or if a group feels that regardless of the kinds of pressure applied the cost of resistance is too high for the rewards, then the probability is great that it *will not* take steps to challenge the racial order. In the final analysis, a group's beliefs regarding its ability or inability to produce change are based on perceptions of both its own relative power resources and the magnitude of the problem to be solved.

Perceptions of power resources often are related to judgments concerning the degree or type of pressure needed to produce the best results, ranging from the employment of formal procedures such as litigation and the exercise of political franchise to the use of open rebellion or revolution. Two major factors operate to explain the utilization of the latter, more violent forms of protest: (1) "a prolonged period of rising expectations and rising gratification followed by a short period of sharp reversal during which the gap between expectations and gratification quickly widens and becomes intolerable"[7] and (2) a belief that the desired change can only be successfully accomplished by accelerating and intensifying the protests. The first factor incorporates the central hypothesis of Davies' "J-curve" theory of revolution and rebellions[8]; however, it provides only a necessary condition for the outbreak of these forms of protest. In order to predict whether the revolt will in fact occur, whether it will escalate to the level of a rebellion or to that of a revolution, consideration also must be given to the second factor.[9] A minority group's faith in the efficacy of violent tactics can be traced to its assessment of both the dominant group's possession of power resources and its willingness to mobilize these resources in order to suppress a revolt.

Although it could be argued that some rebellions are spontaneous and do not involve calculated and rational decisions, nonetheless even in such cases the participants are cognizant of the possible consequences. There is little evidence to support the thesis that the oppressed strike out blindly with suicidal fervor and with little regard for their personal and group welfare. Planned revolts such as revolutions or organized rebellions quite clearly are based on an assessment, accurate or inaccurate, of the prospects of success and the possible returns. In fact, the more the rebellious group has to lose by the use of violent forms of protest, the less likely it is willing to take the necessary risks. Even those who argue that little is to be lost and everything to be gained by a violent uprising must confront the distasteful possibility that they could lose their lives, however miserable their lives might be.

The more restrictive the social structure, the greater are the risks minority members take when they attempt to protest. In very restrictive social structures, e.g., autocratic slavery systems, not only is the power discrepancy between the minority group and the dominant group relatively fixed (although in time all structural relations undergo some change), but also any form of collective minority protest is likely to generate rather severe repression from dominant racial members.

Rather than leading to attacks against the racial order, minority response to racial subjugation frequently assumes the form of nationalist or separatist movements. More specifically, in a society where the subordinate and dominant racial groups share the same social order and pursue the same scarce goals (e.g., jobs, land, and capital) and where subordinate racial members find themselves in more of a dependent than an autonomous relationship with the dominant group, minority nationalist sentiment will tend to be high during periods when the struggle for racial equality seems hopeless or when intense frustration and disillusionment follow a span of heightened expectations. Accordingly, the less minority members depend on dominant members for, say, jobs, housing, and education, the more nationalist sentiment will depend on events internal to the minority community, and therefore the less will it be affected by the behavior of dominant racial members (e.g., the development of more virulent racist norms) or events outside of the community.

The major attraction of nationalist movements is that parallel institutions or societies could be established free of, or removed from, dominant-group control. Nationalist movements may range from those proclaiming positive race identity, including elaboration and/or development of the racial group's historical and cultural identity (cultural nationalism), to those that attempt to gain control of minority social, economic, and political institutions and/or establish separate institutions (institutional nationalism). Central to all nationalist movements is a strong emphasis on racial solidarity.

The success of institutional nationalist movements is dependent on (1) sufficient minority resources to develop and sustain autonomous institutions, (2) support of rank and file minority members ready to abandon the struggle to achieve assimilation in the larger society, and (3) support from dominant members who are willing to sacrifice any possible losses from subordinate-group separation (e.g., relinquishing control of minority labor and of institutions serving the minority community). The more minority nationalists renounce all desire to be incorporated into the larger society, the less of a threat they pose to dominant-group claims of prior rights and privileges. It is true that dominant members differ in their responses to various forms of institutional nationalism. Dominant-group entrepreneurs, for instance, are likely to be far less enthusiastic about the voluntary withdrawal of minority participation in the market place than are others who are not directly affected by such action. Moreover, industrialists who depend on subordinate-group labor are likely to resist any efforts to establish a *totally* separate and independent minority society. However, other aspects of institutional nationalism that are not central to dominant-group livelihood, such as the isolation of residential areas and the separation of social events, are not only likely to receive far less resistance from dominant members, but, depending on the level of racism in society, could very well be strongly supported. In short, the less that dominant members suffer from minority withdrawal, the more they will tolerate and sometimes encourage minority separatism.[10]

The basic thesis implicit in this discussion is that social structures vary with regard to the types of minority response to racial subordination they generate and tolerate. This point is amplified and made explicit in the following section.

RESTRICTIVENESS OF THE SOCIAL STRUCTURE AND MOBILIZATION OF POWER RESOURCES

According to Pierre van den Berghe, "it is reasonable to accept [the fact] that basic aspects of the social structure exert a considerable degree of determinism on the prevailing type of race relations"[11] in society. Nowhere is this relationship more clearly demonstrated than in his rather elaborate typology of competitive versus paternalistic systems of race relations. Grounded on both historical and comparative data, this typology is designed (1) to relate interaction patterns between the dominant and subordinate racial groups to basic structural variables (i.e., the economy, division of labor, and social stratification), (2) to provide a basis for analyzing the mode of race relations at a given period of time, (3) to consider the reasons for the changing forms of race relations through time, and (4) to compare patterns of race relations in different cultures.

The paternalistic form of race relations is, according to van den Berghe, "characteristic of fairly complex but preindustrial societies, in which agriculture and handicraft production constitute the basis of the economy."[12] In such societies, the economy is controlled by an aristocratic segment of the dominate group numerically a relatively small part of the total population. Wide discrepancies exist between the dominant and subordinate groups in income, education, occupation, life style, and death and birth rates. These gaps reflect racial divisions that are reinforced and solidified by a caste system prohibiting mobility except within the racial castes. By rationalizing its rule, the dominant group develops an ideology of "benevolent despotism" and regards the members of the minority group "as inferior, but lovable, as long as they stay in 'their place.' "[13]

An elaborate, symbolized etiquette marked by asymmetrical manners of address and speaking, stringent regulations, and continuous manifestations of subservience and dominance maximizes the differences between the roles and statuses of the dominant and subordinate groups and allows for "close symbiosis and even intimacy, without any threat to status inequalities."[14] This sytem of racial differentiation does not give rise to physical isolation: there is no designed attempt by the dominant group to control the minority group via physical separation, because the elaborate procedures of racial etiquette maintain control of the subordinate group.

As long as the system is not challenged by the subordinate racial group, dominant-group racism is likely to be characterized, not by virulent hatred, but by "pseudotolerance." However, overt racial conflict may flare up in infrequent, periodic ways, generally in the form of minority slave revolts or messianistic, revivalistic, or nationalistic movements.

In short, paternalistic regimes are "extreme examples of tyranny over, and exploitation of, the many by the few. The relative stability of these regimes is partly a product of coercion and, at least as importantly, of close, intimate, albeit highly unequal symbiosis."[15]

Competitive race relations, the polar extreme of paternalistic relations, are generally associated with *industrialized and urbanized society*. Here the dominant group may be a numerical majority or constitute more than 20 or 25 per cent of the total population. Because a heavy price in productivity would have to be paid if racial ascription of occupations was maintained, the gap between the castes of dominant and subservient groups tends to narrow, not only in occupation, but consequently also in education, income, and life style.[16] The racial distinction is still present, but "class differences become more salient relative to caste; that is, there is a greater range of class status within castes."[17]

As the line between the castes diminishes and economic competition increases between the subordinate group and lower-class segments of the dominant group, hatred and bigotry are frequently manifested. Physical segregation is introduced to protect the dominant group's position. Thus the amount of contact between the castes is minimized, and the society is increasingly compartmentalized. Segregation becomes spatial.

The political system of the dominant group generally takes the form of a regime that restricts the exercise of de jure as well as de facto power to dominant-group members. Political consciousness on the part of the subordinate group becomes a catalyst for rebellion; "conflict is endemic and frequently erupts in both dominant and subordinate groups in the form of lynchings, pogroms, race riots, and terrorism as well as disciplined mass movements of political opposition ranging from ordinary demonstrations to passive resistance."[18]

With this summary of the central features of van den Berghe's typology of paternalistic and competitive systems of race relations, I will now attempt to spell out the kinds of power relations one would expect to find in both paternalistic and competitive systems.

Power and paternalistic systems. The subordinate group in a paternalistic system of race relations tends to lack control of sufficient power resources to seriously challenge the racial order. The dominant group's position approaches absolute control over the lives of subordinate racial members. Attempts to resist racial subordination do occur but tend to be limited to the exercise of constraint or pressure resources (i.e., resources used to coerce or punish a group to behave in the desired manner), because the minority group lacks inducement or persuasion resources. The fact that some segments of the minority population are inclined to exercise constraint resources (e.g., slave revolts) indicates a degree of alienation from the system and a rejection of its norms.

The frequency, degree, and type of constraint resources used by subordinate members in a paternalistic system are based to some extent on beliefs regarding their ability to change the system to make their lives more satisfactory. Historians have pointed out that slave revolts in the antebellum South (which was characterized by a paternalistic system of race relations) were more likely to occur near large urban areas, where the slaves were more literate and conscious of their oppressed condition and not as rigidly controlled and suppressed as those in servitude on large plantations.[19] Moreover, it has been argued that both the French and Indian War and the War of 1812 increased the probability of slave revolts because the local militia was drafted to fight in these wars, thus leaving the areas they patrolled to prevent slave rebellions unprotected.[20]

Given the rigidity of the paternalistic system, it seems warranted to conclude that the subordinate group's motivation[21] to exert pressure would be low in all but a few paternalistic regimes,[22] primarily because the dominant group's controls are so strong that few would even entertain the possibility of successfully effecting change. In fact, the dominant group in paternalistic systems, recognizing and fearing the possibility that the subordinate group might use its constraint resources, will tend to rely almost solely on coercion as a means of controlling the subordinate group. The relative stability of paternalistic systems is based on unlimited coercion.

Power and competitive systems. Power relations between dominant and subordinate groups in a paternalistic system are in sharp contrast to those typical of a competitive system. There is more power reciprocity or feedback between the superordinate and subordinate groups in a competitive system. Majority-group members in a competitive system frequently find themselves vulnerable to applied minority constraint resources such as sit-ins, boycotts, and riots. In many cases, the use of constraint resources enables minority members to obtain certain competitive resources. Thus political pressures and economic boycotts can be used to effect changes leading to improved housing, upgraded occupations, and higher-quality education. It is also the case, however, that as minority members acquire competitive resources they move into direct competition with some members of the dominant group, particularly those of the lower strata. If the latter feel that their own status or security is in jeopardy, they will tend to manifest hostility and resentment toward the minority group, ranging from verbal assaults to violent attacks against persons and property.

However, the degree to which certain dominant members express their racial hostility is based not only on the vulnerability of the minority group to belligerent attacks but also on the prevailing norms that define proper interracial behavior. If individual or group attacks against the minority race do not bring strong sanctions either from minority members themselves or from dominant authorities, racial violence perpetrated against the subordinate race will continue unabated.

However, a competitive system of race relations may undergo considerable change during a relatively short period of time, and the manner in which racial violence is managed may be consequently altered. Patterns of interracial behavior do not tend to be as immutable as they are in paternalistic systems. For our purposes, therefore, we may place competitive systems of race relations along a continuum from the relatively restrictive to the relatively fluid or open.[23] Examples from American history may help clarify this point. From 1890 to the first two decades of the twentieth century, the period known as the "golden age of racism," race relations in the United States were the epitome of a restrictive competitive system. Although black people theoretically were free to compete with whites, in most areas of life the repressive and often violent Jim Crow system with its inherent policy of discrimination and segregation reinforced by virulent racial norms severely reduced the blacks' chances of developing competitive resources. Moreover, because of the high probability of overwhelming suppressive reactions by the white majority, blacks were unlikely to resort to the use of activist constraint resources such as protest demonstrations or rioting against property. Organized resentment against the racial order more typically assumed the form of separatist or nationalist movements such as those led by Bishop Turner and Marcus Garvey in the late nineteenth and early twentieth centuries, but such movements represented a retreat from rather than an attack against the social order. Since this period, as blacks have been able to accumulate some competitive resources and apply sanctions against the white power structure by exercising constraint resources, race relations in the United States have slowly moved toward the other polar extreme of the competitive system, i.e., fluid competitive race relations.

Although minority members in a fluid rather than a restrictive competitive system are more likely to apply constraint resources to eliminate racial inequities, it is also the case that as their persuasion and inducement resources increase, their reliance on constraint as a means of influence is reduced. In fact, constraint resources tend to be employed only when the minority group does not possess sufficient inducement and persuasion resources to bring about desired changes.[24] In some instances, however, persuasion or inducement resources may be combined with constraint resources. Killian et al. apply this argument to nonviolent resistance movements:

> Non-violent protest constituted a mixed strategy of influence. The rhetoric of the movement emphasized its reliance on persuasion, on appealing to the conscience of white Americans. The demonstration of the capacity of blacks for love and long suffering, even in the face of violent white retaliation, was supposed to love the white man into submission to black demands. At the same time, the strategy involved relied on constraints. Civil rights leaders could be sure that the frantic response of white authorities and white citizens to even the most peaceful sit-in, kneel-in, or freedom ride would disrupt any community in which such a demonstration was staged.[25]

Although some pressure to change the racial order is directed at dominant-group citizens in general, minority protests such as nonviolent resistance are ultimately aimed at dominant authorities, particularly authorities of the administrative branch of the government, who tend to have greater power to satisfy demands for racial justice—depending, of course, on whether the protest is directed at municipal, state, or national authorities. Assuming therefore that minority pressures against the government include the presentation of certain demands, there are theoretically at least three steps governmental authorities may take in response to these pressures: (1) attempt to meet all of the demands, (2) present a conciliatory offer (e.g., grant some but not all of the demands, reject the demands but propose to act on alternative solutions to the basic grievances, or promise to give the matter some thought without commitment to a specific course of action), and (3) invoke some means of social control over the minority partisans by preventing their access to resources and their ability to use them.[26]

The first option is most likely to be exercised (1) if the demands are specific rather than diffuse and if they are consistent with the ideals or values that the government is committed to uphold, (2) if the authorities feel that the dissenting minority possesses resources that could be used to seriously damage their political fortunes, and (3) if the authorities believe that failure to satisfy all of the demands would be more harmful politically than pursuing an alternative course of action. The government's selection of the first option is therefore an indication that the minority partisans possess sufficient resources to accomplish their main objectives.[27]

The second option represents an attempt to relax the pressures without meeting the original demands. Concessions are often granted essentially to maintain the balance of power in the government's favor. As William Gamson has noted, "Social movements may falter on partial success, winning small victories which, while leaving basic dissatisfaction untouched, hamper the members in their ability to mobilize resources for further influence."[28] The extent to which the conciliatory offer approximates or departs from the original set of demands is a function of two major factors: (1) the nature of the original demands—the more diffuse and extreme the original demands, the more the government's offer fails to satisfy them —and (2) the regard the governmental authorities have for the dissenting group—the greater the resources possessed by the minority, the greater the government's concern for the possible political consequences of their action and the more its conciliatory offer satisfies the original set of demands.

Finally, the third option will tend to be chosen by governmental officials if the demands are considered extreme and diffuse and, more importantly, the dissenting minority possesses insufficient resources to persuade or pressure the government to meet the demands or grant concessions. Stated differently, the fewer power resources a group possesses, the more likely is the government to ignore its demands and exert social control to eliminate the pressure. The third option is more frequently exercised in restrictive competitive systems. On the other hand, fluid competitive systems present more the opposite situation. Frequently there are some segments of the minority population in a position to command the respect and attention of the larger community because of their possession and effective utilization of persuasion, inducement, and constraint resources.

Racism and Racial Conflict

As race relations approach a fluid competitive system, beliefs concerning minority cultural or biological inferiority are undermined and their debilitating effects on subordinate racial members are reduced. In other words, if the oppressed minority group can increase its power resources and move into positions once solely occupied by dominant members, institutional racism becomes exposed and is challenged, and individual racism and collective racism are undermined. Because of increasing opportunities for education and skilled training, subordinate members find themselves in a position to challenge the authority of the dominant group and exhibit degrees of competence and expertise that invalidate racist stereotypes. In the face of these changes, therefore, some members of the dominant group, particularly those receiving no direct material benefits from racial stratification, will come to question the legitimacy of an unequal distribution of rights and privileges and either withdraw support of racist norms or join other dominant members in an attack against the system of racism. The greatest threat to any form of racism, then, is the significant entry of minority members into upper-status positions within the larger society.

However, depending on the situation, racism can either heighten or diminish overt conflict. Specifically, racism reduces conflict when its effect on subordinate racial members is so penetrating that they actually suffer from psychic exploitation and hence define themselves as biologically or culturally inferior and attempt to identify with dominant norms and culture. Although often producing negative psychic reactions in subordinate racial members, racism also gives rise to "positive" psychic effects in dominant-group members in that it increases the sense of group position among dominants and contributes to their feeling of superiority. The more that dominant members internalize racist norms and beliefs, the greater is their support for a social structure denying the subordinate group access to positions of power, prestige, and influence and the more likely are they to resist efforts to change the racial order. Thus the combination of dominant-group resolve to conserve racial stratification and minority self-derogation provides the greatest possibilities for the preservation of the racial order and the fewest possibilities for racial conflict.[29]

However, as the power resources of minority members increase so that they are able to challenge the authority of the dominant group, they tend to develop a heightened awareness of and bitterness toward the racial order. This process often leads to open struggle against the system of racism in which efforts are made to revive and perpetuate aspects of the minority's racial or cultural heritage that have been disrupted by racism, thus weakening personal and group identities.

The increased awareness and rejection of racism by members of the minority group produces a kind of racial solidarity that becomes increasingly threatening to dominant-group members. Under these conditions, if the dominant group attempts to reinforce the system of racism or if it fails to take the steps defined by the minority group as necessary to eliminate or reduce racist exploitation, the chances of overt conflict are greatly enhanced.

The irony of the situation is that racial conflict is most likely to occur when the minority racial group experiences some improvement in their condition and senses the possibility for further improvement.[30] It is here that the continued existence of racism in society becomes more of a catalyst for minority rebellion and less of a mechanism for dominant-group social control.

SOCIAL CHANGE AND TYPES OF RACE RELATIONS

The shift from one system of race relations to another (e.g., from paternalistic to restrictive competitive or fluid competitive) is not simply the result of some natural evolutionary process but rather occurs because of fundamental societal changes, often beyond the interracial arena. I have in mind such factors as beginning or growing industrialization, urbanization, internal migration and immigration, political changes resulting from internal or external pressures on the government, revolutions, and civil wars. Because of such changes, racial groups may accumulate or lose resources, and long-term effects on the balance of power between the racial groups may be produced —effects often more significant than any race-related actions undertaken by the respective groups.[31] The more rapid the social change, the greater is the possibility that the social structure will loosen, thus making new resources available for either the dominant or the minority group to use to extend or alter the power balance in their favor.[32]

Although the subordinate racial members frequently are able to improve their absolute position in society (e.g., increased income, improved educational opportunities, upgraded occupations, and greater freedom of movement) as a result of societal changes, their relative position vis-à-vis the dominant group may remain the same because the latter may also experience an upswing in living conditions. Moreover, the absolute gains of minority members may be further neutralized by the dominant group's ability to introduce new mechanisms of social control and thus preserve their power advantage. In other words, a shift in the racial order may occur, but only in a lateral direction, with the dominant group merely transfering its control of the old institutions to new institutions ushered in by societal changes. Let us examine this process by focusing momentarily on the shift from paternalistic to competitive forms of race relations.[33]

In the race relations literature, it is commonly observed that the emergence of industrialization undermines the paternalistic racial order. To be more specific, certain innovations accompany industrialization such as severance of paternalistic dependency relations, dissolution of old and development of new occupations, breakdown of rural areas and villages with concurrent development of large urban centers, and increase of opportunities for vertical mobility as a result of the proliferation of skilled positions. In short, industrialization destroys many of the pillars of the established racial order, dislodges racial groups from their positions in society, and weakens or severs the bonds existing between them.

It has also been argued that in time the intrinsic tendencies of industrialization will undermine racist thinking. These tendencies represent "the structural requirement of industrialization" and include factors such as (1) the emphasis on rational perspectives, (2) the necessity of physical mobility, (3) the primacy of contractual relations, (4) the requirement of an impersonal market, (5) the allotment of resources on the grounds of productive receipts, and (6) the internal pressures that constantly activate the foregoing requirements.

A society undergoing industrialization therefore has a rather distinctive character, in which a premium is placed on rational decisions, in which social mobility is largely a consequence of individual merit and aptitude, hence undermining the importance attached to traditional group affiliation such as race, and in which secular interests form the basis of shifting alignments. In short, "status by achievement" replaces "status by ascription."

Finally, it is often assumed that where established relations between dominant and subordinate members in paternalistic regimes are forced, because of industrialization, to become competitive in areas where dominant members feel they have prior claim, racial tension and conflict ensue.

> The net import of this conventional view—even though it is not well developed—is that industrialisation introduces a transitional stage into race relations—a stage marked by unfamiliar association, competitive contact, and a challenge to previous social standing. Race relations become uncertain and instable. The shifts in them awaken suspicion, arouse resentment, occasion strain and provoke discord.[34]

These arguments constitute the basic postulates of the conventional thesis of industrialization and race relations and have been subjected to a penetrating critique by Blumer. As I understand them, the basic arguments in Blumer's rebuttal are as follows:

1. That it is a serious error to assume that industrialization necessarily leads to a basic transformation or displacement of the established racial order.

2. That in the early stages of industrialization, rational orientation "may compel an adherence to the racial system rather than a departure from it."[35] Employers may decide not to hire or promote minority workers because they fear a possible backlash by certain dominant-group workers that could lead to the disruption of efficient operation.

3. That the change from status relations to contractual relations and the increased possibilities for social mobility due to the proliferation of new occupations may not produce any basic changes in the respective positions of the racial groups. Subordinate racial members may find that certain ceilings are imposed on their job mobility, denying them skilled positions and limiting their options to only the most menial and poorly paid jobs.

4. That the racial conflict and tension attributed to emerging industrialization are not likely to occur in societies with an established racial order but rather in societies (a) where "industrialisation may bring together racial groups which previously have not had relations with each other or only tenuously defined positions with regard to each other" and (b) where "a firmly established racial order is definitely undergoing disintegration"[36] (usually brought about, not by pressures from industrial forces, but by nonindustrial influences).

5. That in the final analysis the "racial alignment is shaped in major measure by nonindustrial influences, that resulting patterns of racial alignment permeate the industrial structure, and that changes in such patterns are traceable mainly to movements in social and political happenings."[37]

As subsequent chapters will show, there is a good deal of empirical support for Blumer's thesis. Even though the shift from paternalistic to competitive race relations is facilitated by industrialization, we should expect to find little change in the racial order if the shift is not also accompanied by political and social pressures of sufficient magnitude to alter the racial alignment.[38] New resources may become available as a result of industrialization, but they are offset by new controls imposed by the dominant group. Race relations become competitive, but only in the narrowest sense. The system remains closed, with restricted minority mobility, restricted interracial competition, and consequently restricted areas of racial conflict.[39]

Although industrialization may not *directly* contribute to a realignment of the established racial order, it can contribute indirectly. We need only recognize that with the growth of industrialization comes the growth of urbanization. As expanding industry lures minority members to urban areas, they find themselves in a much better position to accumulate power resources. There are greater educational and occupational opportunities available in the cities. The usual political, social, and economic imperatives of urban living provide greater opportunities to develop viable minority institutions such as schools, churches, political and labor organizations, and professional and business associations. The physical proximity of large numbers of minority individuals facilitates communication, ideological development, group identity, and collective action. Furthermore, in urban areas the minority members are not as vulnerable to dominant attacks such as pogroms or lynchings as they are in rural areas. For all of these reasons, minority groups concentrated in urban areas are in a far better position to mount an offensive against racial oppression and move into more fluid competitive relations with dominant members.[40]

Because rapid social change tends to loosen the social structure and thereby create new resources for either the dominant or the subordinate group to employ in the interracial power contest, conflict and tension between the two groups may be expected to increase until a new balance of power is stabilized.[41]

The manifold ways in which the power balance is disrupted, stabilized, and disrupted again may be spelled out more easily through concrete examples than by further theoretical discussion. This process has been repeated often enough in the history of interracial behavior in the United States and the Republic of South Africa to provide us with sufficient illustrations to establish the validity of the hypothesis. Indeed, the entire theory outlined in this chapter and the three preceding chapters will be applied to the dynamics of race relations in these two societies. Our major focus, however, will be on black–white relations in the United States, a subject discussed in some detail in the next three chapters.

NOTES

1. Gary T. Marx, *Protest and Prejudice: A Study of Belief in the Black Community* (New York: Harper, 1967); James C. Davies, "The J-Curve of Rising and Declining Satisfactions as a Cause of Some Great Revolutions and a Contained Rebellion," in *Violence in America: Historical and Comparative Perspectives*, ed. by Hugh Davis Graham and Ted Robert Gurr (New York: Bantam, 1969), pp. 690–730; and James A. Geschwender, "Social Structure and the Negro Revolt: An Examination of Some Hypotheses," *Social Forces*, 43:248–256 (Dec. 1964).

2. James C. Davies, "Toward a Theory of Revolution," *American Sociological Review*, 27:5–19 (Feb. 1962).

3. Marx, op. cit., p. 69.

4. Richard Schermerhorn, *Comparative Ethnic Relations: A Framework for Theory and Research* (New York: Random House, 1970), p. 14.

5. H. M. Blalock, Jr., *Toward a Theory of Minority-Group Relations* (New York: Wiley, 1967), p. 126.

6. Ibid., pp. 126–131.

7. Davies, "The J-Curve of Rising and Declining Satisfactions," op. cit., p. 690.

8. Ibid. In Chapter Seven, I discuss the point that Davies' theory has not been fully understood by some writers, who fail to distinguish physical gratification from emotional gratification and hence reject the theory in some cases where it should be accepted. See section entitled "Power and the Changing Character of Black Protest" in Chapter Seven.

9. Designations such as "rebellion" or "revolution" are vague and difficult to apply empirically. Obviously, there are various levels of violence for acts described as rebellions or revolutions. Davies, for instance, states: "If the [oppressed group's] frustration is sufficiently widespread,

intense, and focused on government, the violence will become a revolution that displaces irrevocably the ruling government and changes markedly the power structure of the society. Or the violence will be contained within the system, which it modifies but does not replace. This latter case is rebellion." Ibid., p. 690.

10. In contrast, separatist movements are unlikely to occur in slave regimes because the slaves' movements are restricted and their labor is central to the economy. However, sentiments for group autonomy and independence could be manifested in nativistic or revivalistic movements insofar as they are not viewed by dominant members as posing a distinct threat to the system of slavery.

11. Pierre van den Berghe, *Race and Racism: A Comparative Perspective* (New York: Wiley, 1967), p. 26.

12. Ibid., p. 28.

13. Ibid., p. 27.

14. Ibid., p. 27.

15. Ibid., p. 29.

16. This argument is debatable and will be fully explored in the concluding section of this chapter.

17. van den Berghe, op. cit., p. 29.

18. Ibid., pp. 30–33.

19. See, for example, Herbert Aptheker, *American Negro Slave Revolts* (New York: Columbia U.P., 1943), and Stanley M. Elkins, *Slavery: A Problem in American Institutional and Intellectual Life* (Chicago: U. of Chicago, 1959), p. 138.

20. Aptheker, op. cit., pp. 91–93.

21. The term "motivation," as used here, should not be confused with desire. To desire change in this context is to want an improved position and a better way of life, whereas to be motivated for change is not only to desire change but also to feel that change can, in fact, be brought about. In other words, our concept of "motivation" takes into account both the desire for change and the expectation that meaningful change can be accomplished.

22. History reveals one major exception to this general pattern—slavery in Latin America. In Chapter Five, I will discuss the major differences between slave resistance in Latin America and that in the United States.

23. Philip Mason also feels that the dichotomy between paternalistic and competitive systems of race relations should be expanded. His classification, which is applied to societies that range from the United States and South Africa to Tanganyika and Uganda, includes three categories: domination, paternalism, and competition. See Philip Mason, *Patterns of Domination* (London: Oxford U.P., 1970), pp. 60–65. For a discussion of Mason's notion of fluid competition among racial groups in comparative perspective, see Philip Mason, *Race Relations* (London: Oxford U.P., 1970, chap. 8.

24. William Gamson, *Power and Discontent* (Homewood, Ill.: Dorsey, 1968), pp. 169–170.

25. Lewis M. Killian, James Fendrich, and Michael Pearson, "Alienation and the Crisis in Black Leadership" (unpublished manuscript, 1970), p. 5.

26. The selection of these options is largely dictated by the nature of the power relationship between governmental authorities and minority partisans. In some cases, however, the government's actions are also controlled by its concern with the responses or expected responses of third parties both within and outside its territorial limits.

The ideas developed in the latter part of this section were inspired by Gamson, op. cit., especially chap. 6.

27. On the one hand, the resources used could be the effective utilization of forms of protest and pressure tactics. A threat to mobilize such resources or to continue to mobilize them could produce the desired result. However, constraint or pressure resources cannot be indiscriminately applied and are more effective in one time period than in another. For example, A. Philip Randolph's threat in 1941 to march 100,000 blacks on Washington, D. C., protesting job discrimination in America's defense plants prompted President Roosevelt both to issue an executive order prohibiting employment discrimination in governmental agencies and defense plants and to establish the Fair Employment Practices Commission to implement the order. Because the nation was at war and it was widely felt that the march would divide the black and white citizens of the nation at a time when national unity was essential, Roosevelt had little choice but to meet the demands. It is highly unlikely that he would have moved as swiftly and forthrightly if the threat had been made before the United States became involved in the war. On the other hand, the minority group may possess the types of resources that could persuade the government to meet certain demands without the use of organized protest. For example, a politician who needs black support for reelection could be induced to support or propose certain kinds of legislation designed to improve conditions in the black community. However, in each of the foregoing cases the demands must be specific. Regardless of the resources of the minority group and the fears of the government, diffuse demands beyond the government's capacity cannot be met.

28. Gamson, op. cit., pp. 114–115.

29. Shibutani and Kwan have commented on this point: "Ironically, where the color line is well-established, tension is usually at a minimum. To be sure, the calm of a stable society is occasionally disturbed by a mutiny led by a resourceful rebel who becomes the thorn in the side of the authorities. But such incidents are rare and seldom a serious threat to the ascendancy of the dominant group." Tamotsu Shibutani and Kian M. Kwan, *Ethnic Stratification: A Comparative Approach* (New York: Macmillan, 1965), p. 342.

67

30. See Robin M. Williams, Jr., "The Reduction of Intergroup Tensions" (*Social Science Research Council Bulletin* 57, 1947), p. 61.

31. Richard Schermerhorn, "Toward a General Theory of Minority Groups," *Phylon*, 24:238–246 (1965).

32. Ibid.

33. In the following discussion, I am heavily indebted to Professor Herbert Blumer's excellent paper "Industrialisation and Race Relations," in *Industrialisation and Race Relations: A Symposium*, ed. by Guy Hunter (London: Oxford U.P., 1965), pp. 200–253.

34. Ibid., p. 229.

35. Ibid., p. 232.

36. Ibid., p. 237.

37. Ibid., p. 239.

38. I have in mind pressures from some segments of the dominant population opposed to continued racial oppression, or pressures exerted by governmental officials, or pressures from minority groups themselves. Blumer states: "The picture in the United States in this regard is decisive. In the American South, managerial policy in industry has supported and maintained a racial alignment and a racial code for three-quarters of a century. It is only in very recent years that changes are beginning to appear. These changes, which are still in an early stage, have not sprouted indigenously in Southern industry or for that matter in Southern society. They are the result of pressures emanating outside of both. These pressures are part of the growing movement on behalf of 'desegregation,' a movement which has its geographical roots in the area of politics and in the Federal Government." Ibid., p. 247.

39. Racial conflict in this instance would be limited largely to minority members and lower-class dominant members who have to compete for low-status jobs and housing.

40. For further discussion of these points, see Henry Allen Bullock, "Urbanism and Race Relations," in *The Urban South*, ed. by Rupert B. Vance and Nicholas J. Demerath (Chapel Hill: U. of North Carolina, 1954); Ray Marshall, "Industrialisation and Race Relations in the Southern United States," in *Industrialisation and Race Relations*, op. cit., pp. 61–96; Hylan Lewis, "Innovations and Trends in the Contemporary Southern Negro Community," *Journal of Social Issues*, 10:22–24 (1954); and M. Elaine Burgess, "Race Relations and Social Change," in *The South in Continuity and Change*, ed. by John E. McKinney and Edgar T. Thompson (Durham, N.C.: Duke U.P., 1965), pp. 337–358.

41. Schermerhorn, "Toward a General Theory of Minority Groups," op. cit., p. 245.

PART TWO
Theoretical and Sociohistorical Analyses of Race Relations in the United States and South Africa

CHAPTER FIVE

Slavery in the United States as a Power Relationship

ISTORIANS generally agree that the first blacks to settle permanently in North America arrived in Virginia in
1619 and that others slowly trickled in during the next several decades. Oscar and Mary Handlin have claimed that
these early blacks came as indentured servants—bound by
contract to work for a specified time period—and basically
received the same treatment afforded white indentured servants.[1] Others have maintained that, unlike white indentured
servants, black servants were victims of race prejudice and
white supremacy, that they were relegated to a lower status
from the beginning, and that some were actually enslaved as
early as 1640.[2] However, Winthrop Jordan, in an impressive
study of early American attitudes toward blacks, has concluded that although the available evidence is insufficient to
settle any claims regarding the status of blacks prior to 1640,
the claim that some blacks were being held in permanent servitude between 1640 and 1660 while others were not can be sub-
stantiated.[3] Slavery received statutory recognition in 1661 in
Virginia, in 1663 in Maryland, and shortly thereafter in other
colonies. Clearly, then, regardless of which position is taken
with regard to the actual status of blacks before 1640, within a
few decades after their arrival in the New World some were
forced into a position of lifetime slavery—a position in
marked contrast to the temporary servitude experienced by
white indentured servants.

DIFFERENTIAL POWER AND THE DEVELOPMENT OF RACIAL STRATIFICATION IN AMERICA

There are several factors that explain slavery's replacement of indentured servitude as the source of cheap labor in early America. Although land was plentiful during the colonial period, labor was expensive, and the limited supply of indentured servants did not begin to meet the needs of proprietors desiring large-scale production of rice and tobacco. Even plantation owners with a sufficient supply of indentured servants were ultimately faced with the legal obligation of supplying each servant with money, clothing, and a plot of land on completion of this service. Slaveholders were not legally bound to care for their slaves in this way. The use of slaves was not only less expensive but also more productive in the long run because their service was guaranteed for life.[4] As Jordan remarked in this connection, "Negroes became slaves, partly because there were social and economic necessities in America which called for some sort of bound, controlled labor."[5]

Some critics have questioned the uniform and unqualified application of this argument to colonial America. They have noted that slavery also developed quite early in some Northern colonies where the economic necessity for bound, controlled labor did not exist.[6] Although it is true that slavery was not considered vital to the Northern economy, the few Northerners who owned slaves had nonetheless an economic vested interest in legalized slavery. Indeed, according to Noel,

> For the individual retainer of Negro servants the factual and legal redefinition of Negroes as chattel constitutes a vital economic interest whether or not the number of slaves is sufficient to vitally affect the economy of the colony. Our knowledge of the role of the elite in the establishment of community mores suggest that this constitutes at least a partial explanation of the Northern [slave] laws. In addition, the markedly smaller number of Negroes in the North might account for the fact that "although enactments in the Northern colonies recognized the legality of lifetime servi-

tude, no effort was made to require all Negroes to be placed in that condition." We surmise that the laws were passed at the behest of a few powerful individuals who had relatively many Negro servants and were indifferent to the status of Negroes in general so long as their own vested interests were protected.[7]

Whereas the emergence of slavery can be associated with man's desire to maximize control of scarce resources, factors of a different nature must be taken into account to explain why blacks, and not some other group, ultimately constituted the slave population. In fact, three groups were logical candidates for permanent servitude in the early colonies—blacks, white indentured servants, and Indians. Of the three groups, blacks were the most powerless vis-à-vis white settlers. Involuntarily removed from their home country, separated from their families and tribes, and brought to a land with an alien culture and language, black slaves were immediately forced into a dependent relationship with the settlers—a relationship that provided slaveholders with instant power and facilitated the development and growth of the "peculiar institution." The significance of power with respect to the fate of blacks and white indentured servants has been analyzed by Marvin Harris:

The facts of life in the New World were such . . . that Negroes, being the most defenseless of all the immigrant groups, were discriminated against and exploited more than any others. Thus the Negroes were not enslaved because the British colonists specifically despised dark skinned people and regarded them alone as property suited to slavery; the Negroes came to be the object of virulent prejudices because they and they alone could be enslaved. Judging from the very nasty treatment suffered by white indentured servants, it was obviously not sentiment which prevented the Virginia planters from enslaving their fellow Englishmen. They undoubtedly would have done so had they been able to get away with it. But such a policy was out of the question as long as there was a King and a Parliament in England.[8]

73

In retrospect, however, it should be noted that even if white indentured servants had been without the protection of external legal force, the probability of their enslavement would still have been much lower than it was for blacks. Unlike blacks, white servants had not been previously victimized in the international slave trade and thus were not likely to be automatically associated with slavery. Moreover, there were no sharp differences between the settlers and white servants in language pattern, culture, and skin color, which heighten ethnocentric beliefs, increase alienation and detachment, and thereby clear the path for total subjugation. Be that as it may, the protection of the English Parliament placed them in a far better position to avoid permanent servitude.

In actuality, the increasing pressure for labor in the colonies during the seventeenth century helped to improve conditions for white indentured servants but created further debasement for blacks. Disturbed that further immigration would be frustrated because of widespread reports in Great Britain concerning the harsh treatment of indentured servants, the colonists enacted legislation designed to improve the lot of white servants and enhance their chances of obtaining a meaningful release once their contract expired. This legislation had no effect on the status of black slaves.[9] As Kenneth Stampp has observed, "Neither the provisions of their charters nor the policy of the English government limited the power of colonial legislatures to control Negro labor as they saw fit. Negroes did not have the benefit of written indentures which defined their rights and limited their term of service."[10]

Blacks were also in a more powerless position than the American Indians, who also were without the protection of an external government. Despite the fact that the colonists defeated the Indians in numerous military confrontations, the colonists' perception of the degree to which Indians could be enslaved contrasted markedly with their view regarding the vulnerability of Africans to permanent servitude. Attempts to enslave the Indians were tried (especially in the Carolinas) and promptly abandoned. Essentially, "Indians were in a position to mount murderous reprisals upon the English settlers, while the few scattered Negroes were not."[11] It did not take the average plantation owner long to realize that he was putting both his life and the lives of his family in jeopardy by attempting to use Indian slaves. Unlike blacks, Indians, being indigenous to the American colonies, knew a great deal about the territory in which they might seek refuge,[12] and they were organized tribally and thus better able to resist colonial encroachment. In short, they were far less vulnerable to institutionalized white repression than were blacks, who were forced to live in a foreign land, lacked organization, and were scattered about the countryside.

However, to suggest that blacks were ultimately chosen over Indians to be enslaved because the slave transfer situation made them much more powerless than the American Indians is not to ignore the fact that the American Indians' cultural experience rendered them less suitable as slaves. Eric Foner has discussed this issue: "It is one of the tragic ironies of Afro-American history that Africans were imported to the New World because their level of culture and economic skill made them better slave laborers than the Indians. In fact, African slaves introduced techniques of tropical farming and mining which were adopted by the Europeans."[13]

It is a matter of some speculation as to how heavily each of these factors was weighed by slaveholders in their decision to select blacks rather than Indians for enslavement. Jordan argues that although the culture of the Africans probably meant that they were more enslavable than the Indians, in the long run it was "the different contexts of confrontation" that counted most heavily in the choice of blacks for chattel slavery.[14] Support for this position can be found in the writings of Edgar Thompson:

The planter resorted to the importation of outside laborers not only because the native population was numerically insufficient, but more often, perhaps, because it was difficult or even impossible to obtain a satisfactory degree of control over people who were at home in the local environment. The familyless man or woman recruited in some distant place and transported to a plantation region where he found himself in strange surroundings and among strange people was more easily made dependent upon an employer.[15]

Regardless of which position one takes on this issue, it seems reasonable to conclude that because blacks did not have access to the resources available to the American Indians, they were less able to mount serious resistance to their enslavement. This fact, coupled with a cultural background that had already prepared them for settled agriculture, increased their desirability as slaves and enhanced the growth of slavery. But if the needs of the plantation economy led to the development of slavery, and if the black man's lack of power resources insured its growth, slavery was ultimately reinforced, justified, and defended by an ideology of racism.

DEVELOPMENT OF RACISM AND INSTITUTIONALIZATION OF BLACK SLAVERY

Although biological racism, as we shall see, is fairly well documented as a phenomenon that crystallized in the nineteenth century ostensibly to reinforce slavery, it is difficult to identify the precise point at which cultural racism began to play a major role in the subjugation of blacks. Historians have noted that Englishmen had vague prejudices toward blacks even before they set foot on American soil.[16] Initial contact with Africa and African culture led Englishmen to perceive themselves as being radically different from the Africans. Blacks were described as uncivilized heathens. Their language, patterns of etiquette, methods of warfare, and morals all seemed inferior to the English, judged by Western standards. The sense of group position Englishmen developed vis-à-vis Africans was further heightened by the difference in skin color. In addition to being associated with savagery and heathenism, blackness in the tradition of Western thought and mythology also signified evil, sin, baseness, ugliness, and filth.[17]

Although these early reactions against blacks are indicative of an extreme form of ethnocentrism, they do not necessarily imply that cultural racism existed on a wide scale during this period. Ethnocentric views do not inevitable translate into beliefs supporting the exploitation or suppression of a group because of "inferior cultural behavior."[18] It is probably true that prior to the colonization of America some Englishmen were cultural racists in their outlook and approach to blacks,[19] but the evidence seems to indicate that the widespread ethnocentric view toward blacks did not develop into a form of cultural racism on a significant scale among Englishmen until the international slave trade required justification during the last quarter of the seventeenth century.[20] There is little evidence to suggest the existence of an explicit set of beliefs reinforcing black exploitation prior to the development of slavery in the states. Jordan has concluded that

> From the first, Englishmen tended to set Negroes over against themselves, to stress what they conceived to be radically contrasting qualities of color, religion, and style of life, as well as animality and a peculiarly potent sexuality. *What Englishmen did not at first fully realize was that Negroes were potentially subjects for a special kind of obedience and subordination which was to arise as adventurous Englishmen sought to possess for themselves and their children one of the most bountiful dominions of the earth.*[21] [Italics added.]

However, when we examine the historical facts associated with early black–white contact in the colonies, the line dividing ethnocentrism and cultural racism cannot be easily drawn. Because some blacks were reduced to the status of slaves shortly after their arrival in the colonies, the issue becomes somewhat complicated. To be sure, many of the colonists were influenced by the ethnocentric attitudes toward blacks already firmly established in England, and their contact with early blacks on American soil probably increased these feelings. Because so little is known about black–white contact prior to 1640, it is quite difficult to interpret accurately white attitudes toward blacks during this period. Evidence indicating black enslavement after 1640 certainly raises the possibility that cultural racist attitudes had taken hold even at this early date. However, as Milton Cantor has observed in his study of "The Image of the Negro in Colonial Literature," although the earliest settlers did view the African as alien and different from the European, "they did not seem to care sufficiently to either justify or to lament the philosophical assumptions of slavery. There was good reason for this: slavery was a tenuous innovation, without roots or tradition, in the first half of the seventeenth century."[22] But with the expansion of the international slave trade in the late seventeenth and early eighteenth centuries, some Englishmen felt that it was in their best interest to justify slavery by making explicit reference to the black man's savagery and heathenism.[23] Although some proslavery writers did equate savagery with biological inferiority, this view did not sufficiently develop to indicate that the prevailing philosophy of exploitation in the seventeenth and eighteenth centuries was that of biological racism. For, as Jordan has remarked in this connection,

> Most English commentators seem to have felt that Negroes would behave better under improved circumstances; a minority thought the African naturally wicked, but even these observers often used "natural" only to mean "ingrained" (English accounts of West Africa did not emphasize ingrained stupidity in the natives; defect of "Reason" was seen as a function of savagery). Until well into the eighteenth century there was no debate as to whether the Negro's nonphysical characteristics were inborn and unalterable; such a question was never posed with anything like sufficient clarity for men to debate it.[24]

Thomas Gossett, in a comprehensive study of race theories in America, perceived the situation in much the same way when he reported that prior to the nineteenth century, scientific and informed opinion in the United States generally supported the idea that proper training and a suitable environment could, in time, eliminate any "negative traits" associated with blacks.[25] He also noted "that among the colonists in the seventeenth and early eighteenth centuries it is the heathenism of the Negroes . . . rather than their race, which is emphasized as a basis for their enslavement."[26]

But as heavy criticism was leveled against the institution of slavery, proponents of slavery were forced to shift from cultural racism to a more explicit and, indeed, a more forceful ideology of exploitation. "When the Negro was categorised simply as a black, a heathen, or a savage, he could be no more than an impersonal object that men manipulated for certain purposes," states David Brion Davis. "The growth of antislavery opinion would require a shift in focus from the Negro's generalized qualities to specific actions and capabilities that would at once reveal his individuality and his true humanity."[27] The doctrine of biological racism provided slavery proponents with the weapon they needed.

Biological racism became the dominant philosophy of racial exploitation during the third or fourth decade of the nineteenth century (although, as we have suggested, there were traces of it prior to their period)[28] and emerged at the time when slavery was under heavy attack from antislavery forces. Drawing on the environmentalist theories (i.e., the view that human behavior is determined to a greater extent by environment than by heredity) that emerged during the eighteenth-century Enlightenment period, antislavery forces were able to mount a serious offensive against slavery. As long as the "inferiority" of blacks was not viewed as being innate but rather as the result of unique cultural factors, the environmentalists had a strong case against slavery and cultural racism. They could argue that blacks should be released from servitude and given proper education and training in order that they might achieve a status of equality with whites.

No serious and sustained threat against the institution of slavery developed before the revolutionary era, and slaveholders felt little if any need to justify its existence other than claiming that blacks were savages or heathens. However, after the American Revolution all of this changed. Northern abolitionists, under the influence of the liberal philosophy of the

Revolutionary era, boosted their campaign against slavery to an unprecedented height by the 1830s. They argued that slavery was amoral and that blacks should be emancipated immediately.[29]

In addition to pressures from Northern abolitionists, slaveholders also had to concern themselves with the problem that the ratio of blacks to whites in some Southern states had increased to a point where the threat of slave revolts was very real. "As the black slave's real or imagined ability to disrupt the system increased, so did the importance which whites attached to 'keeping him in his place.' "[30] The widely discussed insurrections of Gabriel Prosser, Denmark Vesey, and Nat Turner in the early nineteenth century and the fear that similar insurrections could duplicate Toussaint L'Ouverture's successful rebellion in Haiti all combined to heighten white anxiety, increase hatred of blacks, and generate a sense of urgency to reinforce the system of slavery.

The combined pressures of Northern abolitionist attacks and the threat of slave insurrections are two important reasons why a forceful philosophy of exploitation was needed to keep blacks suppressed in the state of slavery. Southerners had little difficulty in invoking and cultivating the biological racist view that slavery was a suitable and appropriate condition of life for blacks, who were inherently inferior to whites.

Although increased pressure against slavery created the need for a philosophy of exploitation such as biological racism, its growth was facilitated by emerging currents of thought in the nineteenth century. First, Darwinian thought, with its emphasis on evolutionary stages, hereditary determinism, and survival of the fittest, provided conservative social scientists with a model they presumed to be applicable to *Homo sapiens*. Social Darwinism "dovetailed with the economic liberalism of the early nineteenth century. Although John Stuart Mill and other early liberals were explicitly antiracists, laissez-faire was later reinterpreted as a mandate not to interfere with any form of human inequality and suffering."[31] It was argued that black people were enslaved because they were biologically inferior and natural selection had found the most suitable place for them.[32]

Second, the libertarian and egalitarian ideas of the Enlightenment period following the American and French Revolutions on the one hand confronted slavery supporters with a glaring contradiction between the existence of permanent servitude and the prevailing norms of equality and freedom, whereas on the other hand they gave slavery apologists ammunition with which to defend slavery. In effect, humanity could be divided into two groups—men (whites) and submen (blacks). The egalitarian ideals were restricted to the former. "The desire to preserve both the profitable forms of discrimination and exploitation and the democratic ideology made it necessary to deny humanity to the oppressed group."[33]

Although biological racism did not reach its golden age until the latter part of the nineteenth and early twentieth centuries, it had, by the beginning of the Civil War, made its impact on the lives of both blacks and whites in the United States, as we shall presently see.

POWER, RACISM, AND RACIAL CONFLICT IN THE ANTEBELLUM UNITED STATES

A characteristic feature of paternalistic systems of race relations is the absence of any meaningful power balance between the dominant and subordinate racial groups. Most certainly, slave transfers created an initial situation that severely reduced the black man's possibility of developing sufficient power resources to seriously challenge slave regimes. The fact that blacks were abruptly uprooted from their African homeland, forcibly marched to the sea by the African traders and fed into the international slave trade, brutalized during the "middle passage" (a period of such terror that only one in three Africans survived), dispersed up and down the Atlantic Coast, and dispersed again among the various plantations near their points of disembarkation to begin their "breaking in" process all combined to maximize their vulnerability to control by white slaveholders.[34]

The rigid plantation system of the antebellum South is an example of van den Berghe's notion of a paternalistic regime, in which a small but powerful land-owning aristocracy is able to generate political and legal support for slavery with a view to keeping slaves in a constant state of subjugation. To call such regimes "paternalistic" in the face of the widespread tyranny and exploitation that characterizes them would seem to stretch the meaning of the term. However, as Eugene D. Genovese has noted, paternalism in the antebellum South essentially meant "a special notion of duty and responsibility towards one's charges. Arbitrary power, harshness toward disobedience, even sadism, constituted its other side."[35] Obedience placed the slave in a position to receive favors from the master, and resistance could be severely and legally punished.[36]

As the slave population increased during the seventeenth century and fears of slave uprisings spread, the colonial assembly of Virginia adopted a rigid slave code that restricted the slave's freedom of movement and denied him legal and civil rights. In other colonies, similar codes were passed by legislative bodies as the number of slaves grew. Slave codes tended to be most rigid in colonies such as Maryland, Delaware, Georgia, and South Carolina where the slave population was large.[37]

Some historians have suggested that although the slave codes attest to the fact that there was widespread fear of black uprisings, in the final analysis the fears were exaggerated, because the rigidity of the slave system forced most slaves to be obedient and adopt a sambo-like personality. Other historians reject the sambo image of the slaves by arguing that blacks constantly struggled against their suppressed status. Let us focus momentarily on this controversy.

Those who maintain that the North American slaves were basically docile often draw comparisons between the relative infrequency of slave revolts in the United States and the proliferation of violent slave uprisings in Latin America. It is true that slave revolts in Latin America occurred much more often, but it is also true that slaves in Latin America were in a far better position to stage revolts. To be more specific, slave trading in Latin America first of all continued well into the nineteenth century and insured a constant supply of newly imported slaves. Unlike slaves born into servitude who never had experienced freedom, recently arrived slaves who had had their freedom abruptly taken away were much more apt to stage a revolt.[38] Demographic factors in the South American tropics and Latin America necessitated a continual flow of imported slaves. The slave population had a low natural growth rate because of a very low birth rate. As Philip Curtin has observed, "this was tied directly to the low real cost of slaves in Africa. Planters wanted more men than women on their estates, calculating that it was cheaper to buy young African men of working age than it was to import African women, who would sit idle raising families."[39] Not only was this demographic factor reversed in the North, where the higher birth rate produced a large indigenous slave population and thereby reduced the need for imported slaves,[40] but slave trading terminated in 1801 (although a few slaves were illegally imported after that date). "In the United States the great majority of slaves during the antebellum period had been born and raised on Southern plantations. Their ranks received little reinforcement from newly enslaved and aggressive Africans."[41]

Second, the slaveholding population in Latin America and South America was relatively small—in many cases, too small to discourage or suppress a revolt. Moreover, the white planters were often in conflict with one another, thus weakening the slave-control apparatus. However, in North America slaves were generally outnumbered by whites, who cooperated in establishing a strong defense to discourage slave uprisings.

Third, in South America the combination of a weak state with suitable terrain allowed runaway slaves to establish maroon colonies, thus keeping alive any inclination toward armed resistance. In North America, such colonies for the most part could not be established because once runaway slaves left the plantation they were surrounded by the whites who inhabited most of the region. "Death, not refuge, lay beyond the plantation."[42]

Finally, as Genovese has said, "a substantial revolt presupposed the formation of ideology and leadership."[43] These components were far more possible in the Caribbean and in Brazil, where the large sugar plantation had a slave labor force averaging two hundred persons or more and where the white population was small. Under these conditions, a positive group identity and nationalistic ideologies, which promote resistance, could easily develop. In the United States, on the other hand, half of the slaves lived and worked in groups of twenty or less with a majority of the other half living and working on plantations in groups of fifty or less. In most cases, these relatively small units were closely supervised, not only by white planters, but also by nonslaveholders who supported slavery. For all these reasons, blacks in the Caribbean and Brazil were far more openly rebellious than the slaves in North America. The former had possession of the power resources that generated the necessary motivation to stage a revolt and enhanced the possibility of a successful revolt.

However, although these arguments do help in accounting for the greater frequency of slave insurrections in Latin America and South America, they cannot be used to establish the claim that blacks in North America were basically docile sambo types who tacitly accepted the norms of slavery.[44] Although it is true that blacks were forced to openly conform to the system of slavery, they were not so dehumanized as to fail to exercise any form of protest.[45] They did engage, as already indicated, in subtle or indirect day-to-day resistance such as destroying property, slowing up of work, malingering, self-mutilation, inadequate workmanship, sabotage and running away.

The most dramatic form of resistance, of course, was the armed revolt. The actual number of slave revolts has been debated by historians, but they tend to dismiss Herbert Aptheker's claim that over two hundred slave insurrections took place in North America between the seventeenth and nineteenth centuries.[46] According to Jordan, "it now seems clear that there were many more rumors than revolts and that the number of actual revolts was small; if it takes a score of persons to make a 'revolt' the number all-told before 1860 was probably not more than a dozen."[47] Certainly the number of revolts actually documented suggest that North American slaves were far less inclined to stage insurrections than were slaves in Latin America. However, the revolts that did occur generated considerable hysterical anxiety among the colonists.

In this connection, Stanley Elkins argues "that although the danger of slave revolts (like Communist conspiracies in our day) was much overrated by touchy Southerners, the revolts that actually did occur were in no instance planned by plantation laborers but rather by Negroes whose qualities of leadership were developed well outside the full coercion of the plantation authority-system."[48] However, Earle E. Thorpe maintains that this argument does not necessarily uphold the thesis that blacks on plantations were sambos lacking in leadership qualities; rather, it may indicate that "the opportunity to plan revolts was greater in or near towns or cities."[49] But Thorpe's statement actually supports Elkins' contention that in areas where industrialization and urbanization had taken place, slaves tended to be more literate and to have a greater awareness of their oppressed state. Moreover, urbanized areas attracted freed blacks who, in some cases, agitated for an end to slavery and generated discontent among blacks in servitude.[50]

Thus the rigid paternalistic regimes not only discouraged attempts to organize slave insurrections but also virtually eliminated the possibility of successful insurrections. The few revolts tried were all violently suppressed. This suggests that the slave insurrectionists severely miscalculated both their own resources to stage a revolt and the resources of the slaveholders to suppress a revolt. It is significant to note that after the violent suppression of the Nat Turner rebellion, no subsequent slave revolts occurred. The South was literally an armed camp, and the life of any slave or freed black even remotely suspected of contemplating a revolt was in very real danger.

In summary, blacks in North America were forced to openly comply with slavery, the few slave revolts notwithstanding. Such compliance, however, does not necessarily indicate widespread internalization and acceptance of slavery. Slaves did not possess the power resources that would permit open resistance; they were forced to role-play, as some historians have suggested, to give the appearance of being faithful to the master, and their means of resisting and protesting against slavery were for the most part indirect.[51]

But it would be difficult to argue that a paternalistic system as rigid as the slave regimes in the antebellum South did not have some debilitating effects on the personalities of the slaves. Most certainly, some slaves were influenced by racist thought, questioned their own humanity, and internalized the norms of slavery. The power discrepancy between masters and slaves was far too great to allow blacks the degree of independence and self-assertion typically found in the more fluid competitive systems of race relations.

Slavery and racism also had a rather pervading influence on the behavior of whites. One of the remarkable paradoxes of United States history is that although only a small percentage of whites enjoyed the social prestige and economic benefits of slave ownership,[52] slavery received overwhelming support from white Southerners. To some extent, this is a testament to the power of the slaveholders—they were able to influence and direct patterns of thought among whites. Their characterization of slaves as either uncultured savages or inferior human beings in public discussion helped to strengthen the sense of group position among whites as well as to secure both formal and informal support for slavery. Even the poorest white non-slaveholder derived some psychic benefit from his identification with a "superior" caste. Thus he shared in the responsibility of keeping the slave "in his place"—he could punish slaves while on patrol duty and could arrest runaway slaves. As long as both slaves and freed blacks were denied the privileges enjoyed by the white caste, the nonslaveholder was assured a position above the bottom of the social ladder. The stronger the nonslaveholder's sense of group position, the greater was his hatred of blacks and the more intense his fear that freed blacks would attempt to claim equality with him.[53]

In addition to his concern to preserve his superior social position, the nonslaveholder supported slavery because he thought it was a means of controlling the economic competition from blacks. Actually, slaves proved to be "more ruinous economic competitors of white labor than they were as freemen."[54] White workers found, in almost every occupation, that their bargaining power was greatly restricted because it was cheaper for employers to take slaves and retain them at a subsistence level.[55] But the yearning to be superior was far too great; racism had so affected the minds of poor Southern whites that there was never a time when their support for slavery significantly wavered.

With the outbreak of the Civil War, slavery abruptly came to a halt. However, the norms of biological racism and the philosophy of racial exploitation had so contaminated the country that the freed blacks, struggling to overcome the effects of slavery, soon found themselves confronted with a new and almost equally debilitating system of exploitation, Jim Crow segregation.

NOTES

1. Oscar and Mary F. Handlin, "Origins of the Southern Labor System," *William and Mary Quarterly*, 3rd ser., 7:199–222 (Apr. 1950).

2. Carl N. Degler, *Out of Our Past* (New York: Harper, 1959), and "Slavery and the Genesis of American Race Prejudice," *Comparative Studies of Society and History*, 2:49–66 (Oct. 1959); and W. F. Craven, *Southern Colonies in the Seventeenth Century, 1607–1689* (Baton Rouge: Louisiana State U.P., 1949).

3. Winthrop D. Jordan, *White Over Black: American Attitudes Toward the Negro 1550–1812* (Chapel Hill: U. of North Carolina, 1968).

4. Benjamin Quarles, *The Negro in the Making of America* (New York: Macmillan, 1964), p. 34.

5. Jordan, op. cit., p. 61. This argument is consistent with the position taken by Kenneth Stampp. He states: "The use of slaves in southern agriculture was a deliberate choice (among several alternatives) made by men who sought greater returns than they could obtain from their own labor alone, and who found other types of labor more expensive." Kenneth Stampp, *The Peculiar Institution: Slavery in the Ante-Bellum South* (New York: Knopf, 1956), p. 5.

6. Degler is quite emphatic on this point; he states that "Because of the small number of Negroes in the northern provinces, the development of a form of slavery, which left a caste in its wake, cannot be attributed to pressure from increasing numbers of blacks, or even from an insistent demand for cheap labor. Rather it seems clearly to be the consequence of the general social discrimination against the Negro. For in

the northern region, as in the southern, discrimination against the Negro preceded the evolution of a slave status and by that fact helped to shape the form that the institution would assume." Degler, "Slavery and the Genesis of American Race Prejudice," op. cit., p. 59. As I shall attempt to show later, however, the existence of slavery in the North cannot be solely explained in terms of "the consequence of the general social discrimination against the Negro."

7. Donald L. Noel, "A Theory of the Origin of Ethnic Stratification," *Social Problems*, 16:167 (Fall 1968). Noel introduces a second factor that helps to account for the existence of slavery and may be associated with the growth of slavery in the South—the factor of prestige. There is reason to believe that prestige competition played a major role in the growth of slavery in both the North and the South. As Stampp has put it, "No other profession gave a Southerner such dignity and importance as the cultivation of soil with slave labor." There was often a struggle among slaveholders to own as many slaves as possible. "Because masters enjoyed status from the ownership of a large force," continues Stampp, "they sometimes supported more fieldhands and domestics than they could employ with maximum efficiency." Stampp, op. cit., pp. 385–386.

8. Marvin Harris, *Patterns of Race in the Americas* (New York: Walker, 1964), pp. 69–70.

9. Handlin and Handlin, op. cit.

10. Stampp, op. cit., p. 22. Also see Joseph Boskin, "Race Relations in Seventeenth Century America: The Problem of the Origins of Negro Slavery," *Sociology and Social Research*, 49:446–455 (July 1965).

11. Jordan, op. cit., p. 89. Jordan further states: "When English–Indian relations did not turn upon sheer power they rested on diplomacy. In many instances the colonists took assiduous precautions to prevent abuse of Indians belonging to friendly tribes. Most of the Indians enslaved by the English had their own tribal enemies to thank. It became a common practice to ship Indian slaves to the West Indies where they could be exchanged for slaves who had no compatriots lurking on the outskirts of English settlements. In contrast, Negroes presented much less of a threat—at first." Ibid., pp. 89–90.

12. As Stampp has put it, "Unlike Negroes, Indian slaves found it relatively easy to escape along familiar forest trails to the protection of their own people." Stampp, op. cit., p. 23.

13. Eric Foner, *America's Black Past* (New York: Harper, 1970), p. 29. For another study that stresses the importance of blacks' unique cultural experiences as a factor in their enslavement, see Eugene D. Genovese, *The Political Economy of Slavery* (New York: Pantheon, 1965), pp. 70–84.

14. Jordan, op. cit., p. 89. Also see Noel, op. cit., especially pp. 169–171.

15. Edgar T. Thompson, "The Plantation: The Physical Basis of

Traditional Race Relations," in *Race Relations and the Race Problem,* ed. by Edgar T. Thompson (Durham, N.C.: Duke U.P., 1939), p. 185.

16. George M. Fredrickson, "Toward a Social Interpretation of the Development of American Racism," in *Key Issues in the Afro-American Experience,* ed. by Nathan I. Huggins, Martin Kilson, and Daniel M. Fox (New York: Harcourt, 1971), vol. 1, pp. 240–255; Jordan, op. cit.; and David Brion Davis, *The Problem of Slavery in Western Culture* (Ithaca, N.Y.: Cornell U.P., 1966).

17. Jordan, op. cit., chap. 1, and Fredrickson, op. cit.

18. See Earl Raab and Seymour Martin Lipset, "The Prejudiced Society," in *American Race Relations Today: Studies of the Problems Beyond Desegregation,* ed. by Earl Raab (New York: Anchor, 1962), pp. 29–55.

19. A few may even be described as biological racists, but the documentation on this is very sketchy.

20. Jordan, op. cit., chap. 2; also see Davis, op. cit., p. 453. However, Finley has argued that because it was decreed in the Southern colonies "as early as the 1660's . . . that henceforth all Negroes who were imported should be slaves, but whites should be indentured servants and not slaves," we have evidence to refute the view that racism developed out of slavery (M. I. Finley, "On David Brion Davis, *The Problem of Slavery in Western Culture,*" in *American Negro Slavery,* ed. by Allen Weinstein and Frank Otto Gatell [New York: Oxford U.P., 1968], pp. 348–354). This argument is shortsighted, however, because it ignores the fact that blacks were in a much more vulnerable position to be enslaved than were white indentured servants. Fredrickson, for example, maintains that when blacks arrived in most colonies they were easily seen as enslavable because their source was the international slave trade. Moreover, the combination of the black vulnerability to permanent servitude, the need for bound, controlled labor, and the absence of a strong bias against slavery as an institution is sufficient to explain the emergence of slavery in the colonies. Fredrickson, op. cit., p. 245. Also see Eric Williams, *Capitalism and Slavery* (Chapel Hill: U. of North Carolina, 1944).

21. Jordan, op. cit., p. 43.

22. Milton Cantor, "The Image of the Negro in Colonial Literature," *New England Quarterly,* 36:453 (1963).

23. Jordan, op. cit., chap. 2, Davis, op. cit., p. 453, and Wilbert E. Moore, *American Negro Slavery and Abolition: A Sociological Study* (New York: Third Press, 1971), pp. 81–85.

24. Jordan, op. cit., p. 26.

25. Thomas F. Gossett, *Race: The History of an Idea in America* (Dallas: Southern Methodist U.P., 1963), p. 41.

26. Ibid., p. 31. In illustrating the types of beliefs and rationalizations that prevailed among early proslavery advocates, Davis states: "De-

fenders of slavery could rely on the Christian horror of paganism and idolatry: how fortunate was the African who was rescued from savagery and given the wholesome discipline of a Christian country." Davis, op. cit., p. 473.

27. Davis, op. cit., p. 473.

28. Fredrickson states: "The view that blacks were created permanently unequal was enunciated by a minority of theorists in the eighteenth century, including the Englishmen Lord James and Charles White and the negrophobic Jamaican physician Edward Long. But, despite the fact that Jefferson speculated in the 1780's about the possibility that blacks were inherently inferior in some respects to whites, no one in the United States actually defended institutionalized inequality on the basis of racial theory until well into the nineteenth century." Fredrickson, op. cit., p. 251. For a discussion of the colonial legislation that implied the biological inferiority of blacks in the eighteenth century, see Wilbert E. Moore, op. cit., pp. 85–92.

29. Ibid., p. 252.

30. Bryan T. Downes and Stephen W. Burks, "The Historical Development of the Black Protest Movement," in *Blacks in the United States*, ed. by Norval D. Glenn and Charles M. Bonjean (San Francisco: Chandler, 1969), p. 324.

31. Pierre van den Berghe, *Race and Racism: A Comparative Perspective* (New York: Wiley, 1967), p. 17.

32. Ibid., p. 17.

33. Ibid., p. 18.

34. See Joel R. Williamson, "Black Self-Assertion Before and After Emancipation," in *Key Issues in the Afro-American Experience*, op. cit., pp. 213–240, and Stampp, op. cit.

35. Eugene D. Genovese, "The Roots of Black Nationalism," in *Americans from Africa: Old Memories, New Moods*, ed. by Peter I. Rose (New York: Atherton, 1970), p. 34.

36. Ibid., p. 34.

37. John Hope Franklin, *From Slavery to Freedom*, 3rd ed. (New York: Knopf, 1967), p. 74.

38. In my discussion of Latin American slavery, I am heavily indebted to Genovese, "The Roots of Black Nationalism," op. cit. Also see Carl N. Degler, *Neither Black Nor White* (New York: Macmillan, 1971), especially pp. 47–61, and H. Orlando Patterson, *The Sociology of Slavery* (London: McGibbon & Kee, Ltd., 1967), pp. 273–283.

39. Philip D. Curtin, "The Slave Trade and the Atlantic Basin," in *Key Issues in the Afro-American Experience*, op. cit., p. 89.

40. On this point, Curtin states: "A total immigration of only about 430,000 slaves produced a slave population of about four and a half million by 1863, the year of emancipation. In short, with less than about 5 percent of the total immigration from Africa, the United States came to

have one of the largest Afro-American populations in the present-day Americas." Ibid., p. 92.

41. Genovese, "The Roots of Black Nationalism," op. cit., p. 33.

42. Ibid.

43. Ibid., p. 53.

44. Stanley M. Elkins, *Slavery: A Problem in American Institutional and Intellectual Life* (Chicago: U. of Chicago, 1959). Elkins maintains that, unlike slavery in Latin America where the Church, royal officials, and federal laws restricted the slaveholders' power by granting the slaves the right of appeal when their fundamental rights were violated, slavery in North America was a system of absolute power and degradation. The slave was unprotected by law and therefore completely at the mercy of his master. Drawing on an analogy between North American slave plantations and German concentration camps, Elkins argues that the system of slavery in the colonies was so dehumanizing that slaves began to "identify with the aggressor." The typical slave was a docile child, a sambo who instead of rebelling against the system internalized the norms of the slaveholders.

45. See, for example, R. S. Bryce-Le Porte, "The American Slave Plantation and Our Heritage of Communal Deprivation," *American Behavior Scientist*, 2–8 (Mar.–Apr. 1969); Richard C. Wade, *Slavery in the Cities: The South 1820–1860* (New York: Oxford U.P., 1964); Earle E. Thorpe, "Chattel Slavery and Concentration Camps," *Negro History Bulletin*, 25:171–176 (May 1962); Mina Davis Caulfield, "Slavery and the Origins of Black Culture: Elkins Revisited," in *Slavery and Its Aftermath*, ed. by Peter I. Rose (New York: Atherton, 1970), pp. 171–193; Herbert Aptheker, "Slave Resistance in the United States," in *Key Issues in the Afro-American Experience*, op. cit., pp. 161–173; Alice and Raymond Bauer, "Day to Day Resistance to Slavery," *Journal of Negro History*, 27(4):388–419 (Oct. 1942); Stampp, op. cit.; and Herbert Aptheker, *American Negro Slave Revolts* (New York: Columbia U.P., 1943).

46. Aptheker, *American Negro Slave Revolts*, op. cit.

47. Jordan, op. cit., p. 113.

48. Elkins, op. cit., p. 138. August Meier and Elliot Rudwick have commented on this point: "Some support is given to the Elkins thesis by a recent statistical analysis of the geographical distribution of slave revolts, which concludes that they tended to occur near cities or in rural areas of paternalistic traditions. On the large plantations of the Deep South where conditions were worst, slave revolts were extremely rare. Yet it is well to point out that no insurrection erupted in New England, the section of the country where the slave system was the least repressive." August Meier and Elliot Rudwick, *From Plantation to Ghetto: The Interpretative History of American Negroes* rev. ed. (New York: Hill and Wang, 1970), p. 70.

In private conversations, I discussed this point with Professor Elkins, and he observed that there were so few blacks in New England that this militated against the possibility of collective organized resistance despite the fact that the atmosphere was more relaxed.

Additional support for Elkins' arguments is found in Gerald Mullin's recent study of Gabriel's Insurrection. Mullin states: "The conspirators were probably freer, more autonomous, than any other type of slave, they were at least a step or two away from their masters. . . . Allowing slaves to hire their own time (or simply hiring them out) was an illegal but highly profitable practice in this period of economic readjustments and diversification. Some conspirators were so far removed from their owners that their provenance was difficult to determine." Gerald W. Mullin, "Gabriel's Insurrection," in *Americans From Africa: Old Memories, New Moods*, op. cit., p. 66.

49. Thorpe, op. cit., p. 160.

50. Aptheker, *American Negro Slave Revolts*, op. cit., and Wade, op. cit.

51. For a discussion of the indirect technique of slave protest as revealed through an analysis of black folk tales and songs, see Sterling Stuckey, "Through the Prism of Folklore: The Black Ethos in Slavery," *The Massachusetts Review*, 9:417–437 (1968).

52. "Nearly three-fourths of all free Southerners had no connection with slavery through either family ties or direct ownership. The 'typical' Southerner was not only a small farmer but also a nonslaveholder." Moreover, the great majority of slaveholders were not part of the planter class, which required ownership of at least 20 slaves. "For 88% of the owners held less than that number, 72% held less than ten, and almost 50% held less than five." Stampp, op. cit., p. 30.

53. Ibid., p. 426.

54. Ibid.

55. Ibid.

CHAPTER SIX

Jim Crow Segregation and the Growth of Biological Racism

T IS one of the paradoxes of race relations in the United States that biological racism reached its peak several decades after the emancipation of slaves in 1861. As the twentieth century began, an overwhelming majority of whites in all sections of the country strongly endorsed the philosophy of biological racism. The basic argument of this chapter is that the demise of slavery and the subsequent shift from paternalistic to competitive race relations increased the need for biological racism as a line of defense against black encroachment in areas where whites claimed prior rights and advantages.

RACISM AND RACIAL OPPRESSION OF FREE BLACKS

To some extent, an indication of what could be expected once increasing numbers of blacks moved into competitive relations with whites was demonstrated in the states above the Mason–Dixon Line after they passed laws freeing the slaves in the late eighteenth and early nineteenth centuries.[1]

The freeing of Northern slaves several decades prior to the Civil War raises the question of just how profitable slavery was in the North. However, as Litwack has pointed out in his brilliant analysis of blacks in the free states from 1790 to 1860, "It took legal action to force many slaveholders to part with their human chattel. Such reluctance would seem to suggest that the slaves at least performed some useful and profitable services."[2] Northern slaves did in fact perform a variety of services (skilled and unskilled, mechanical and agricultural) in a varied economy.[3]

Unlike in the South, however, only a minority of the elite population in the North benefited directly from slave labor; and whereas the slave population in the South exceeded several million, in the North there were no more than 70,000 slaves at any one time. Furthermore, there was considerable opposition to slavery from white laborers, not because they believed in equality for the slaves, but because the use of slave labor reduced their own bargaining power when seeking skilled and unskilled positions. Unlike Southern nonslaveholders, white nonslaveholders in the North were not conditioned to accept slavery uncritically. Certainly, this was due to the fact that slavery was not central to the Northern economy; many elite leaders had no direct interests in slaves, and therefore the few families who owned slaves were hardly able to control the economy and the social and political thought of the region.[4] White workers' resentment of slaves was so intense that many Northern proprietors feared that the continued use of slave labor would precipitate violent attacks. For all of these reasons, it was much easier for antislavery proponents to mold public opinion against Northern slavery.

Although all states north of the Mason–Dixon Line had either passed antislavery laws or provided measures for gradual emancipation by 1804, Northern blacks had little reason to feel optimistic about a significant reduction in racial oppression. Indeed, in the first part of the nineteenth century Northern whites had come to accept the racist view that blacks were biologically inferior and therefore could not be meaningfully assimilated with the white race. Whites rejected slavery as an acceptable institution in the North but were unwilling to endorse the view that blacks should receive social, economic, and political equality. What is significant to note here is that the biological racist thought perpetuated by Southern slavery apologists received widespread acceptance not only from the nonslaveholding masses of the South but from many Northerners as well. Perhaps Fredrickson comes closest to explaining this phenomenon:

> In a period when the sweeping egalitarism associated with the age of Jackson was undermining most social and political distinctions, frightened Northern conservatives were led to emphasize racial distinctions as one remaining barrier that could be defended, and they were often aided and abetted by insecure lower-class whites who longed for some assurance of their own status, a sense that they were superior to someone, if only by virtue of the color of their skin. When, by the 1850's, an expansive Southern "slavocracy" was seen as a threat to the Northern way of life, the tentacles of racist thought and feeling had gained such a stranglehold that most Northern opponents of the extension of slavery carefully disassociated themselves from the abolitionists and their ideal of racial fraternity and argued that theirs was exclusively a white man's cause. The fact that Northerners could oppose slavery without a commitment to racial equality helps explain why the Civil War resulted in the emancipation of the Negro from slavery but not from caste discrimination and the ravages of racism.[5]

Following their emancipation, in the years preceding the Civil War Northern blacks were denied service on juries, were prohibited from marrying whites, were often refused public-school education in the new states of the Northwest, were barred from entering the states of Illinois, Indiana, and Oregon, were forced away from the polls, and were relegated to the most unskilled, menial jobs in Northern cities. To compound their precarious situation, Northern blacks had the misfortune of competing for housing and jobs with many of the nearly five million European immigrants who entered the United States between 1830 and 1860.[6] The German and Scandinavian immigrants who settled on farmlands in the Midwest did not pose a direct threat to blacks, but the penniless and poverty-stricken Irish crowded into the slum areas of Northern cities eventually forced blacks out of many cheap labor positions.[7]

The Irish, also victims of discrimination and prejudice when they arrived, found some psychic relief in the ideology of biological racism, which allowed them to identify with white supremacy and to discharge their anger and frustrations against blacks. In direct competition with blacks for lower-status jobs, the Irish repeatedly voted against any proposals to extend political rights to blacks and often took vigorous steps to drive blacks out of many of the low-paid occupations. For example, Herman D. Bloch reports that in New York City in 1862 a "group of Irish longshoremen informed their employer that all Afro-American longshoremen, dockhands, and other types of workers must be dismissed summarily, otherwise the Irish would tie up the port."[8] In time, Irish workers dominated canal and railroad construction and put an end to the black man's monopoly of the service occupations.[9]

The situation of blacks living in free states increasingly deteriorated during the twenty years preceding the Civil War. Competitive relations became more restrictive: the Irish immigrants were driving them out of the menial occupations they had at one time monopolized; they were completely or practically disfranchised in all but the New England states (where only 7 per cent of the free black population above the Mason–Dixon Line resided); they were discouraged by the Dred Scott Decision and the anti-immigration laws in certain Midwestern states; and their very existence was threatened by the Fugitive Slave Act.

It is instructive to examine the thoughts and reactions of free blacks in the face of worsening conditions. Although racist ideology had so warped many blacks that they either consciously or unconsciously placed a positive value on white standards of beauty while denigrating their own skin color,[10] others promoted race pride and were actively involved in efforts to overcome their oppressed status. To understand the efforts of the latter, it is important to note that they occurred in a context of restrictive competitive race relations, a situation in which blacks were severely limited in the kinds of pressures they could apply.

The most notable and representative purveyor of black thought during this period was the Negro Convention Movement. Beginning in 1830, black leaders periodically met at state and national conventions to devise plans to eliminate racial oppression.[11] These conventions were attended by the most distinguished leaders of the black race, including newspaper editors, clerics, businessmen, and orators such as Frederick Douglass. At first, convention delegates followed the approach of the white abolitionist William Lloyd Garrison and emphasized moral persuasion and nonresistance as techniques to both improve the plight of Northern blacks and abolish slavery in the South. But as the black man's position in the North began to deteriorate, a number of black leaders became disillusioned with this approach and began to push for direct political action around 1840. Blacks pressed candidates for political office to take a stand against slavery; they launched suffrage campaigns and spoke out against political oppression; and they supported the Liberty Party in 1843 and the Free Soil Party in 1848. However, during the disheartening years of the 1850s a number of blacks had reached the conclusion that meaningful integration into American society was no longer possible and that blacks should press for separation. Among them was the black leader Martin R. Delany, who "advised his followers to turn their backs on American society and seek their destiny in immigration."[12] Although Frederick Douglass and most other black leaders continued to argue for integration into American society, sentiment for separatism clearly reached a peak shortly before the Civil War. A pattern was unfolding that, as we shall see, was to repeat itself time and time again: a push for integration during periods when blacks are optimistic about meaningful assimilation and a drive for separatism during periods of disillusionment and resignation.

In the final analysis, however, free blacks in the antebellum North had little reason to develop widespread optimism. So clearly prevalent was the pattern of racism and racial oppression in the North that the observant and perceptive French nobleman Alexis de Tocqueville was led to conclude that

> Race prejudice seems stronger in those states that have abolished slavery than in those where it still exists, and nowhere is it more intolerant than in those states where slavery was never known.[13]

In the absence of the institution of slavery to severely restrict both the horizontal and the vertical mobility of blacks, whites in the North had to rely all the more strongly on an ideology of biological racism to define and reinforce patterns of racial subordination. Tocqueville, touring the United States in the early nineteenth century, actually forecasted that the South would have to confront the same problem in the future:

> If I absolutely had to make some guess about the future, I should say that in the probable course of things the South would increase the repugnance felt by the white population toward the Negroes. I base this opinion on analogy with what I have previously noticed in the North. I have mentioned that the white northerners shun Negroes with all the greater care, the more legislation has abolished any legal distinction between them; why should it not be the same in the South? In the North the white man afraid of mingling with the black is frightened by an imaginary danger. In the South, where the danger would be real, I do not think the fear would be less.[14]

The manner in which the South adjusted to the abolition of slavery and the emergence of competitive race relations is the central subject of the following section.

RACISM AND THE EMERGENCE OF JIM CROW SEGREGATION IN THE SOUTH

The emancipation of slaves following the Civil War marked the dissolution of paternalistic forms of race relations in the

South, although some patterns of the master–servant model lingered on for several years. Because Presidents Lincoln and Johnson were willing to give the South some freedom in adjusting to a way of life in which the economy was no longer based on slave labor, competitive race relations immediately assumed a very restrictive pattern. Southern leaders hastened to reestablish their control over the freedmen through the passage of special legislation known as the Black Codes. Although their provisions varied among states, the Black Codes essentially prevented the freedmen from voting or holding office, made them ineligible for military service, and disbarred them from serving on juries or testifying in court against whites. Moreover, blacks were forbidden to travel from place to place without passes, were not allowed to assemble without a formal permit from authorities, and could be fined and bound out to labor contractors if they were unwilling to work.[15]

Partly because of the Southern states' enactment of the Black Codes and their rejection of the Fourteenth Amendment as it applied to blacks and partly because Northern Republicans were dependent on black votes to remain in power, Congress instituted a series of Reconstruction Acts in 1867 that, among other things, divided the ten Southern states into five military districts under Northern supervision and gave blacks voting rights.[16] Reconstruction drastically modified race relations in the South and created a brief period in which the restrictive competitive race relations of the Black Codes era were replaced by a somewhat more fluid pattern. However, Reconstruction concomitantly intensified racial tension, especially between poor whites and blacks, forced, for the first time, into large-scale competition.

By taking advantage of both the competition between the two groups and the traditional racist attitudes of poor whites, the planter and propertied classes of the South effectively prevented any cooperation between blacks and poor whites. The latter were constantly bombarded with propaganda that reinforced their sense of group position and emphasized their obligation to preserve the "purity and supremacy" of the Caucasian race.[17] Because the governments established under military rule of the South did not eliminate the landowning white aristocracy, the great mass of impoverished and illiterate blacks were still quite dependent on them for their livelihood. For many blacks, the traditional master–servant relationship continued to exist via the system of sharecropping. This economic dependency was complicated by the fact that poor blacks had to compete with white tenants and sharecroppers for diminishing positions on the land. Ray Marshall comments that

> though the white croppers were given no better terms than their coloured competitors, there appears to have been little class feeling, since the planters were apparently considered public benefactors, while the white cropper's hatred and frustration was vented on his Negro competitor. Indeed, one motive for the Ku Klux Klan movement of these years was a desire by low-class whites to remove the Negro as a competitor, especially in the renting of land.[18]

Unlike the period of slavery, in which racial tension was kept to a minimum by the rigid color line that restricted black mobility and prevented black encroachment in areas where whites had prior claim, the decade of Reconstruction was plagued with racial tension. Many blacks refused to acknowledge the traditional patterns of racial etiquette and "remain in their place." By exercising their voting rights, running for political office, attending school, acquiring land, and often failing to exhibit "proper" respect when encountering whites, blacks posed a serious challenge to the white man's sense of superior group position. Biological racist thought as a line of defense intensified, and violence against blacks was reported on a wide scale.

Despite the violence perpetrated against blacks, black thought during "the decade of Reconstruction was characterized by a hopefulness that was in marked contrast to the deepening pessimism of the 1850's."[19] Articulate blacks were optimistic about their future in the United States, and the overwhelming sentiment was one of support for full integration into white society.[20] This optimism, of course, was based on the few advances blacks made during Reconstruction that placed them in a more competitive position with whites: the Fifteenth Amendment had given them the right to vote; many blacks were political officeholders in the South; and the Civil Rights Act of 1875 provided equal rights in theaters, inns, conveyances, and juries.

However, the black optimism during Reconstruction proved to be unfounded. The Compromise of 1877 marked the end of the Reconstruction period and opened the doors for a resurgence of white supremacy and more restrictive competitive relations. The pattern had already been set in 1872, when the North stopped sending troops to the South to enforce federal election laws and gradually reduced its commitment to uphold the civil rights of blacks. The acquiescence of Northern liberalism is traceable to the larger social and economic changes of the last quarter of the nineteenth century. As Meier has observed,

> The Compromise of 1877 was itself rooted in the growth of industrialism in the New South and in the increasing domination of Southern politics by industrial rather than agrarian interests, which ended the necessity of depending on Negro votes for an economic program favorable to the banking and industrial interests of the North which had come to control the Republican party. Northern capitalists, allied with and dominating Southern industry, not only found Negro votes unnecessary, but were interested in securing a stable, semiskilled labor force with which to exploit Southern resources and develop Southern industry rather than in securing justice and social reform for the benefit of the ex-slaves and their descendants.[21]

Several years after the demise of the Reconstruction governments and the Compromise of 1877, the ideology of biological racism increased to such a degree that it virtually engulfed the thoughts and actions of whites. With the withdrawal of support from the federal government, Southern blacks were left defenseless against assaults on their political and civil rights.

Because of the manipulation of voting and registration procedures and the widespread use of intimidation, violence, and
fraud, black political influence diminished. Formal racist laws,
as in the separation of the school systems in the 1870s and
1880s and railroad segregation in the 1880s and 1890s, generally followed informal racist norms. The 1896 Supreme Court
decision on *Plessy v. Ferguson,* which gave legal sanction to
separate facilities, accelerated the passage of Jim Crow laws.
By 1900, blacks in the South were completely segregated in
public conveyances, cemeteries, restaurants, and theaters.
School appropriations for black children were cut.[22] Job mobility was severely restricted to the most menial and poorly
paid work, and blacks were denied service on "lily-white" juries. Lynchings (mostly in the South) reached their peak in the
late nineteenth century, reaching a high of 235 in 1892 and averaging 150 a year in the 1880s and early 1890s.[23]

This oppressive system of Jim Crow segregation did not immediately develop after the collapse of the Reconstruction
regimes.[24] Blacks continued to exercise their voting rights for
several decades as both conservative Democrats and Republicans competed for the black vote. The shift from limited tolerance of black participation in the larger society to a virulent
ideology of biological racism and extreme segregation is directly related to the growth of a political power conflict between lower- and upper-status whites in the South.

In the post Civil War years, blacks were the victims of the
struggle between Southern industrialists who promoted the
drift toward monopoly and finance capitalism and the workers
of the agrarian and labor reform movements who attempted to
halt or alter the economic drift. Blacks were often used as
pawns in the power struggle. Both the Populist Movement and
the Southern Alliance courted the black man and identified
with his cause when it was politically feasible. However, they
then proceeded to shun him when they saw they could not influence his vote in the plantation belts (where Democratic politicians regulated the election process and filled ballot boxes
with fraudulent black votes to defeat the Populists)[25] and when
they realized that "the election laws, as they stood, might ac-

tually be turned against poor, ignorant whites if the Democrats became vindictive and sought to disfranchise the Populists as well as their Negro allies."[26] In time, both factions in this power struggle came to the conclusion that "It was much better to have clear-cut constitutional disfranchisement of the Negro and to leave the white group to fight elections out among themselves."[27]

Thus most whites favored black disfranchisement because they feared that if whites split along economic lines blacks would hold the balance of political power.[28] It is ironic, therefore, that the rise of lower-class whites to power and political consciousness contributed to black disfranchisement. In fact, C. Van Woodward has suggested "that political democracy for the white man and racial discrimination for the black were often products of the same dynamics."[29] As lower-class whites were able to assert their own political power, they began to press for Jim Crow laws—laws designed to reduce or eliminate black competition for subsistence wages in the mines, cottonfields, and wharves and to restrict white contact with blacks who had invaded the new industrial and mining towns of the uplands and thus were forced into closer and more frequent association with lower-class whites.[30]

If the rise of white democracy helped to increase racial intolerance after Reconstruction, the resurrection of racism and racial exploitation in the North aided and abetted Jim Crow segregation once it moved into full operation.

RACISM AND THE REVIVAL OF JIM CROW SEGREGATION IN THE NORTH

The segregation pattern of the antebellum period had broken down slightly in the North during the two decades following the Civil War partly because of the efforts of Radical Republicans, who in their power struggle with the Democrats attempted to enhance the status of blacks in the nation,[31] and partly because the German and Irish immigrants were able "to elevate their economic status in the trades and municipal employment,"[32] thus removing themselves from direct competition with blacks, largely restricted to the lower rungs of the occupational ladder. During this period, blacks were enfranchised, school systems were desegregated, segregation in public accommodations was declared illegal (although it continued in practice in many areas), and civil rights laws were passed in Massachusetts in 1865, in New York in 1874, and in eleven other Northern states by 1885.[33] Furthermore, between 1870 and 1890, although housing discrimination existed, racially mixed residential areas were commonly found,[34] and although discrimination in employment prevailed, some blacks were able to prosper in the professions and business.[35] "The North between 1870 and 1890 was hardly a paradise of interracial amity," states Allan Spear, "but there was probably more contact between the races during these years than at any other time before or since."[36]

After 1890, competitive race relations in the North abruptly shifted from a mixed fluid–restrictive pattern to one that became increasingly restrictive. Residential segregation increased sharply as blacks were forced to leave white communities "by neighborhood improvement associations, economic boycotts, frequent acts of violence, and, later, restrictive covenants."[37] Because of lack of enforcement or the refusal by white juries to uphold them, civil rights laws proved ineffective. The old black business class who had direct contact with whites was replaced by a new middle class with business and social ties exclusively in the black community. Residential concentration increased the black man's voting potential, but the possibility of a white constituency's electing a black man for public office, as was the case in the 1880s and 1890s, virtually disappeared after 1900.[38] Biological racist themes were more loudly proclaimed in public characterizations of the black. Racist books such as Charles Carroll's *The Negro a Beast* (1900), William P. Calhoun's *The Caucasian and the Negro in the United States* (1902), William B. Smith's *The Color Line* (1905), and Robert W. Shufeldt's *The Negro, A Menace to American Civilization* (1907) were widely read in the South. Northern liberal magazines in the latter part of the nineteenth century (e.g., *Nation, North American Review, Har-*

per's Weekly, and the *Atlantic Monthly*) also expressed views supporting white supremacy and postulating the biological inferiority of the black race. Furthermore, scholarly opinion in the biological sciences lent support to biological racist beliefs. Political scientists and historians reinterpreted the Reconstruction period and the resurgence of white supremacy in a manner supportive of racist apologists.[39]

The fact that the hardening of race relations in the North and the resurgence of white supremacy in the South paralleled the United States' new imperialistic domination and exploitation of Puerto Ricans, Filipinos, and other peoples of color suggests that a general mood fostering racial intolerance existed in the country.[40] Even more fundamentally, this was a period of laissez-faire capitalism, industrial strife, and urban dislocation, which combined to heighten the economic and social anxieties that manifested themselves not only in discrimination and exploitation of blacks but also in anti-Semitism, and anti-Catholic and anti-immigrant pogroms in the East, and anti-Oriental attacks on the West Coast.[41] In the face of this general anxiety and intolerance, probably the most important factor in the growth of biological racism and racial conflict in the North was the increased migration of blacks from the South to Northern urban centers in the late nineteenth and early twentieth centuries.

Black migration to Northern urban areas after 1890 began slowly but reached significant proportions between 1915 and 1920. Although the repressive Jim Crow system probably motivated many blacks to leave the South, economic pressure was the major impetus. Cotton production was drastically reduced by a series of floods and boll weevil infestations from 1914 to 1917, thereby generating widespread unemployment and wage cuts not only among poor rural blacks but also among urban blacks whose jobs depended on a healthy cotton economy.[42] At the same time, the drastic curtailment of immigration from Europe during World War I caused an acute labor shortage in Northern factories. Northern industrialists, in dire need of unskilled and semiskilled labor, began a heavy campaign to attract black labor from the South in order to meet the demands of the Allies in Europe. Labor recruiters spread throughout the South offering impoverished black laborers free transportation and high wages if they agreed to migrate. These efforts were bolstered by personal letters from friends in the North who wrote about high wages and fair treatment from whites and by black newspapers such as the *Chicago Defender* that depicted the North as the promised land and the South as the land of tyranny, violence, and racism.[43] In the face of inducements to migrate to the North and the economic pressures in the South, it is little wonder that so many Southern blacks viewed the North as the promised land. As Spear has put it,

> The offer of an agent, an encouraging letter from a friend in the North, or the appeal of the militant Negro press, coming after years of smoldering discontent, sparked the final decision to migrate. Through these media, tenant farmers and sharecroppers, displaced by agricultural reorganization or disastrous floods, or merely weary of their marginal economic status and the proscription of the southern caste system, learned of the opportunities that awaited them in Chicago, Detroit, and Cleveland. Each Southern Negro who chose to migrate made a highly personal decision, but he was frequently influenced by the power of mass suggestion.[44]

The increased number of blacks in the North drastically altered race relations in that area. As the percentage of blacks in urban areas increased, white hostility and tensions intensified, particularly among immigrant ethnics, whose communities tended to be adjacent to black neighborhoods.[45] If the problems blacks experienced in their encounters with the older immigrant ethnics (Germans and Irish) were temporarily relieved during the 1870s and 1880s by the latter's upward mobility, they were soon replaced by the efforts of the newer Eastern European ethnics to restrict low-status housing and job competition. Bloch describes the problems faced by Northern black Americans because of the arrival of new immigrants:

106

Prior to this influx of new immigrants, it was traditional for Southern Afro-Americans to perform . . . seasonal type of work. Colored Americans were displaced by Greeks and Italians in the shoeshining and catering trades. During this same period, young Germans and Frenchmen were fast monopolizing the barber trade. . . . After white immigrants had accommodated themselves to their new conditions and found segments of a trade no longer economically and socially advantageous, they permitted Afro-Americans to enter.[46]

As long as a sufficient supply of white labor existed, Northern industrialists were not disposed to hire blacks, especially in skilled and semiskilled positions. Open immigration from Europe before World War I virtually eliminated a labor shortage, and industrialists saw little need to antagonize white workers by hiring black labor. Moreover, blacks were denied equal participation in labor unions. Some labor unions excluded blacks through clauses in their constitutions. Others admitted them but restricted their participation to segregated and subordinate black unions under the control of parallel white groups who ostensibly negotiated and bargained for them. But in many cases the parent white unions either excluded blacks from special projects or made little effort to seek employment for them.[47]

Because labor leaders failed to encourage or support black unionization, industrialists who ignored blacks during periods of normal employment persuaded some blacks to become strikebreakers. There was little resistance in the black community against such policies. Black leaders such as Booker T. Washington, upset by the exclusionist policies of the labor unions, encouraged blacks to cross the picket lines and seek employment usually denied to them. However, the use of blacks as strikebreakers further aggravated the racial tensions already produced by increased black visibility in the North. Blacks were used to help break the Chicago stockyard strikes of 1904 and 1916, the Chicago teamster strike of 1905, the East St. Louis Aluminum Ore Company strike of 1917, and the national steel strike of 1919. Employers intentionally "played upon social fears in order to deflect the white workers' hostility from themselves to the black strikebreakers."[48] According to Spear, "often both black and white workers were but pawns in the efforts of the economic and political elite to weaken any threat to its own hegemony."[49] Racial violence often followed in the wake of these incidents; in fact, nearly all of the racial violence in the early twentieth century involved lower-class whites and blacks.[50]

Violent racial conflict between blacks and whites reached its peak during 1919, when more than twenty riots or racial incidents erupted in cities across the nation.[51] The typical riot began after black retaliation against white violence or persecution of individual blacks. Upset by what they perceived to be a premeditated and organized black conspiracy to "take over," whites responded with armed attacks by mobs and police. In the Chicago riot, for example, a black crowd, infuriated because police refused to take any action when they charged that a black man had been stoned by whites and subsequently drowned, attacked several white men. Rumor that a full-scale race riot was taking place quickly spread over Chicago's South Side. Whites retaliated in the next few days by beating, stabbing, or shooting blacks who had wandered accidentally into white neighborhoods, attacking black workers departing from the stockyards, and assaulting blacks in streetcars. Meanwhile, black mobs responded with attacks against whites who rode trolleys through or worked in the black belt.[52]

A number of factors caused these incidents of violence across the nation. The mass recruitment of thousands of blacks to work in the industrial plants during the white labor shortage of World War I created serious housing problems, because many cities were unable to absorb the large influx of blacks. As blacks spilled over ghetto boundaries and confronted and displaced whites, hostilities between the two groups increased.[53] Landlords were quick to play one race against the other as they raised rents.[54] Black encroachment was threatening to whites who felt that they had prior claim to certain rights and advantages. As Rudwick has observed,

Whites . . . resented increased contacts with Negroes after the black ghetto gradually expanded or "invasion" took place. Improvement Associations held indignation meetings, and, when warnings were ignored, violent measures were sometimes taken. During the two years before the Chicago riot, bombs wrecked an average of one Negro dwelling a month. . . . Disputes occurred when Negroes attempted to use parks, playgrounds, or bathing beaches which were controlled by whites.[55]

Moreover, because of the economic cutback immediately following World War I, job insecurity and unemployment were high, and competition for employment became increasingly racial in character. Furthermore, many whites were upset that blacks did not follow the segregation pattern and racial etiquette of the South: they felt that blacks were taking advantage of their Northern freedom.[56]

Finally, the increased militancy of the black population made it unlikely that blacks would passively sit by while whites attacked them. Because blacks often retaliated against white violence, interracial tension was further heightened. Although the victims in the riots of 1919 were mostly blacks, who were often unable to protect themselves or their families, these outbursts marked the first time that blacks engaged on a wide scale in retaliatory violence against white attacks and sometimes took the initiative in attacking whites.[57] This more aggressive response to white attacks represented a change in blacks' perception of their power resources and their ability to resist unrestrained white violence.

DIFFERENTIAL BLACK RESPONSE TO WHITE POWER AND BIOLOGICAL RACISM

As I have stated previously, during much of the Reconstruction period black Americans were generally optimistic about their future in American society, and the dominant pattern of thought was that of strong support for meaningful integration into American society. The Negro Convention Movement in the early 1870s placed a great deal of emphasis on civil rights, protest against increasing white violence and discrimination, and ways to enforce the Fifteenth Amendment.[58] Moreover, in 1872 blacks successfully carried out a boycott of segregated streetcars in Savannah, Georgia. Nonviolent black demonstrations and protest produced desegregation of streetcars in New Orleans, Charleston, and Richmond in 1867, and in Louisville in 1870–1871.[59] That these demonstrations occurred and were successful indicated that blacks had acquired the power resources that allowed them openly to attack Jim Crow segregation. The black man's position had been strengthened with the adoption of the Fourteenth and Fifteenth Amendments and various civil rights legislation and by the Radical Republicans' commitment during the Reconstruction to uphold his civil rights, thus making it all the more likely that black leaders would not only stress political action and pressure for civil rights in the Negro Convention Movement but would also attempt to confront Jim Crow segregation directly and achieve some success.

However, as conditions for blacks began to deteriorate after the Reconstruction period and as racist beliefs intensified in both the North and South, black protest was replaced by accommodation to Jim Crowism, and black social thought shifted from a dominant emphasis on integration to a defensive ideology of self-help and racial solidarity. Lynchings, pogrom-like attacks against the black community, Jim Crow laws, racist Supreme Court decisions, disfranchisement, and exclusionist labor policies all combined to diminish black optimism and faith in the American system. "When Booker T. Washington made his famous speech in Atlanta in 1895 in which he announced his widely quoted formula for the accommodation of the two races," states Frazier, "the Negro had already been gradually forced to accept an inferior status in the South and the period of acute race conflict was drawing to a close."[60]

The ascendancy of Booker T. Washington during this period can only be fully understood in relation to the abrupt shift from a restrictive–fluid pattern of competitive race relations to a very restrictive pattern in all parts of the nation. As Meier eloquently states,

> Not only did his espousal of economic advancement and self-help make sense to a substantial and growing element, not only did Southern Negroes find an opportunistic accommodation advantageous if not necessary, but many leaders in all sections, even those who basically nourished a deep-seated protest philosophy, discouraged as they were by the trend of events, hopefully supported the Tuskegeean and his program in their eagerness to somehow stem the seemingly irresistible tide of racial proscription.[61]

Despite the prominence of Booker T. Washington, black protest against increased racism did not completely disappear during this period. The first years of the twentieth century witnessed a proliferation of black boycotts of segregated streetcars; blacks staged boycotts in twenty-six cities between 1900 and 1907.[62] These protests were conservative by contemporary standards. Because they took place during a period in which white hegemony and biological racism were in ascendancy, the boycotters "avoided a direct confrontation with the laws, such as would have occurred if Negroes had insisted on sitting in the white section."[63] Unlike the earlier demonstrations against segregated streetcars during the Reconstruction period and the later Montgomery bus boycott in 1955, which occurred during periods of more fluid competitive race relations, the boycotts of 1900–1907 had little chance for success and eventually collapsed, with few concrete gains. As Meier and Rudwick have stated,

> In some cities, like Atlanta, Memphis, Natchez, Richmond, and Savannah, leadership cleavages undoubtedly hastened the demise of the protests. But more than anything else, what undoubtedly caused their decline was a feeling of discouragement—a realistic pessimism—that must in time have come over the demonstrators as they saw that their withdrawal of patronage produced no results. It is not

surprising that, in the end, the boycott movements against Jim Crow trolleys failed in all of the cities where they were initiated. They occurred at a time when southern racism was reaching its crest and when the white South had gained a respectful hearing in the North. With the Supreme Court endorsing the separate-but-equal doctrine and with Negroes in most places virtually disfranchised, the boycotts were the only way of protesting realistically open to them. In retrospect, it is easy to see that their failure was inevitable, the remarkable thing is not that the boycotts failed, but that they happened in so many places and lasted as long as they often did.[64]

There were, of course, other black responses to the system of racism and Jim Crow segregation. Bishop Henry McNeal Turner attempted to organize an emigration movement to Africa during the 1890s and the first decade of the twentieth century, "but he was never able to launch a successful emigration plan, even though individuals and small groups occasionally migrated to Africa."[65] W. E. B. DuBois organized the Niagara Movement in 1905 to combat Booker T. Washington's policy of accommodation and to provide aggressive action for the elimination of racial oppression. However, the movement lasted only four years, and although it generated considerable publicity, "beyond agitation its accomplishments were relatively little."[66]

In 1911 and 1914, white liberals and educated blacks, respectively, founded the National Association for the Advancement of Colored People and the National Urban League. Working through controlling institutional channels and relying heavily on education and persuasion, these organizations did not make a significant impact before 1930, although the NAACP did achieve some limited success in awakening politicians and the general public to the evils of lynchings in the 1920s. But in the early twentieth century black protest organizations were severely restricted in the resources they could apply in the face of virulent racism and Jim Crow segregation, and, having little impact on the white power structure, they achieved few concrete gains.

Although black Americans were not in a position to aggressively and successfully press for civil rights during this period, the mass migration of blacks to Northern urban centers between 1910 and 1920 and their subsequent concentration in black ghettoes provided a new potential for mass action not available to them in the rural South.[67] At first, this new resource did not manifest itself in organized and disciplined movements against racial stratification but rather was reflected in the fact that blacks felt secure enough in large ghetto communities to fight back when attacked by whites. Whereas previous large-scale confrontations between black and white citizens had consisted largely of pogrom-like attacks in which whites assaulted blacks in a one-way battle (e.g., the Irish attacks on the black community during the New York draft riots in 1863), the riots in East St. Louis in 1917 and in Northern urban centers in 1919 were two-way battles. In fact, very few whites dared to venture into the black community to attack blacks. Most blacks were killed or injured on the periphery of the black ghetto or in white neighborhoods.

The period immediately following the violent outbreaks in 1919 brought little change in the status of black Americans. The general economic prosperity of the roaring twenties improved the employment opportunities of whites, thereby alleviating the tensions and fears that precipitated the riots in 1919, but had little effect on blacks. Frustrated by the bloody riots of 1919 and continued racial discrimination that virtually closed every avenue of assimilation, black social thought shifted further away from integration and moved closer to black nationalism. Among the black elite, nationalist sentiment was manifested in the Harlem Renaissance after World War I. The Harlem Renaissance was basically a period of black self-discovery and of ardent interest in black experience.[68] The art and literature of the Harlem Renaissance rejected racist stereotypes and white values regarding race and sought to create a new race consciousness.

Among the black lower-class masses, however, nationalist sentiment was reflected in the widespread support for Marcus Garvey's "Back to Africa" movement. Drawing on the disillusionment and frustration of the urbanized black masses, many of them recent migrants from Southern rural areas who soon discovered that the North was not the promised land, Garvey launched the first significant black mass movement in the United States.[69] Garvey received little support from the black intelligentsia, who denounced him as a demagogue and argued that his program to ship blacks back to Africa was impractical. But Garvey provided lower-class blacks with a dream, a new promised land in Africa. Inventing honors and distinctions, he made lower-class blacks feel that they were participating in a great cause.[70] There are no exact figures on the total membership of Garvey's movement, but various writers have suggested numbers ranging from one million to six million.[71] Beginning in 1914 and reaching its peak during the post World War I period, the movement finally collapsed in 1923 when Garvey was convicted for mail fraud and subsequently deported. But the movement indicated "the extent to which Negroes entertained doubts concerning the hope for first-class citizenship in the only fatherland of which they knew."[72]

So the 1920s marked a period of little black optimism and extended the disillusionment that had gripped black social thought as far back as 1890. The ideology of biological racism had crystallized, segregation and discrimination were institutionalized, and an overwhelming majority of the black population was in a struggle for survival with little hope for any immediate improvement in their impoverished state. But as we shall see in the next chapter, the period of restrictive competitive relations was soon challenged, and for a brief period of time black social thought once more moved from a deep pessimism and support for racial solidarity, self-help, and black nationalism to a burgeoning optimism and support for interracial cooperation and political protests.

NOTES

1. Because of the relatively large number of free blacks in the North (e.g., in 1790 there were 21,108 free blacks and 40,370 slaves in the states of New Hampshire, Vermont, Rhode Island, Connecticut, New York, New Jersey, and Pennsylvania; there were 5,463 free blacks in Massachusetts and 538 free blacks in Maine, both states having previously

abolished slavery) (see Peter M. Bergman, *The Chronological History of the Negro in America* [New York: Harper, 1969], p. 68.), the pattern of race relations in the North could not be adequately described as a paternalistic system but rather as a system with both competitive and paternalistic features.

2. Leon F. Litwack, *North of Slavery: The Negro in the Free State, 1790–1860* (Chicago: U. of Chicago, 1961), p. 5. Also see Wilbert E. Moore, *American Negro Slavery and Abolition: A Sociological Study* (New York: Third Press, 1971), pp. 22–23.

3. Litwack, op. cit., p. 5.

4. On this point, Noel states: "In contrast to the Northern situation, the men of power in the Southern colonies were predominantly planters who were unified in their need for large numbers of slaves. The margin of profit in agricultural production for the commercial market was such that the small landholders could not compete and the costs of training and the limitation on control (by the planter) which were associated with indentured labor made profitable exploitation of such labor increasingly difficult. Hence, it was not the need for labor *per se* which was critical for the establishment of the emerging economic system of a particular kind of labor. In short, the Southern power elite uniformly needed slave labor while only certain men of power shared this need in the North and hence the latter advocated slave laws but lacked the power (or did not feel the need) to secure the all-encompassing laws characteristic of the Southern colonies." Donald L. Noel, "A Theory of the Origin of Ethnic Stratification," *Social Problems*, 16:167 (Fall 1968).

5. George M. Fredrickson, "Toward a Social Interpretation of the Development of American Racism," in *Key Issues in the Afro-American Experience*, ed. by Nathan I. Huggins, Martin Kilson, and Daniel M. Fox (New York: Harcourt, 1971), vol. 1, p. 253.

6. See Robert Ernst, *Immigrant Life in New York City, 1825–1863* (Port Washington, N.Y.: Kings Crown Press, 1949).

7. Litwack, op. cit., chap. 5.

8. Herman D. Bloch, *The Circle of Discrimination: An Economic and Social Study of the Black Man in New York* (New York: New York U.P., 1969), p. 34. Irish resentment against blacks reached its peak in 1863 with the New York draft riots. Essentially, the Irish were upset about being drafted into a war they felt would free the blacks, who would in turn flood the cities and take away their jobs. The riots lasted from July 13 to 16, and many blacks were beaten to death and had their homes destroyed. These assaults were described as pogrom attacks against blacks.

9. Litwack, op. cit., p. 166.

10. See Ibid., pp. 182–183, for a discussion of this point.

11. For a discussion of the Negro Convention Movement, see William H. and Jane H. Pease, "The Negro Convention Movement," in

Key Issues in the Afro-American Experience, op. cit., pp. 191–205; also see *Negro Convention Proceedings,* reprint ed. (New York: Arno, 1970).

12. Pease and Pease, op. cit., p. 201.

13. Alexis de Tocqueville, *Democracy in America,* ed. by J. P. Mayer (New York: Doubleday, 1969), p. 343. Tocqueville goes on to state: "In the South, where slavery still exists, less trouble is taken to keep the Negro apart: they sometimes share the labors and the pleasures of the white men; people are prepared to mix with them to some extent; legislation is more harsh against them, but customs are more tolerant and gentle.

"In the South the master has no fear of lifting the slave up to his level, for he knows that when he wants to he can always throw him down into the dust. In the North the white man no longer clearly sees the barrier that separates him from the degraded race, and he keeps the Negro at a distance all the more carefully because he fears lest one day they be confounded together." Ibid., p. 343.

14. Ibid., p. 357.

15. Thomas F. Gossett, *Race: The History of an Idea in America* (Dallas: Southern Methodist U.P., 1963), pp. 256–257, and August Meier and Elliot Rudwick, *From Plantation to Ghetto: The Interpretative History of American Negroes,* rev. ed. (New York: Hill and Wang, 1970), pp. 138–139.

16. E. Franklin Frazier, *The Negro in the United States,* rev. ed. (New York: Macmillan, 1957).

17. Ibid., p. 135.

18. Ray Marshall, "Industrialisation and Race Relations in the Southern United States," in *Industrialisation and Race Relations,* ed. by Guy Hunter (London: Oxford U.P., 1965), p. 66.

19. August Meier, *Negro Thought in America, 1880–1915: Racial Ideologies in the Age of Booker T. Washington* (Ann Arbor: U. of Michigan, 1964), p. 3.

20. Nowhere was this optimism reflected more than in the speeches of Frederick Douglass during this period. "We are no longer property, but persons. We are not aliens, but citizens. We are not only men, but men among men. If any people may have a future, a prosperous and happy future, such a future is possible to us, and I hope it will be the business of every man who hears my voice to-day, to contribute his full share to the sum of the common welfare of our race." Frederick Douglass, "Address Before the Tennessee Colored Agricultural and Mechanical Association" (Sept. 18, 1873), in *Negro Social and Political Thought, 1850–1920,* ed. by Howard Brotz (New York: Basic Books, 1966), p. 297.

21. Meier, op. cit., p. 22.

22. On this point, Meier states: "By 1910 in most Southern states at

least twice as much was spent per pupil on whites as on Negroes. Conservatives acceded to the desirability of industrial education for the uplift of a 'backward race,' but extremists like Governor Vardamon of Mississippi objected to any sort of education for Negroes." Ibid., pp. 162–163.

23. Ibid., p. 20.

24. See C. Van Woodward, *The Strange Career of Jim Crow* (New York: Oxford U.P., 1966), p. 35.

25. Eric Foner, *America's Black Past* (New York: Harper, 1970), p. 234.

26. John Hope Franklin, *From Slavery to Freedom*, 3rd ed. (New York: Knopf, 1967), p. 337.

27. Ibid.

28. Ray Marshall, *The Negro Worker* (New York: Random House, 1967), pp. 12–13.

29. C. Van Woodward, *Origins of the New South, 1877–1913* (Baton Rouge: Louisiana State U.P., 1951), p. 211.

30. Ibid., p. 221.

31. As John Hope Franklin put it: "Many Republicans, whatever their altruistic motives, were moved to adopt the cause of the Negro almost solely by considerations of political expediency and strategy. It would have been unnatural for them not to have strengthened their party by enfranchising the Negroes and enlisting them as loyal voters." Franklin, op. cit., p. 325.

32. Bloch, op. cit., p. 38.

33. Allan Spear, "The Origins of the Urban Ghetto, 1870–1915," in *Key Issues in the Afro-American Experience*, Vol. II, op. cit., pp. 158–159. Also see Allan Spear, *Black Chicago: The Making of a Negro Ghetto* (Chicago: U. of Chicago, 1967).

34. In describing Chicago during this period, Spear states: "Most Negroes, although concentrated in certain sections of the city, lived in mixed neighborhoods." Spear, *Black Chicago*, op. cit., p. 7.

35. Spear, "The Origins of the Urban Ghetto," op. cit., p. 154.

36. Ibid.

37. Ibid., p. 159.

38. Ibid. "In Chicago, for instance, blacks had been elected to the state legislature and to the county board of commissioners by predominantly white constituencies in the 1880's and the early 1890's. In 1906, however, when a black attorney ran for the municipal court, he aroused vigorous white opposition and was the only Republican candidate to lose what was otherwise a Republican sweep."

39. For further discussion of many of these points, see Meier, op. cit., pp. 161–163; C. Van Woodward, *The Strange Career of Jim Crow*, op. cit., pp. 52–53; Gossett, op. cit., chap. 11; and Rayford W. Logan, *The Betrayal of the Negro* (New York: Macmillan, 1954), chap. 13.

40. See Spear, "The Origins of the Urban Ghetto," op. cit., p. 161; Meier, op. cit., p. 22; Pierre van den Berghe, *Race and Racism: A Comparative Perspective* (New York: Wiley, 1967), p. 87; and Franklin, op. cit., pp. 425–432.

41. van den Berghe, op. cit., and John Highan, *Strangers in the Land* (New Brunswick, N.J.: Rutgers U.P., 1955).

42. Reynolds Farley, *Growth of the Black Population: A Study of Demographic Trends* (Chicago: Markham, 1970), p. 46, and Chicago Commission on Race Relations, *The Negro in Chicago, A Study of Race Relations and a Race Riot* (Chicago: U. of Chicago, 1922), p. 81.

43. Spear, *Black Chicago*, op. cit., chap. 7.

44. Ibid., p. 136.

45. Spear, "The Origins of the Urban Ghetto," op. cit., p. 162.

46. Bloch, op. cit., p. 41.

47. See Ray Marshall, *The Negro and Organized Labor* (New York: Wiley, 1965), and *The Negro Worker* (New York: Random House, 1967); Sterling D. Spero and Abram L. Harris, *The Black Worker* (New York: Columbia U.P., 1931); Charles H. Wesley, *Negro Labor in the United States, 1850–1925: A Study in American Economic History* (New York: Vanguard, 1931), Spear, *Black Chicago*, op. cit.; and Herbert G. Gutman, "Blacks and the Labor Movement: A Case Study," in *America's Black Past*, ed. by Eric Foner (New York: Harper, 1970).

48. Spear, "The Origins of the Urban Ghetto," op. cit., p. 163. Spero and Harris comment on management's use of black strikebreakers: "But when all is said and done, the number of strikes broken by black labor have been few as compared with the number broken by white labor. What is more, the Negro has seldom been the only or even the most important strike-breaking element. Employers in emergencies take whatever labor they can get and the Negro is only one of many groups involved. But the bitterness of American race prejudice has always made his presence an especially sore point and not infrequently a signal for exceptional disorder." Spero and Harris, op. cit., p. 131.

49. Spear, "The Origins of the Urban Ghetto," op. cit., p. 163.

50. Ibid., p. 163.

51. Arthur I. Waskow, *From Race Riot to Sit-In* (Garden City, N.Y.: Doubleday, 1966), pp. 1–218.

52. Spear, *Black Chicago*, op. cit., pp. 214–219; Chicago Commission on Race Relations, op. cit.; and Morris Janowitz, "Patterns of Collective Racial Violence," in *Violence in America: Historical and Comparative Perspectives*, ed. by Hugh Davis Graham and Ted Robert Gurr (New York: Bantam, 1969), pp. 416–417.

53. Bryan T. Downes and Stephen W. Burks, "The Historical Development of the Black Protest Movement," in *Blacks in the United States* ed. by Norval D. Glenn and Charles M. Bonjean (San Francisco: Chandler, 1969), p. 24.

54. Elliot Rudwick, *Race Riot at East St. Louis, July 2, 1917* (New York: World, 1966), p. 219.

55. Ibid., p. 219.

56. Ibid., p. 220.

57. Downes and Burks, op. cit., p. 331.

58. Meier, op. cit., pp. 9–10.

59. August Meier and Elliot Rudwick, "A Strange Chapter in the Career of 'Jim Crow,'" in *The Making of Black America: Essays in Negro Life and History,* ed. by August Meier and Elliot Rudwick (New York: Atheneum, 1969), pp. 14–19; Joel R. Williamson, *After Slavery: The Negro in South Carolina During Reconstruction, 1861–1877* (Chapel Hill: U. of North Carolina, 1965), pp. 281–283; and Marjorie M. Morris, "An Early Instance of Non-Violence: The Louisville Demonstrations of 1870–1871," *Journal of Southern History,* 25:487–504 (Nov. 1966).

60. Frazier, op. cit., p. 162.

61. Meier, op. cit., p. 166.

62. August Meier and Elliot Rudwick, "The Boycott Against Jim Crow Streetcars in the South, 1900–1906," *Journal of American History,* 55:756–759 (Mar. 1969).

63. Ibid., p. 771.

64. Ibid., p. 775. Blacks also participated in boycotts of segregated schools in the North between 1897 and 1925, but all to no avail. See August Meier and Elliot Rudwick, "Negro Boycotts of Jim Crow Schools in the North, 1897–1925," *Integrated Education,* 5:1–12 (Aug.–Sept. 1967).

65. Edwin S. Redkey, "The Flowering of Black Nationalism: Henry McNeal Turner and Marcus Garvey," in *Key Issues in the Afro-American Experience,* Vol. II, op. cit., p. 115. Also see Edwin S. Redkey, *Black Exodus: Black Nationalism and Back-to-Africa Movements, 1890–1910* (New Haven, Conn.: Yale U. Press, 1969).

66. Meier, op. cit., p. 179.

67. Downes and Burks, op. cit., p. 331, and Allen D. Grimshaw, "Lawlessness and Violence in America and Their Special Manifestations in Changing Negro–White Relationships," *Journal of Negro History,* 64:52–72 (Jan. 1959).

68. Robert A. Bone, "The Negro Novel in America," in *America's Black Past,* op. cit., p. 383.

69. See Harold Cruse, *The Crisis of the Negro Intellectual* (New York: Morrow, 1967), and E. U. Essien-Udom, *Black Nationalism: A Search for an Identity in America* (New York: Dell, 1962).

70. Franklin, op. cit., p. 529.

71. Essien-Udom, op. cit., p. 49.

72. Franklin, op. cit., p. 492.

CHAPTER SEVEN

Competitive Race Relations and the Proliferation of Racial Protests: 1940–1970

ISTORY will record the mid-twentieth century as one of the most dynamic periods of black–white contact. It was a period that witnessed the proliferation of black protests, ranging from the essentially nonviolent to the violent. It was a period when competitive race relations reached their most fluid pattern and when biological racism declined and cultural racism was revived primarily in institutional form. Fundamentally, however, it was a period when blacks experienced their most significant growth of power resources. Because of black migration to cities, increased urbanization, expanded industrialization, basic shifts in the national economy, and changes ushered in by World War II and the Cold War, new resources became available to black Americans that placed them in greater competition with whites. In the next several sections of this chapter, I shall attempt to describe in some detail the way these various aspects of social change have influenced the growth of black power resources.

THE GROWTH OF BLACK COMPETITIVE RESOURCES

Black citizens' struggle for survival continued well into the 1930s as they were hit hard by the Depression. The last to be hired and the first to be fired, twice as many blacks as whites required public assistance. In some cities of the South, about three fourths of the black population was on relief.[1]

The upturn for blacks came with the New Deal policies of the Roosevelt administration, which were developed to soften the impact of the Depression. The New Deal programs extended federal securities and benefits to all citizens, especially the poor. Despite the fact that New Deal agencies often practiced racial discrimination in the allocation of services and funds, black citizens, overwhelmingly represented in the poverty-stricken segment of the population, benefited materially from this federal commitment to improve the plight of the poor.

In the New Deal's efforts to assist blacks, black leaders participated in federal governmental affairs as never before.

Many relief programs included elementary education and training classes as part of the regimen. Negro colleges and universities received funds for buildings. The Office of Education, along with other agencies, began an important study of Negro education.

Professional opportunities opened up in government, although not at the rate which Negroes were graduating from colleges. For the first time, Negroes were employed as architects, lawyers, engineers, economists, statisticians, interviewers, office managers, case aids, and librarians. Nonprofessional white collar jobs now became available to trained stenographers, clerks, and secretaries. While many of these jobs centered around programs for Negroes within the government, such as Negro slum clearance projects, Negro NYA offices, and the like, they broke down the dam which had hitherto kept Negroes out of these kinds of positions.[2]

It was no mere coincidence that this new concern of federal officials for the plight of blacks occurred at a time when the black vote in the key Northern states had become a significant factor of politics. As John Hope Franklin has put it,

In consequence of the concentration of Negroes in the Northern cities there developed a political resurgence on the part of Negroes that placed them once more in the thick of American politics and gave them the kind of strength that they had not exercised since the period of Reconstruction.[3]

The black vote has been used as a form of political pressure for decades. Since the elections of the 1920s, blacks have analyzed the voting records of Congressmen and monitored the actions of Presidents in order to identify their political adversaries.[4] The lure of the black vote has often prompted the promises of politicians to work for racial equality, as did the Democratic and Progressive candidates of 1928. At other times, politicians have granted token concessions in the hope of preserving or gaining black support, as did Roosevelt in 1940 when he took steps to increase black participation in the Armed Forces within a segregated context. It was clear by 1940 that the black vote was large enough in pivotal Northern states to decide close national elections.[5] In fact, President Truman, overwhelmingly picked by political observers to lose the Presidential election to Governor Dewey of New York, recognized that he could not possibly defeat his Republican rival without the support of black Americans. For the first time since Reconstruction, the status of the black man was a central issue in a Presidential campaign, and much to the chagrin of its Southern members the Democratic Party in 1948 adopted a civil rights plank as part of its party platform. That same year, President Truman issued an executive order banning racial segregation in the Armed Forces—satisfying a demand originally introduced by black leaders in 1940. Such actions proved to be effective. Truman, with the overwhelming support of black voters, narrowly defeated Dewey.[6]

Furthermore, it was during the New Deal period that blacks

made their first real breakthrough in the labor movement. The Congress of Industrial Organization (CIO) broke with the American Federation of Labor (AFL) and adopted a policy explicitly egalitarian toward blacks. Unlike the craft unions, which had organized workers on the basis of individual craft, the CIO attempted to unionize already employed workers on an industry-wide basis—thus the union had little control over the racial makeup of membership.[7] Moreover, CIO officials realized that during a period of labor surplus it was indeed difficult to organize workers effectively by ignoring blacks and thereby forcing them to become strikebreakers.[8] However, it would be incorrect to assume that blacks did not experience discrimination in gaining membership, because some CIO locals tolerated segregation and relegated blacks to inferior jobs and others barred blacks altogether.[9] Nevertheless, August Meier and Elliot Rudwick have concluded that "the CIO contribution to the changing pattern of race relations has been incalculable. It made interracial trade unionism truly respectable. It gave black and white workers a sense of common interest, a solidarity, that transcended racial lines."[10]

In the face of changes involving increased voting power and greater participation in labor unions, a new wave of optimism and sense of power were reflected in black leadership. Once again, black leaders engaged in direct political action in an effort to improve the civil rights and economic conditions of black Americans. As early as 1940, A. Philip Randolph, Walter White, T. Arnold Hall, and other outstanding black leaders submitted to President Roosevelt a seven-point program outlining minimal standards for giving blacks fair consideration in the national defense program. The government responded by allowing blacks to enter the Armed Forces in proportion to their percentage of the population—but they were to remain in segregated units, and, with the exception of chaplains or medical officers, no black officers were to be used in the black units commanded by whites. Black leaders were dissatisfied with these limited changes and openly denounced Roosevelt in the press. Roosevelt's appointment of Colonel Benjamin O. Davis as Brigadier General in 1940 was dismissed as a political move immediately before national elections.[11] At this point, the overall impression of black leaders was that the federal administration had committed itself to a segregated army to fight the threat of worldwide racism and fascism.

While blacks were segregated in the Armed Forces, they were also experiencing widespread discrimination in the nation's defense plants. Cognizant of the skyrocketing wages in industrial plants holding defense contracts and aware that the rigid antiblack policy in industry had undergone minor change, blacks organized a program for direct action. Early in 1941, A. Philip Randolph, president of the Brotherhood of Sleeping Car Porters, promoted the idea that one hundred fifty thousand blacks should march on Washington, D.C., to protest racial discrimination in the nation's defense plants. This idea proved to be immediately effective, partly because it was overwhelmingly endorsed by the black community and partly because the government was vulnerable to massive demonstrations during wartime (in Washington the question was repeatedly asked "What will Berlin think?") and hence more willing to negotiate to settle black demands. As thousands of blacks were making plans to participate in the march and after repeated pleas failed to get Randolph to call off the march, President Roosevelt agreed to issue an executive order banning discrimination in defense plants and in governmental agencies. Following this historic act, Roosevelt established the Fair Employment Practices Committee to implement the order. "Though it worked unevenly and in many cases not at all, it nevertheless was a major basis for advance above sustenance for Negroes. By war's end, some 2 million blacks were employed in war industry, and the FEPC reported that 1,300,000 of these had gotten jobs in consequence of its efforts."[12]

The economic status of blacks significantly improved during the war. The President's executive order, which removed many racial barriers, combined with the acute labor shortage enabled many blacks to move into positions heretofore denied them.[13] It is true that many black workers experienced losses in occupational status following the war because defense industries declined, the Fair Employment Practices Committee

ended in 1946, and competition with white veterans returning to the civilian labor force increased.[14] However, as Leonard Broom and Norval D. Glenn have stated,

> Not all wartime gains were lost, the conditions remained
> more favorable for Negro advancement than they had been
> before the war. Negro servicemen and workers in war indus-
> tries gained valuable training and experience that enabled
> them to compete more effectively and their employment in
> large numbers in the unionized industries during the war left
> them in a stronger position in the labor movement.[15]

Because the government took steps to avoid a postwar recession, blacks (as well as whites) continued their economic gains.
Although the relative position of blacks with respect to whites
changed very little in the decade following World War II,
expanding occupational opportunities, particularly in urban
areas, enabled a relatively small but significant number of
blacks to upgrade their occupations, increase their income, and
improve their standard of living. As more and more blacks at-
tained middle-class status, expectations and aspirations increased, and, as we shall see, dissatisfaction with continued racial oppression became more intense. However, if black
expectations were raised because of improved economic conditions, greater representation in labor unions, and increased voting strength, they were reinforced and further heightened by
the emergence of the newly independent African states and
the 1954 Supreme Court decision.

The new African states broke up the old colonial empires
and significantly altered international politics, with both Eastern and Western powers competing for the support of the new
regimes. Racial violence and tension in the United States therefore were embarrassing to government officials. Meanwhile,
identifying with the successful efforts of African nations in
achieving liberation, blacks in the United States were strengthened in their own struggle against racial oppression. Commenting on these developments, James W. Vander Zanden writes
that

Although the United States had for decades been more or less willing to allow the South a measure of sovereignty on the race issue, it has become increasingly unwilling to do so since World War II. There has been a growing insistence, reinforced by international pressures, that the racial norms of the South give way to the democratic norms of the American creed. Middle-class Negroes, in particular, have found their status as middle-class Americans conflicting with the dictates of a racial-caste order.[16]

The 1954 Supreme Court decision against mandatory school segregation overturned the "separate but equal" doctrine established by *Plessy v. Ferguson* in 1896 and defined blacks as first-class citizens in the most formal and authoritative fashion.[17] "The Supreme Court's antisegregation decisions and the emergence of the African nations created a new self-image for many Negroes; accommodation to Jim Crow no longer could be an acceptable response to the enduring and aggravated frustrations of the racial order."[18]

WHITE REACTION TO INCREASED BLACK COMPETITIVE RESOURCES

The growth of black competitive resources after World War II was not immediately accompanied by severe white hostility. Except for the South's attempt to resist desegregation in the late 1950s, black advancement prior to 1960 occurred with relatively little white resistance. Black encroachment in the economic sphere did not generate the kind of racial violence that disrupted the country in the early twentieth century. In order to fully understand why the immediate postwar period was spared the intense racial tension that sometimes accompanies changes in competitive race relations, attention must be directed to the fundamental shifts that took place in the national economy and in the structural relations that determined black–white contact. Specifically, whereas the total employed labor force increased 37 per cent between 1941 and 1960, the total number of employed white-collar workers expanded by 81 per cent (by almost twelve million).[19] Even though blacks were virtually excluded from the highest-status positions (e.g., managers, officials, and proprietors), they were able to fill the intermediate-level jobs vacated by hundreds of thousands of upwardly mobile whites who were moving into upper-level positions.[20] Broom and Glenn conclude that

> Because Negro gains could occur without loss to whites, white resistance to Negro advancement was less than it otherwise would have been. Expansion of jobs at the upper levels is not a new trend; it goes back to the start of industrialization, but until recently the upward movement of workers generated by this change did not greatly benefit Negroes. As long as large numbers of European immigrants were entering the country, they, rather than Negroes, replaced most of the native-born whites who moved up. World War I slowed European immigration and the Immigrant Act of 1924 reduced it to a mere trickle, so that by the 1940's there was no longer a large pool of immigrants at the lowest occupational levels to replace the upward-moving native workers. The opportunity for the first great occupational advancement of Negro Americans was at hand.[21]

However, the moment the dominant group perceives particular minority gains as constituting a *distinct* threat to its sense of superior position, racial tensions intensify. Nowhere is this more clearly demonstrated than in the resistance to desegregation exhibited by Southern whites following the 1954 Supreme Court decision. Efforts to implement this decision were viewed by Southern whites as the most serious challenge to their way of life and proprietary claims to rights and privileges since Reconstruction, and they reacted accordingly. To mention a few of the incidents: White Citizens Councils sprang up all over the South, imposing drastic sanctions on blacks who signed integration petitions; the Ku Klux Klan made its reappearance in Alabama, Florida, Georgia, and South Carolina; Southern politicians attempted to outdo each other in racist militant statements; a black woman, Autherine Lucy, was confronted with a rioting mob when she attempted to enroll in the University of Alabama in 1956; the Alabama Chapter of the NAACP was fined a hundred thousand dollars and slapped with a court injunction that prohibited its operating in the state (for the next two years the NAACP was inactive in Alabama); and national guardsmen joined white mobs to prevent integration of a high school in Little Rock, Arkansas, in 1957.[22] It was clear by the late 1950s that Southern whites were quite optimistic about their ability to defeat desegregation. The Supreme Court decision had been passed, the NAACP had taken steps to implement it with hundreds of suits in courts, but segregation remained well entrenched. Southern whites had little reason to believe that they would soon face the most serious threat in the twentieth century to their group position—the proliferation of black protest movements during the 1960s.

POWER AND THE CHANGING CHARACTER OF BLACK PROTEST

Throughout our discussion of black social thought and protest in the United States, one pattern of behavior seems to emerge: *the changing goals of black advancement tend to be associated with the changing definition of black despair, and both the defined problem and the conceived goal are ultimately associated with the choice of possible pressure or constraint resources that blacks can mobilize in pressing for the desired solution.* However, it should be noted that despite the definition of the problem and the conception of the goal, the choice of pressure resources is influenced or determined by the extent to which blacks find themselves in competitive relations with whites. The now more conservative black protest movements, such as the NAACP and the National Urban League, developed and gained momentum when racial accommodations were undergoing change but when the dominant-group controls were so strong that the pressure tactics of the mid-twentieth century activist movements would not have been tolerated.[23]

Before the emergence of the activist black protest movements, the drive for civil rights was therefore in the hands of a few professionals competent to work through controlling legal and educational channels.[24] The NAACP achieved great success through these agencies, and its definition of the problem facing black people signified its planned strategy. Specifically, prior to 1960 the NAACP tended to define the racial problem as legal segregation in the South, and its major goal, popularized by the slogan "free by 1963," was the elimination of all state-enforced segregation. Although the officials of the NAACP have lacked a power orientation, the mobilization of their legal machinery has represented a display of power—the power of litigation—in this instance, a power resource of high liquidity. Working through prevailing institutional channels, the NAACP was able to win an overwhelming number of cases in the Supreme Court and thus helped to produce laws designed to improve racial conditions in America, although white Southerners ingeniously circumvented the new laws and thus usually prevented their implementation. Lewis M. Killian has discussed this matter:

> It is ironic that the white South was extremely successful in minimizing the impact of the desegregation decision of the federal court without arousing the indignation of the rest of the nation. As much as the White Citizens Council and the Ku Klux Klan are invoked as symbols of the southern resistance, they and their extra-legal tactics did not make this possible. Far more effective were the legal strategems, evasions, and delays that led Negroes to realize that although they had won a new statement of principle they had not won the power to cause this principle to be implemented.[25]

White procrastination made it apparent to many black leaders that both the goal and the problem had been too narrowly defined. A new definition of the problem thus emerged— token compliance to the newly created laws—and a corresponding new goal—the elimination of both de facto and de jure segregation. Litigation, no longer an effective pressure resource in the face of white procrastination, was replaced by passive or nonviolent resistance. The fact that the power balance between blacks and whites had undergone some alteration also helped bring about the shift to nonviolent direct-action protest. As blacks increased their political and economic resources, as the Supreme Court rendered decisions in favor of desegregation, and as the United States government became increasingly sensitive to world opinion of its racial situation, black expectations were heightened, continued white resistance became more frustrating, and consequently support for direct-action (albeit nonviolent) protests quickly mushroomed. Although some writers have identified the successful Montgomery bus boycott of 1955–1956 as the beginning of the black revolt,[26] Meier and Rudwick have maintained that "the really decisive break with the pre-eminence of legalistic techniques came with the college student sit-ins that swept the South in the spring of 1960."[27] These demonstrations set a chain of nonviolent resistance movements to desegregation into motion that subsequently swept the country from 1960 to 1965. Even though the initial emphasis was on persuasion resources rather than constraint resources, the technique of nonviolence was in reality an aggressive manifestation of pressure. Its twofold goal was to create and to implement civil rights laws. Even though many of the nonviolent protests were not specifically directed at the federal government, they were in many cases intended to apply indirect pressure on it. Black leaders recognized that because of their political and pressure resources and because of the United States' concern for world opinion, the government was not in a position to ignore their stepped-up drive for civil rights.

For a brief period of time, the nonviolent resistance strategy proved to be highly effective. In addition to forcing local governments and private agencies to integrate facilities in numerous Southern cities and towns, the nonviolent demonstrations pressed the federal government into passage of civil rights legislation in 1964 and voting rights legislation in 1965—acts that satisfied many of the black demands of the early 1960s. There are several reasons why the federal government responded favorably to many of the demands emanating from the nonviolent protest movement: (1) the demands that accompanied the protests tended to be fairly specific, e.g., "end discrimination in voting," and hence the government was able to provide "remedies" that clearly approximated the specifications in the demands; (2) the attempt to satisfy these demands did not call for major sacrifices on the part of whites, and hence there was little likelihood that a significant political backlash against the government would occur in sections of the country other than the South; (3) the demands were consistent with prevailing ideals of democracy and freedom of choice, and hence they could not be easily labeled "extreme" either by the white citizens or by governmental authorities; (4) the more blacks pressed their demands and carried out their protests, the more violent was the Southern response, and because these developments were receiving international attention, the government became increasingly concerned; (5) the government was sensitive to the political resources blacks had developed and became cognizant of the growing army of Northern whites sympathetic to the black cause; (6) blacks' political strength seemed to be magnified by the united front they presented, as groups ranging from the relatively conservative NAACP to the radical Student Nonviolent Coordinating Committee all joined in nonviolent protests to effect change.

To understand why many blacks shifted away from nonviolence both as a philosophy of life and as a technique to achieve racial equality, it is necessary to recall our earlier theoretical discussion of minority protest: if an extended period of increased expectations and gratification is followed by a brief period in which the gap between expectations and gratifications suddenly widens and becomes intolerable, the possibility of violent protests is greatly increased. Davies applies this analysis to the black rebellion of the 1960s:

> In short—starting in the mid-1950's and increasing more or less steadily into the early 1960's—white violence grew against the now lawful and protected efforts of Negroes to gain integration. And so did direct action and later violence

undertaken by blacks, in a reciprocal process that moved into the substantial violence of 1965–67. That 3 year period may be considered a peak, possibly the peak of the violence that constituted the black rebellion. It merits reemphasis that during this era of increased hostility progress intensified both the white reaction to it and the black counteraction to the reaction, because everytime a reaction impeded the progress, the apparent gap widened between expectations and gratification.[28]

Even though there was no sudden or sharp increase in black unemployment and no sudden reversal in the material gains blacks had accumulated during the prosperous 1960s,[29] "there was, starting notably in 1963, not the first instance of violence against blacks but a sudden increase in it. This resurgence of violence came after, and interrupted, the slow but steady progress since 1940. It quickly frustrated rising expectations."[30] For the first time, there was a real sense of apprehension among blacks that, not only would conditions stop improving, but gains already achieved could very well be lost unless steps were taken to counteract mounting white violence.

Birmingham, Alabama, in 1963 was the scene of this initial wave of white violence and black counterreaction. In April, Birmingham police used high-pressure water hoses and dogs to attack civil rights marchers, and blacks retaliated by throwing rocks and bottles at the police; in May, segregationists bombed the homes of black leaders, and blacks retaliated by rioting, setting two white-owned stores on fire and stoning police and firemen; on September 15, whites enraged by school desegregation bombed a black church, killing four small girls and injuring twenty-three other adults and children, and blacks angrily responded by stoning police.[31]

However, racial violence was not restricted to Birmingham, Alabama, in 1963. Medger Evers, an NAACP official in Jackson, Mississippi, was shot to death in front of his home on May 28, 1963. Whites and blacks in Cambridge, Maryland, engaged in a gun battle after blacks had stormed a restaurant to rescue sit-in demonstrators beaten by whites; the black quarter in

Lexington, North Carolina, was attacked by a white mob after blacks had attempted to obtain service at white restaurants, and in the ensuing gun battle a white man was killed; mounted police at Plaquemine, Louisiana, galloped into a group of civil rights demonstrators and dispersed them with electric cattle prods—fifteen demonstrators were injured; police used tear gas, shotguns, and high-pressure water hoses in Savannah, Georgia, to break up a protest demonstration that turned into a riot—at least ten whites and thirteen blacks were injured; and mass arrests of civil rights activists took place in Athena, Georgia; Selma, Alabama; Greensboro, North Carolina; Orangeburg, South Carolina, and several other Southern towns.[32]

The gap between expectations and emotional gratifications[33] increased black support for violent protest and was reflected, not only in the way blacks responded to white attacks beginning with the Birmingham incident in 1963, but also in the changing philosophy of younger civil rights activists. In the early months of 1964, members of the Student Nonviolent Coordinating Committee (SNCC) and the Congress of Racial Equality (CORE) openly challenged the philosophy of nonviolence and called for more belligerent forms of protest.[34] It was during this same period that Malcolm X, shortly after he resigned from the Nation of Islam, called for blacks to arm themselves and abandon nonviolence and that the Brooklyn chapter of CORE attempted to tie up New York traffic (on April 22, the opening of the World's Fair) by emptying the fuel tanks of 2000 automobiles and abandoning them on the freeways leading to the fairgrounds (lacking support, the strategy failed).[35] Continued white violent acts such as the murder of civil rights workers by white terrorists in Mississippi in 1964, Ku Klux Klan terrorism in Mississippi and Alabama in 1965, attacks against CORE organizers in Bogalusa, Louisiana, in 1965, the beating and murder of civil rights activists in Selma, Alabama, in 1965, and police brutality that precipitated rioting in Northern ghettoes in 1964 deepened the militant mood in the black community and widened the gap between expectations and emotional gratification.

In the face of these developments, the call by some black

134

leaders for greater militancy was based on the optimistic belief that the larger society was more likely to respond properly to black demands backed by belligerent and violent protests than to those reinforced by nonviolent resistance. Our earlier theoretical analysis suggests either that blacks believed they possessed sufficient resources not only to disrupt the larger society but also to prevent an all-out repressive reaction by whites, or that they felt that by the mid-1960s the system had developed a high tolerance for minority protests.[36] However, it was lower-class urban blacks who dramatically demonstrated that a more belligerent mood had gripped the black community when they rocked the nation with a proliferation of ghetto revolts from 1964 to 1968. In the early 1960s, nonviolent protests were heavily populated by middle-class or higher-educated blacks, who were far more likely at this period to participate in a drive for social justice that was disciplined and sustained.[37] Ghetto blacks for the most part were not directly involved in the nonviolent resistance movement of the early 1960s, and many of the gains achieved did not materially benefit them (the civil rights movement up to 1965 produced laws primarily relevant to privileged blacks with competitive resources such as special talents or steady income)[38]; nevertheless, the victories of the nonviolent movement increased expectations among all segments of the black population.[39] In the age of mass communication, Northern ghetto blacks, like blacks throughout the country, were very much aware of and identified with the efforts of Martin Luther King, Jr., and other civil rights activists. By the same token, they were also cognizant of the white violence that threatened to halt the gradual but steady progress toward racial equality.

Accordingly, ghetto rebellions cannot be fully explained in isolation or independently of the increasingly militant mood of the black community. However, what made the situation of ghetto blacks unique was the fact that the gap between expectations and emotional gratification was combined with concrete grievances over police brutality, inferior education, unemployment, underemployment, and inadequate housing. It is true that these conditions have always existed in ghetto life

135

and did not suddenly emerge during the 1960s, but the important point is that increased expectations and greater awareness of racial oppression made these conditions all the more intolerable.[40] Charles Silberman was essentially correct when he stated that "it is only when men sense the possibility of improvement, in fact, that they become dissatisfied with their situation and rebel against it. And 'with rebelling' as Albert Camus put it 'awareness is born,' and with awareness, an impatience 'which can extend to everything that [men] had previously accepted, and which is almost always retroactive.' "[41] Likewise, as the number and intensity of ghetto revolts increased, black complaints about human suffering became more explicit and focused.

The Harlem revolt in 1964 actually marked the beginning of ghetto uprisings of the 1960s (where groups of blacks looted stores, burned buildings, and attacked firemen and police in the black community), but the most serious revolts occurred in 1965 in Watts (resulting in 34 deaths, 900 injuries, 4000 arrests, and an estimated property damage of $100,000,000), in 1967 in Detroit (43 deaths, 1500 injuries, 5000 arrests, and $200,000,000 in property damage), and Newark (26 deaths, 1200 injuries, 1600 arrests, and $47,000,000 in property damage). The assassination of Dr. Martin Luther King, Jr., precipitated the final series of ghetto rebellions in the spring of 1968. During that four-year period (1964–1968) of intense racial violence, thousands of persons, mostly black, were killed or injured, and the property damage was estimated in the billions of dollars.

In addition to these manifestations of greater black militancy, the emergence of the Black Power Movement in 1966, with its shift in emphasis to racial solidarity and its explicit repudiation of nonviolence as a strategy of protest and way of life, can also be associated with the sudden gap between rising expectations and emotional gratification. In a fundamental sense, however, the Black Power Movement represented a return to the self-help philosophy and emphasis on black solidarity that usually occurs "when the Negroes' status has declined or when they experienced intense disillusionment following a period of heightened but unfulfilled expectations."[42]

Unlike the self-help nationalistic philosophies that developed in the 1850s following increased repression in the free states, in the Booker T. Washington era as a response to the growth of biological racism and resurgence of white supremacy, and in the post World War I period as a reaction to white violence perpetrated against black urban immigrants in the North, the Black Power Movement developed during a period when blacks had achieved a real sense of power.

Killian has commented on this new feeling of power:

The nonviolent demonstrations of SCLC, CORE, and SNCC . . . had not solved the bitter problems of the Negro masses, but they had shown that the Negro minority could strike terror into the hearts of the white majority. They had produced concessions from white people, even though the triumph of winning these concessions had soon turned to despair because they were never enough. Watts and other riots reflected no clearly formulated demand for new concessions. They did reflect the basic truth that Negroes, mobilized in ghettoes to an extent never before experienced and made confident by earlier victories, were no longer afraid of white power. Within a few months after Watts, they would begin to proclaim their faith in Black Power.[43]

This new sense of power was reflected not so much in the programs actually introduced under the banner of Black Power as in the revolutionary rhetoric used to articulate Black Power philosophy. That certain black radicals dared, through national media, to call openly for the use of violence to overthrow racial oppression was a clear indication that blacks felt secure enough to threaten the very stability of the larger society. In actual fact, however, although Black Power advocates often disagreed about the aims and purposes of the movement, their various demands and programs were more reformist in nature than revolutionary[44] (e.g., programs emphasizing black capitalism, the running of black candidates for political office, self-help in the area of jobs and housing, black studies in high schools and colleges, and black culture and identity). Some of the programs introduced by Black Power spokesmen were an extension of the conservative separatism advocated by the Nation of Islam (Black Muslims) under the leadership of Elijah Muhammad. From the 1950s to the first half of the 1960s, when black social thought continued to be overwhelmingly supportive of integration,[45] the Nation of Islam served as the major medium for a black nationalist philosophy.[46] Commenting on Muslim philosophy, Cruse wrote that the

> Nation of Islam was nothing but a form of Booker T. Washington economic self-help, black unity, bourgeois hard work, law abiding, vocational training, stay-out-of-the-civil-rights-struggle agitation, separate-from-the-white-man, etc., etc. morality. The only difference was that Elijah Muhammad added the potent factor of the Muslim religion to race, economic, and social philosophy of which the first prophet was none other than Booker T. Washington. Elijah Muhammad also added an element of "hate Whitey" ideology which Washington, of course, would never have accepted.[47]

The most significant influence on the radical flank of the Black Power Movement was ex-Muslim minister Malcolm X. Because of differences with Elijah Muhammad, Malcolm X resigned from the Muslim organization and moved beyond its program of territorial separation and bourgeois economic nationalism. Shortly before he was assassinated in 1965, he had begun to formulate a philosophy of revolutionary nationalism (that "views the overthrow of existing political and economic institutions as a prerequisite for the liberation of black Americans, and does not exclude the use of violence[48]) subsequently adopted by militant Black Power leaders such as Stokely Carmichael and H. Rap Brown and incorporated into the philosophy of the newly emerging Black Panther Party in the late 1960s.

Yet, of all the philosophies of nationalism or racial solidarity that emerged under the banner of Black Power, none has received as much support from black citizens as has cultural nationalism.[49] Cultural nationalism is concerned mainly with positive race identity, including the development and/or elaboration of black culture and history. One of the most illustrative statements of this theme has come from Blauner:

> In their communities across the nation, Afro-Americans are discussing "black culture." The mystique of "soul" is only the most focused example of this trend in consciousness. What is and what should be the black man's attitude toward American society and American culture has become a central division in the Negro protest movement. The spokesmen for black power celebrate black culture and Negro distinctiveness; the integrationists base their strategy and their appeal on the fundamental "American-ness" of the black man. There are nationalist leaders who see culture building today as equal or more important than political organization. From Harlem to Watts there has been a proliferation of black theater, art, and literary groups; the recent ghetto riots (or revolts, as they are viewed from the nationalistic perspective) are the favored materials of these cultural endeavors.[50]

But certainly we must not lose sight of the fact that cultural nationalism, like other forms of nationalism, has become popular during certain periods in history—periods when black disillusionment follows a brief interval of black optimism and commitment to integration. It is not so important that structural assimilation,[51] especially for middle-class blacks, is occurring at a greater rate than ever before (a point we will explore more fully in the following section); what is important is the black perception of the racial changes that are occurring. Black awareness has been heightened by the efforts of both the civil rights and the Black Power activists, and impatience and frustration with the pace of racial equality have become more intense. Whereas the cultural nationalism of the 1850s and of the Harlem Renaissance period was largely confined to segments of the black intelligentsia,[52] the cultural nationalism of the late 1960s and early 1970s has transcended class lines. Awareness of the evils of racial oppression and of white resistance to racial equality is characteristic of all segments of the black population; support for racial solidarity with emphasis on black culture and racial identity has reached unprecedented heights.

We shall have occasion to return to a consideration of cultural nationalism's role in the development of black political awareness. For the moment, however, it is important to examine the extent to which the ideology of racism has withstood both the onslaught of black protest and the drift toward more fluid competitive race relations.

FROM BIOLOGICAL RACISM TO CULTURAL RACISM

The ideology of biological racism, which received its greatest support in the late nineteenth and early twentieth centuries, has steadily declined as a rationale for black subordination. Although the manifestation of black skills and abilities in a more fluid competitive system has helped to destroy many racist stereotypes, probably the most significant factor in the demise of biological racism has been the unwillingness of most elite leaders and public spokesmen to openly utter racist statements reinforcing public opinion in support of black oppression. Ever since blacks developed political resources and the federal government became increasingly sensitive to world opinion of United States race relations, public remarks by influential political leaders have been designed more to promote racial harmony than to create greater racial cleavages. Moreover, since 1940 thousands of scholarly studies and a significant number of novels sympathetic to black citizens have "disseminated information about the Negro problem and helped to make criticism of the caste system respectable."[53] Current scientific opinion overwhelmingly rejects the validity of arguments equating race with innate intelligence. Even the widely heralded Jensen report,[54] which questioned the native intelligence of blacks, has come under rather devastating criticism from social and biological scientists.[55] Finally, individual attitudes as measured by public opinion polls indicate a decline of white beliefs in the biological inferiority of blacks. By the late

1960s, a majority of whites supported the view that blacks and whites are equal in innate mental ability.[56] Accompanying the decline of such beliefs has been a reduction in support of social norms favoring racial exclusion. By 1970, a large majority of whites verbally supported racial integration in public transportation, public facilities, and schools, and although responses toward neighborhood integration and mixed marriages continue to divide the white population, the trend is unmistakably in the direction of more tolerant attitudes in these two areas.[57]

Taken together, the reduction of support for beliefs in the biological inferiority of blacks and the decreasing support for norms of subordination indicate, it seems safe to conclude, that the ideology of biological racism is on the decline. However, attitudes, like overt behavior, are often a function of existing structural arrangements in society. Glenn has argued that

> White resistance to Negro advancement is almost certainly reduced in periods of rapid economic growth and rapid upward shifts in the occupational structure, when Negroes can advance without whites incurring any absolute losses in income or occupational status. Even at such times, closing the Negro–white gap entails loss of a white competitive advantage, but whites who nevertheless are moving up are likely to be less aware of and less concerned about this loss.[58]

Indeed, research on white public opinion indicates that liberal and tolerant attitudes toward blacks exist among those who occupy upper-status positions and are thus furthest removed from direct competition with blacks heavily concentrated in lower-status positions. Thus despite the overall reduction of white racist attitudes and increasing support for racial equality, any sudden shift in the nation's economy that would throw whites into greater competition with blacks for, say, housing and jobs could create and intensify racial tension and, at least for the whites who feel threatened by black advancement, reverse the trend toward increasing racial tolerance. In analyzing the situation in the United States, Jan Dizard is insightful when he suggests that

What we are confronted with, then, is a society whose stability rests on its ability to maintain inequality while at the same time acknowledging as legitimate subordinate groups' demands for more. The answer to this dilemma has been economic growth. When growth does not obtain, stability is threatened from two directions. Those at or near the bottom find their demands for more implicitly requiring a redistribution, thus challenging extant arrangements of power and privilege. At the same time, groups enjoying even a modicum of comfort respond to the squeeze in a typically defensive fashion, thus becoming available for the demagogic mobilization of nativism and racism.[59]

Probably the most effective way that the society of the United States is able "to maintain inequality while at the same time acknowledging as legitimate subordinate groups' demand for more" is through the pervasive and persistent practice of institutional discrimination. Even though racist norms that directed the systematic exclusion of blacks from full participation in stable, patterned, and organized procedures are no longer fervently supported, the fact that many procedures originally based on these norms continue to persist is testimony to the lasting influence of institutional racism. For example, black children continue to be crippled by inferior education, with schooling in the large urban ghettoes being conducted mostly in dilapidated and overcrowded buildings. As Kenneth Clark, Charles Silberman, and others have pointed out, IQ and achievement scores typically drop as black youngsters "progress" through school.[60] A study of ghetto schools in Harlem in the early 1960s revealed that a majority of black youngsters never finish high school.[61] Also, there continues to exist a very high degree of residential segregation of blacks and whites in urban areas. As Karl and Alma Taeuber have said, "Negroes are by far the most residentially segregated urban minority in recent American history. This is evident in the virtually complete exclusion of Negro residents from most new suburban developments of the past fifty years as well as in the block-by-block expansion of Negro residential areas in the central

portions of many large cities."[62] It is true that the black suburban population has increased slightly during the past decade
(by roughly 1.1 million persons); however, this population
shift was heavily concentrated in black suburbs ("Negroes
comprised only about 5 percent of the suburban population in
1970.").[63] What seems to be clear from an analysis of indexes
of residential segregation around the nation is that economic
factors play a relatively minor role in the physical separation
of whites and blacks.

> Regardless of their economic status, Negroes rarely live in
> "white" residential areas, while whites, no matter how poor,
> rarely live in "Negro" residential areas. In recent decades,
> Negroes have been much more successful in securing im-
> provements in economic status than in obtaining housing on
> a less segregated basis. Continued economic gains by Ne-
> groes are not likely to alter substantially the prevalent pat-
> terns of residential segregation.[64]

Although such forms of discrimination persist, a fundamental change has occurred in racist norms. Specifically, in the last
several decades racist institutional norms that were based on
belief in the biological inferiority of blacks are now more
heavily dependent on the postulation of black cultural inferiority. For instance, arguments that black children cannot learn
because of "deficiencies in cultural and social background"
have not only been used as an alibi for educational neglect but
have also been invoked by many white parents and school officials opposed to busing and other efforts to desegregate
schools.[65] As Clark has noted, earlier explanations that attempted to account for black children's poor average perfor-
mance in terms of inherent racial inferiority have recently
been replaced by arguments focusing on general environmental
disabilities.[66] Such explanations tend to stress the point that the
deleterious environment of black children renders them incapable of successfully performing in the school system. The
contemporary version of the environmentalist approach falls
under the general category of "cultural deprivation." As an

answer to the biological racist's theories of the early twentieth century, the cultural deprivation approach is viewed by many social scientists as a quite reasonable explanation of black retardation in the school system.[67] Although it would most certainly be unreasonable to assert that social scientists who rely on such theories are themselves cultural racists, it is true that their explanations have been used by others to support institutional discrimination. Clark was one of the first social scientists to question whether cultural deprivation theories were reinforcing institutional racism and discrimination:

> To what extent are the contemporary social deprivation theories merely substituting notions of environmental immutability and fatalism for earlier notions of biologically determined educational unmodifiability? To what extent do these theories obscure more basic reasons for the educational retardation of lower-status children? To what extent do they offer acceptable and desired alibis for the educational default: the fact that these children, by and large, do not learn because they are not being taught effectively and they are not being taught because those who are charged with the responsibility of teaching them do not believe that they can learn, do not expect that they can learn, and do not act toward them in ways which help them to learn.[68]

Arguments that blacks should be excluded from certain labor unions and apprentice programs, from white residential areas, from institutions of higher learning, and from social clubs and gatherings have also become more cultural racist than biological racist in nature. This is not to say that forms of institutional racism and discrimination have been impenetrable to the proliferation of black protests. Although many discriminatory practices continue to exist, others have undergone significant alteration to allow some modicum of black participation. It goes without saying that blacks have accumulated more competitive resources than they had at the turn of the century, thus facilitating greater participation in the institutional processes. But it is necessary to fully understand the nature of the improved competitive position of blacks vis-à-vis whites, because the changing structural relations between the two groups have not been evenly distributed. Specifically, although most segments of the black population find themselves in a more fluid competitive position with whites, others have either experienced no change in position or have actually fallen further behind in recent years. The net effect is that by 1970 there were very definite signs of a deepening economic schism in the black community.[69] A brief description of recent census data will serve to highlight this problem.

The fact that competitive relations between some blacks and whites are becoming more fluid is reflected in the data presented in Table 1. Whereas the number of whites employed in the white-collar, craftsmen, and operatives occupations—the higher-paying positions—increased by 24 per cent to

TABLE 1

Employment by Broad Occupational Groups: 1960, and 1966 to 1970
(numbers in millions, annual averages)

Year	Total		White-collar workers, craftsmen, and operatives		All other workers *	
	Black and other races	White	Black and other races	White	Black and other races	White
1960	6.9	58.9	2.9	46.1	4.0	12.8
1966	7.9	65.0	4.0	52.5	3.9	12.0
1967	8.0	66.4	4.3	53.6	3.7	12.7
1968	8.2	67.8	4.6	54.9	3.6	12.8
1969	8.4	69.5	4.9	56.4	3.5	13.1
1970	8.4	70.2	5.1	57.0	3.4	13.2
Change, 1960 to 1970 (percent)	+22	+19	+72	+24	−15	+3.2

* Includes private-household and other service workers, laborers and farm workers. Median usual weekly earnings were $50–$100 a week for these workers, compared with $100–$170 a week for white–collar workers, craftsmen, and operatives in March 1970.

Source: U.S. Department of Labor, Bureau of Labor Statistics.

(57.0 million) between 1960 and 1970, "Negro and other races"[70] recorded an increase of 72 per cent (from 2.9 million to 5.1 million). Equally as significant is the fact that the heavily disproportionate representation of blacks in the lower-paying positions (private-household and other service workers, laborers, and farm workers) has declined by 15 per cent (from 4 million to 3.4 million) since 1960, whereas the number of whites in these same occupations has increased by 3.2 per cent (from 12.8 million to 13.2 million).[71]

Black penetration into institutions of higher learning has also been impressive. Table 2 includes data on black college enrollment between 1964 and 1970. It is significant to note that the total black college enrollment has increased by 127 per cent (from 234,000 in 1964 to 522,000 in 1970), with 133 per cent of this growth occurring in institutions other than predominantly black colleges.[72] The fact that the percentage of black college students enrolled in institutions other than predominantly

TABLE 2
Black Students Enrolled in Colleges by Type of Institution:
1964 to 1968, and 1970
(numbers in thousands)

Subject	1964	1965	1966	1967	1968	1970
Enrollment in predominantly black colleges*	120	125	134	144	156	144
Percent of total	51.3	45.6	47.5	38.9	35.9	27.6
Enrollment in other colleges (not predominantly black)*	114	149	148	226	278	378
Percent of total	48.7	54.4	52.5	61.1	64.1	72.4
Total, black college enrollment	234	274	282	370	434	522

* Data on colleges are for four- and two-year institutions and professional schools, both private and public (including community colleges). Statistics for 1966 to 1970 include enrollment figures for nondegree-credit students. Prior to 1966, only degree-credit students are included.
Source: U.S. Department of Commerce, Bureau of the Census, and U.S. Department of Health, Education and Welfare.

black colleges has increased from 48.7 per cent in 1964 to 72.4 per cent in 1970 is indicative of the efforts of white institutions to overcome many of the traditional barriers imposed by institutional racism.[73] Finally, the overall ratio of black to white family income has risen from about 53 per cent in 1961–1963 to roughly 64 per cent in 1970.[74]

Nevertheless, as already indicated, not all segments of the black population have experienced a relative increase in competitive resources vis-à-vis whites. Despite the fact that "Negro and other races" have moved out of such low-paying occupations as private-household workers, laborers, and farm workers more rapidly than whites during the last decade, in 1970 they still held one fifth (about 1.5 million) of the service occupations other than those in private households (jobs that require little skill), about the same proportion as in 1960. Moreover, in the semiskilled operative jobs (primarily in factories) the number of "Negro and other races" expanded by 42 per cent (to slightly over 2 million) compared with an increase of only 13 per cent (to 11.9 million) for whites. By 1970, these two categories of low-skill jobs comprised 42 per cent of the total employment of "Negro and other races," whereas in 1960 their share was only 38 per cent.[75] Furthermore, although the unemployment rate for "Negro and other races" declined from a high of 12.4 in 1961 (during the recession period) to a low of 6.5 in 1969 (but then increased to 8.2 in 1970 and 8.6 in 1971), throughout the 1960s their unemployment rates were about double those for whites, including a disproportionate representation in the long-term unemployment category.[76]

Moreover, blacks have not escaped the category of poverty as rapidly as whites.[77] Whereas "Negro and other races" constituted 29 per cent of all officially poor family members in 1959, by 1969 their percentage had increased to 35 per cent. Even more important, "Negro and other races" accounted for 41 per cent of all the children (under 18 years) in poor families in 1964, whereas in 1959 they accounted for 34 per cent. In poor families headed by women, the number of "Negro and other races" children increased by 756,000 from 1959 to 1969. "Children of Negro and other races accounted for 52 per cent

147

of all children in these families."[78] In 1959, they constituted 42 per cent of the total number of children in households below the poverty level headed by females.

It is clear therefore that although most blacks have improved their socioeconomic position relative to whites, a significant minority have experienced no gain or have fallen behind. In fact, as Andrew Brimmer has observed, by the late 1960s the income distribution among black families was considerably more unequal than the distribution among white families (the lowest two fifths among families of "Negro and other races" contributed only 15.3 per cent of the total black income in 1969, whereas the lowest two fifths of white families contributed 18.7 per cent of the total white income; conversely, the upper two fifths among white families contributed 63.7 per cent, whereas the upper two fifths among families of "Negro and other races" contributed 68.2 per cent). And, unlike for whites, the income schism in the black community does not seem to be narrowing.[79] I shall reserve a final comment about this problem until the latter part of the following section.

FROM PROTESTS TO POLITICS

I have used Davies' "J-curve" theory to explain violent black protest during the middle 1960s. However, as indicated in my previous theoretical discussion, the sudden gap between expectations and gratifications is not sufficient for violent protest to occur, because it is also necessary for the subordinate group to have faith in the efficacy of such protests. Crucial to this consideration is the minority group's assessment of the dominant group's tolerance of protest and its ability to successfully suppress a revolt. By 1970, there was some indication that not only had black expectations for short-term racial gains been lowered but also that greater concern existed among blacks concerning the possibility of national repression of black protesters.[80] A riot-control amendment and civil-order clause were added to the 1968 civil rights bills, allowing the government to play a more active role in controlling the militant segments of the black community.[81] Whereas the government had, during the 1960s, responded to black pressure by satisfying demands and offering concessions, in 1968, faced with the threat of continued violent protest, it had taken steps to suppress and isolate the militant segments of the black community. The theme of "law and order" that permeated the nation, the confrontations between black militants and police, and the arrests and killings of leaders of the militant Black Panther Party all contributed to a growing fear in the black community that the continuance of belligerent protest would ultimately generate violent white repression.

However, the event that probably contributed most to the lowering of black expectations as well as increasing concern about racial oppression was the election of Richard Nixon as President in 1968 and the policies he pursued during his first term in office. As Thomas Pettigrew has observed,

> Nixon ran on a so-called "Southern strategy" (better termed a "segregation strategy"), and true to his word, behaved accordingly once in the White House. Negro Americans understandably expected little of him or his administration; and they were not disappointed. This had the effect of lowering black expectations for short run gains.[82]

The facts that the pattern of ghetto revolts was broken after 1968 and that early in 1972 the Black Panther Party (which became the dominant symbol of black militancy after SNCC faded and CORE retreated to a philosophy of black capitalism) nationally announced a shift from "the rhetoric of the gun" to the goal of politically organizing the black community indicate that beliefs in the efficacy of violent protest had declined in an atmosphere strongly supportive of "law and order."[83]

Although black protest as a pressure resource had all but subsided in early 1970, there developed increasing reliance on black political activity. However, unlike the civil rights politics of the 1960s, in the early 1970s black politics had begun to integrate various facets of nationalistic philosophy. Drawing on the widespread cultural nationalism in the black community, the new breed of black politicians has increasingly relied on

symbols of black pride and black solidarity in their public ut-
terances.[84] It may not be coincidental that black pride and
identity are flourishing at the same time that we are witnessing
an unprecedented degree of cooperation between black middle-class politicians and ghetto blacks.[85] In addition, as an out-
growth of the Black Power Movement there exists a growing
thrust to increase black control of the social, economic, and
political institutions in black communities. If the conditions associated with the ebb and flow of black nationalist development in the past are any indication,[86] its continued growth
may very well depend on the extent to which black competitive resources expand over the next several years.

We have already emphasized that the economic advancement of blacks is heavily dependent on national economic
prosperity. Michael Flax's comments in this regard provide
some basis for a less than optimistic outlook as the nation en-
ters the 1970s:

> Equality of income distribution, rising wages and salaries,
> and special programs to improve future income for non-
> whites have all been dependent upon rapid rates of eco-
> nomic growth and low national unemployment rates, both
> of which conditions existed during the decade of the 1960's.
> There is, therefore, little ground for optimism or compla-
> cency if the national growth rates decline and unemploy-
> ment rates rise, as they did in 1970, unless alternative means
> are found to narrow the income gaps. The effect of such a
> deteriorating situation will be relatively more serious for
> nonwhites than for whites and the gains seen may well be
> lost in a period of economic decline.[87]

Furthermore, as I have indicated, racial intolerance tends to
be greater in periods of economic decline, particularly for
whites unable to advance themselves and forced by economic
strains to compete more heavily with minority groups. Accordingly, not only is it possible that the gains experienced by
middle- and upper-income blacks could decline, but it is also
possible that the deteriorating circumstances of many lower-

150

class blacks could worsen, further widening the economic schism.

In the short run, if declining expectations and fears of racial oppression are combined with major economic setbacks, black nationalist themes of racial solidarity will intensify. In the long run, there is every reason to believe that violent confrontations between blacks and whites will flare up again and again. We have seen throughout this volume that race relations are extremely variable, shifting back and forth from periods of accommodation (or peace in feud) to periods of overt conflict. Until factors that produce racial conflict are eliminated (such as differential power, racism, strong sense of group position, and intergroup competition for scarce resources), this pattern will continue to persist.

However, racial conflict and tension are not unique to the United States. In many respects, a more severe and potentially more explosive situation exists in the Republic of South Africa. Although there are some distinct differences, both countries nonetheless have evidenced similar historical patterns of racial power and racism. Indeed, the value of comparing the historical patterns of race relations of one society to another is that one can see that the forces operating to produce racial friction are not necessarily unique. And the sheer act of comparison often produces greater understanding of race relations in a single society. I shall attempt therefore to systematically contrast these two racially ordered societies in Chapter Nine vis-à-vis my theoretical framework; but first let me undertake to describe and explain the major historical patterns of South African race relations in the next chapter.

Notes

1. John Hope Franklin, *From Slavery to Freedom*, 3rd ed. (New York: Knopf, 1967), p. 496.

2. Leslie H. Fishel, Jr., and Benjamin Quarles, *The Negro American: A Documentary History* (Glenview, Ill.: Scott, Foresman, 1967), pp. 448–449.

3. Franklin, op. cit., p. 523.

4. Ibid.

5. Henry L. Moon, *Balance of Power: The Negro Vote* (Garden City, N.Y.: Doubleday, 1948).

6. In subsequent national elections, the black vote provided the margin of victory for Kennedy in 1960, helped produce the Johnson landslide in 1964, and almost led to a Nixon defeat in 1968. Furthermore, the outcome of many Congressional elections may be traced to the decisions of black voters. Finally, fear of the black vote produced enactment of public accommodation laws and fair employment practice laws in Northern and Western municipalities and states.

7. Ray Marshall, *The Negro Worker* (New York: Random House, 1967), pp. 24–35.

8. August Meier and Elliot Rudwick, *From Plantation to Ghetto: The Interpretative History of American Negroes*, rev. ed. (New York: Hill and Wang, 1970), p. 213.

9. Marshall, op. cit., p. 26, and Meier and Rudwick, op. cit., p. 213.

10. Meier and Rudwick, op. cit., p. 242.

11. Franklin, op. cit., p. 577.

12. James C. Davies, "The J-Curve of Rising and Declining Satisfactions as a Cause of Some Great Revolutions and a Contained Rebellion," in *Violence in America: Historical and Comparative Perspectives*, ed. by Hugh Davis Graham and Ted Robert Gurr (New York: Bantam Books, 1969), p. 719.

13. Meier and Rudwick, op. cit., p. 218. It should be pointed out that as blacks migrated to the North and West in search of employment and housing during the war they confronted many whites also migrating from rural to urban areas. According to John Hope Franklin, "Among the Midwestern cities that witnessed an influx of Negroes and whites, Detroit showed the greatest strains in the problem of achieving adjustment. Approximately 50,000 Negroes had come into the city, along with 450,000 other persons in the three years preceding 1943. The lack of housing, the presence of race-baiters and demagogues, the problem of organizing newly arrived workers, and the impotence of the government created an ideal atmosphere in which a riot could flourish." Franklin, op. cit., p. 597.

In June 1943 the most serious interracial riot of the war period broke out in Detroit as twenty-five blacks and nine whites were killed. "Other Northern cities feared that they would have the same experience as Detroit, and numerous efforts were made to stem the tide toward interracial clashes. New York City and Los Angeles did not escape completely, but many communities were able to avert riots by making intelligent and careful approaches to the solution of the problems that created riots." Ibid., p. 598.

14. Leonard Broom and Norval D. Glenn, "The Occupations and Income of Black Americans," in *Blacks in the United States*, ed. by Norval D. Glenn and Charles M. Bonjean (San Francisco: Chandler, 1969), p. 24.

15. Ibid.

16. James W. Vander Zanden, *Race Relations in Transition: The Segregation Crisis in the South* (New York: Random House, 1965), p. 61.

17. Ibid., p. 60.

18. Ibid., pp. 60–61.

19. Broom and Glenn, op. cit., p. 24.

20. Ibid. "For instance, of white males 25 through 34 years old in 1950 who were employed as clerical and kindred workers, 61,000—or 9 percent—had moved out of these occupations or died by 1960 and had not been replaced by other white males of the same cohort . . . some of these white males were replaced by younger whites, but many were replaced by Negroes." Ibid.

21. Ibid.

22. Peter M. Bergman, *The Chronological History of the Negro in America* (New York: Harper, 1969), pp. 535–554.

23. See Clarence E. Glick, "Collective Behavior in Race Relations," *American Sociological Review*, 13:287–293 (June 1947).

24. James H. Laue, "The Changing Character of Negro Protest," *Annals of the American Academy of Political and Social Science*, 357:120 (Jan. 1965).

25. Lewis M. Killian, *The Impossible Revolution?: Black Power and the American Dream* (New York: Random House, 1968), p. 70.

26. See, for example, Louis Lomax, *The Negro Revolt* (New York: Signet, 1962).

27. Meier and Rudwick, op. cit., p. 227.

28. Davies, op. cit., p. 721.

29. These points will be discussed in the following section.

30. Davies, op. cit., p. 723.

31. Keesing's Research Report, *Race Relations in the USA, 1954–68* (New York: Scribner's, 1970), pp. 152–153.

32. Ibid., pp. 154–155.

33. A number of writers have not made full use of Davies' "J-curve" theory because they have restricted the notion of "gratification" to material gains or physical gratification and have ignored the factor of "emotional gratification." See, for example, James A. Geschwender, "Social Structure and the Negro Revolt: An Examination of Some Hypotheses," *Social Forces*, 43:248–256 (Dec. 1964), and Thomas F. Pettigrew, *Racially Separate or Together?* (New York: McGraw-Hill, 1971), chap. 7.

34. Keesing's Research Report, op. cit., pp. 164–165.

35. Ibid., p. 164.

36. For a discussion of this latter point, see L. H. Massotti and D. R. Bowen, eds., *Riots and Rebellion: Racial Violence in the Urban Community* (Beverly Hills, Calif.: Sage, 1968), and Pettigrew, op. cit., chap. 7.

37. As M. Elaine Burgess observed in 1965, "Neither the lower class nor the upper class could have mounted the resistance movement we are now witnessing throughout the South. The former does not possess the resources, either internal or external, essential for such a movement, and the latter is much too small and, very frequently, too far removed from the masses to do so. Such activity had to wait the development of an ample middle class that was motivated to push for validation of hard-won position, thus far denied by the white power structure. The question of unequal distribution of status and power between Negroes and whites would consequently appear as a special case of the more basic problems of order and change. By no means are we saying that all challenges to established social structures or power distributions are class oriented, or directly concerned with relative social position. Nevertheless, it is true that one of the major sources of tension and therefore of change and potential change in the South, as in the broader society, stems from the new middle-class Negro's disbelief in past rationales for inequality and the desire for substitution of new rationales." M. Elaine Burgess, "Race Relations and Social Change," in *The South in Continuity and Change*, ed. by John C. McKinney and Edgar T. Thompson (Durham, N.C.: Duke U.P., 1965), p. 352.

38. As Martin Luther King, Jr., once observed, "What good is it to be allowed to eat in a restaurant if you can't afford a hamburger?"

39. See, for example, William Brink and Louis Harris, *Black and White: A Study of U.S. Racial Attitudes Today* (New York: Simon & Schuster, 1966), p. 42; H. Cantrell, *The Pattern of Human Concerns* (New Brunswick, N.J.: Rutgers U.P., 1965), p. 43; and Pettigrew, op. cit., chap. 7.

40. See *Report of the National Advisory Commission on Civil Disorders* (New York: Bantam, 1968), and Nathan S. Caplan and Jeffrey Paige, "A Study of Ghetto Rioters," *Scientific American*, 219:15–21 (Aug. 1968).

41. Charles Silberman, *Crisis in the Classroom* (New York: Random House, 1970), pp. 19–20.

42. John H. Bracey, August Meier, and Elliot Rudwick, eds., *Black Nationalism in America* (Indianapolis: Bobbs-Merrill, 1970), p. xxvi. It is true, as John Bracey has argued, that black nationalist philosophy has always existed among some segments of the black population (see "John Bracey Sketches His Interpretation of Black Nationalism," Ibid., pp. lvi–lix), but what available research there is clearly establishes the fact that support for this philosophy increases and declines during certain periods in history.

43. Killian, op. cit., pp. 105–106.

44. Harold Cruse, *Rebellion or Revolution* (New York: Apollo, 1968), chap. 13, and *The Crisis of the Negro Intellectual* (New York: Morrow, 1967), pp. 554–565.

45. According to Bracey et al., "The proliferation of nationalist ideologies and organizations that reached a climax during the 1920's was followed by a thirty year period in which nationalism as a significant theme in black thought was virtually nonexistent. From the thirties until the sixties, with few exceptions, leading Negro organizations stressed interracial cooperation, civil rights, and racial integration. Among the chief reasons for the temporary demise of nationalism were the effects of the Depression and the consequent necessity of relying on the New Deal for survival, and the influx of trade Unionists and Communists into the black community preaching and practicing racial equality and brotherhood. The principal ideological concerns of articulate blacks during the Depression decade focused on very practical aspects of the Negro's relationship to New Deal agencies and the Roosevelt Administration, on the role of industrial unions in the advancement of the race, and on the relevance of Marxist doctrines of the Negro's problem." Bracey et al., op. cit., p. xiv.

46. Founded in the early 1930s, the Nation of Islam became a viable institution around 1950. It achieved its greatest popularity after the late Malcolm X became a convert to the Muslim sect and one of its most influential ministers until he resigned in 1964.

47. Cruse, *Rebellion or Revolution*, op. cit., p. 111.

48. Bracey et al., op. cit., p. xxviii. Also see *The Autobiography of Malcolm X* (New York: Grove, 1964).

49. For example, the Opinion Research Corporation survey in 1968 revealed that 86 per cent of the blacks in their sample felt that black people should be taught subjects in school that added to their feeling of pride in being black. In their study of black attitudes in fifteen American cities, Angus Campbell and Howard Schuman have found that "There is a strong trend in the data that is related to, but different from and much stronger than 'separation.' It concerns the positive cultural identity and achievements of Negroes, rather than their political separation from whites. The finding appears most strikingly in the endorsement by 42 percent of the Negro sample of the statement 'Negro school children should study an African Language.' Two out of five Negroes thus subscribe to an emphasis on 'black consciousness' that was almost unthought of a few years ago." Angus Campbell and Howard Schuman, "Racial Attitudes in Fifteen American Cities," in *The National Advisory Commission on Civil Disorders, Supplemental Studies* (Washington, D.C.: G.P.O., 1968), p. 6.

Despite the strong sentiment for cultural nationalism in the black community, institutional nationalism—i.e., the efforts of black citizens to gain control of the political, economic, and social institutions in their community and/or to establish separate institutions free of control by the dominant white society—although increasing in popularity, still receive support from only a minority of blacks. See, for example, Brink and Harris, op. cit.; *Report of the National Advisory Commission on Civil Disorders*, op. cit.; Campbell and Schuman, op. cit.; Caplan and Paige, op. cit.; and Gary T. Marx, *Protest and Prejudice: A Study of Belief in the Black Community*, rev. ed. (New York: Harper, 1970).

50. Robert Blauner, "Black Culture: Myth or Reality?" in *Americans from Africa: Old Memories, New Moods*, ed. by Peter I. Rose (New York: Atherton, 1970), pp. 417–418.

51. Following Milton M. Gordon, "structural assimilation" is defined as "large scale entrance into cliques, clubs, and institutions of host society on primary group level." Milton M. Gordon, *Assimilation in American Life* (New York: Oxford U.P., 1964), p. 71.

52. As Robert A. Bone has noted, "Even at the peak of Renaissance nationalism the middle-class writers could never muster more than token enthusiasm for a distinctive Negro culture." Robert A. Bone, "The Negro Novel in America" in *Americas' Black Past*, ed. by Eric Foner (New York: Harper, 1970), p. 385.

53. Arnold M. Rose, "Race and Ethnic Relations," in *Contemporary Social Problems*, ed. by Robert K. Merton and Robert A. Nisbet (New York: Harcourt, 1966), p. 452.

54. Arthur R. Jensen, "How Much Can We Boost IQ and Scholastic Achievement?" *Harvard Educational Review*, 39:1–123 (Winter 1969).

55. For three of the many excellent critiques of Jensen's thesis, see Martin Deutsch, "Happenings on the Way Back to the Forum: Social Science, IQ, and Race Differences Revisited," *Harvard Educational Review*, 39:523–557 (Summer 1969); Arthur L. Stincombe, "Environment: The Cumulation of Effects Is Yet to Be Understood," *Harvard Educational Review*, 39:511–522 (Summer 1969); and Richard A. Goldsby, *Race and Races* (New York: Macmillan, 1971), chap. 7. For a less direct but, nonetheless, important critique of the importance given to genetic factors in accounting for black IQ scores, see Sandra Scarr-Salapatek, "Race, Social Class and IQ," *Science*, 174:1285–1295 (Dec. 24, 1971). It is of course possible that arguments raised by Jensen (and other scientists such as William Schockley and Richard Herrnstein who draw a connection between race and innate intelligence) could become widely accepted in the long run; especially if, as indicated later, demogogic racism becomes widespread.

56. See, for example, Opinion Research Corporation, *White and Negro Attitudes Towards Race Related Issues and Activities*" (Research Park, Princeton, N.J., 1968), and Richard T. Morris and Vincent Jeffries, *The White Reaction Study* (University of California, Los Angeles: Institute of Government and Public Affairs, 1967).

57. Andrew M. Greeley and Paul B. Sheatsley, "Attitudes Toward Racial Integration," *Scientific American*, 225:13–19 (Dec. 1971). Also see Frank R. Westie, "Race and Ethnic Relations," in *Handbook of Modern Sociology*, ed. by Robert E. L. Faris (Chicago: Rand McNally, 1963), pp. 576–618.

Some readers may question the extent to which public opinion polls reflect true feelings. However, the important point to remember is that there has in fact been a change in the degree to which people are openly willing to express intolerant views toward blacks.

58. Norval D. Glenn, "White Gains from Negro Subordination," in *Blacks in the United States*, ed. by Norval D. Glenn and Charles M. Bonjean (San Francisco: Chandler, 1969), p. 291.

59. Jan E. Dizard, "Response to Aggression and the American Experience," paper read at the Annual Meeting of the American Sociological Association, Denver, Colo. (Sept. 1971), pp. 9–10.

60. Kenneth B. Clark, *Dark Ghetto: Dilemmas of Power* (New York: Harper, 1965), chap. 6, and Charles Silberman, *Crisis in Black and White* (New York: Random House, 1964), chap. 9. Also see James S. Coleman, *Equality of Educational Opportunity* (Washington, D.C.: G.P.O., 1966).

61. Clark, op. cit., p. 124. In 1970, 44 per cent of black males aged 19 were high school dropouts. See U.S. Bureau of the Census, "The Social and Economic Status of Negroes," *Current Population Reports*, ser. P-23, No. 38 (Washington, D.C.: G.P.O., 1970), p. 77.

62. Karl E. and Alma F. Taeuber, *Negroes in the Cities* (Chicago: Aldine, 1965), p. 2

63. U.S. Bureau of the Census, "Social and Economic Characteristics of the Population in Metropolitan and Nonmetropolitan Areas: 1970 and 1960," *Current Population Reports*, ser. P-23, No. 37 (Washington, D.C.: G.P.O., 1971). Also see Reynolds Farley, "The Changing Distribution of Negroes Within Metropolitan Areas: The Emergence of Black Suburbs," *American Journal of Sociology*, 75:512–529 (Jan. 1970), and Karl E. and Alma F. Taeuber, "The Negro Population in the United States," in *The American Negro Reference Book*, ed. by John P. Davis (Englewood Cliffs, N.J.: Prentice-Hall, 1966), pp. 96–160.

What seems apparent is that the nation's central cities are becoming increasingly black. The white urban population actually decreased by 2.6 million and the black population increased by 3.1 million during the past decade. In a study by David Birch, evidence is advanced that the rate of the black population's increase in the central cities had actually begun to decline from 400,000 a year in the early 1960s to 262,000 a year in the late 1960s, whereas the black suburban population's yearly increase of 52,000 in the early 1960s had risen to 85,000 by the end of the decade. Birch uses these data to suggest that the pattern of increasing racial imbalance in the central cities may be ultimately reversed (David L. Birch, *The Economic Future of City and Suburbs* [Committee for Economic Development, New York, 1970]). However, it should be noted that Birch does not address the problem of residential segregation in suburbs. Furthermore, definitive statements concerning the future racial makeup of the nation's central cities will have to await analyses of data gathered from subsequent censuses.

64. Taeuber and Taeuber, *Negroes in the Cities*, op. cit., pp. 2–3. Nor can the argument be advanced that blacks prefer to live in all-black neighborhoods. Recent studies reveal that blacks, despite their widespread acceptance of cultural nationalism, overwhelmingly prefer to live in racially integrated communities. See, for example, Campbell and Schuman, op. cit.

65. This is not to say that all opponents of school desegregation rely on cultural racist arguments but rather to indicate that belief in the cultural inferiority of blacks is one of the major arguments used against school desegregation.

66. Clark, op. cit., chap. 6.

67. Even so perceptive a social analyst as Charles Silberman accepted this approach uncritically when he published his insightful book *Crisis in Black and White*, op. cit., see chap. 9, only to later repudiate the position in his latest book *Crisis in the Classroom*, op. cit., p. 81.

68. Clark, op. cit., p. 131.

69. Andrew Brimmer, "Economic Progress of Negroes in the United States: The Deepening Schism," paper read at the Founders' Day Convocation, Tuskegee Institute, Tuskegee, Ala. (Mar. 22, 1970), and "The Black Revolution and the Economic Future of Negroes in the United States," *The American Scholar*, 629–643 (Autumn 1969).

70. "Negro and other races" is a United States Census Bureau designation, and is used in those cases where data are not available solely for blacks. However, because about 90 per cent of the population "Negro and other races" is black, statistics reported for this category generally reflect the condition of the black population.

71. It is interesting to note racial changes in the technical and professional positions and in the managers, officials, and proprietors occupations. Whereas the number of whites in technical and professional positions increased by 45 per cent (to 10,374,000) from 1960 to 1970, "Negro and other races," on the other hand, netted an increase of 131 per cent (to 766,000). Whereas the number of white managers, officials, and proprietors (the second highest paying category) increased by only 16 per cent (to 7,991,000), "Negro and other races" expanded by 67 per cent (to 296,000). See U.S. Bureau of the Census, "The Social and Economic Status of Negroes in the United States, 1970," *Current Population Reports*, ser. P-23, No. 39 (Washington, D.C.: G.P.O., 1971).

72. In order to contrast black gains in higher education with white gains, I have analyzed the census data on the college enrollment of persons 18 to 24 years of age between 1965 and 1970. This analysis shows that blacks have increased their percentage of the total college enrollment in this category from 4.7 per cent in 1965 to 7.3 per cent in 1970.

73. See William J. Wilson, "The Quest for a Meaningful Black Experience on White Campuses," *The Massachusetts Review*, 10:737–746 (Autumn 1969).

74. U.S. Bureau of the Census, "The Social and Economic Status of

Negroes in the United States, 1970," *Current Population Reports*, ser. P-23, No. 38 (Washington, D.C.: G.P.O., 1971), p. 1. However, as Brimmer has pointed out, such data failed to take into account the fact that black families tend to be substantially larger than white families. An analysis of 1967 family income adjusted to a per capita basis reveals that "the median income data unadjusted for differences in family size may have overstated the relative economic status of nonwhite families by something on the order of 11 per cent" (Brimmer, "Economic Progress of Negroes in the United States," op. cit., p. 11). Accordingly, the gap between white and black per capita income, although slowly closing, is probably still very wide indeed. In this connection, it was also reported by the Bureau of the Census that young black and white husband–wife families (35 years and younger) in the North had reached parity in income by 1970. Nevertheless, when the analysis included work experience of the wife it was found that "young Negro families in which only the husband worked were making only about three-fourths as much as many or comparable white families in both 1959 and 1970" (U.S. Bureau of the Census, "Differences Between Incomes of White and Negro Families by Work Experiences by Work Experience and Region," *Current Population Reports*, ser. P-23, No. 39 [Washington, D.C.. G.P.O., 1971], p. 1).

75. U.S. Bureau of the Census, "The Social and Economic Status of Negroes in the United States, 1970," op. cit., p. 59. For a similar analysis of 1960 to 1969 data, see Brimmer, "Economic Progress of Negroes in the United States," op. cit.

76. In 1970, 1.3 per cent of the "Negro and other races" labor force and 0.7 per cent of the white labor force had been unemployed for 15 weeks or more. See U.S. Bureau of the Census, "The Social and Economic Status of Negroes in the United States, 1970," op. cit., p. 56.

77. "The poverty concept developed by the Social Security Administration classifies a family as poor if its income is not roughly three times as great as the cost of an economy food plan for a family of that particular size and farm or nonfarm residence." Brimmer, "Economic Progress of Negroes in the United States," op. cit., p. 14.

78. U.S. Bureau of the Census, "24 Million Americans—Poverty in the United States: 1969," *Current Population Reports*, ser. P-60, No. 76 (Washington, D.C.: G.P.O., 1970), p. 4.

79. Brimmer states that "in the last few years, the distribution of income within the nonwhite community has apparently run counter to the trend among white families. In both the 1961–65 period and the 1965–68 period, the income distribution for white families became more equal. For nonwhite families, the same trend toward greater equality was evident in the first half of the decade. However, it remained roughly constant in the 1965–68 years." Brimmer, "Economic Progress of Negroes in the United States," op. cit., p. 13.

80. Pettigrew, op. cit., p. 160.

81. Specifically, the riot-control clause stipulated that "It would be a Federal crime for any person to travel from one state to another, or to use any form of inter-State facility, including the mails, television, radio, and telephone, with intent to incite, organize, or participate in a riot." The civil-order amendment stipulated that "It would be a Federal offense to manufacture, transport between States, or demonstrate the use of firearms, bombs, or other explosive devices intended for use in a riot or other forms of civil disorder. It would also be a Federal crime for any person to obstruct firemen or police officers engaged in controlling a riot" (Keesing's Research Report, op. cit., p. 210). The bill also specified maximum penalties for persons interfering with the federally protected rights of blacks and civil rights workers, and an amendment prohibited discrimination in housing.

82. Pettigrew, op. cit., p. 160.

83. Huey P. Newton, founder and leader of the Black Panther Party, said in an interview in February 1972, "We've rejected the rhetoric of the gun; it got about 40 of us killed and sent hundreds of us to prison. Our goal now is to organize the black communities politically." John Peterson, "Huey Newton," *The National Observer*, 7:1 (Feb. 12, 1972).

84. This was most clearly revealed at the National Black Political Convention held at Gary, Indiana, in the spring of 1972, where several nationally recognized black politicians were openly endorsing black nationalist themes.

85. Martin Kilson, "Black Politicians: A New Power," *Dissent*, 333–345 (Aug. 1971). The new breed of black politicians such as Richard Hatcher of Gary, Thomas Atkins of Boston, Shirley Chisholm of New York, Kenneth Gibson of Newark, and Julian Bond of Atlanta are rather intimately associated with problems and needs of the black urban community. By 1971, there were "1,500 elected Negro politicians or officials, 62 per cent of them outside the South, representing overwhelmingly city constituencies. They are located in 41 of the 50 states and include, among others, 12 congressmen, 168 state legislators, 48 mayors, 575 other city officials, 362 school board members, and 144 judges and magistrates." Ibid., p. 340.

86. Bracey et al., op. cit.

87. Michael J. Flax, "*Blacks and Whites: An Experiment in Racial Indicators*" (Washington, D.C.: Urban Institute, 1971), p. 43.

CHAPTER EIGHT
Power, Racism, and Privilege in South Africa

I F RACE relations in the United States have become more fluid during the twentieth century, in South Africa they have become increasingly rigid. Although apartheid[1] has been a characteristic feature of South African life, only since 1948 has it received sufficient legal backing to be fully implemented. Cultural and biological racism have played major roles in the development of apartheid, but the most significant factor has been differential power. The power contrast between the white population and the subordinate racial group comes into sharp focus when one considers, not only the widening gap in political, social, and economic resources, but also the fact that the 3.8 million whites constitute only 17.5 per cent of the total population.[2] To some extent, the overwhelmingly strong sense of group position South African whites have developed is a consequence of their smaller population size. Apartheid apologists argue that racial supremacy must be maintained in South Africa so that whites will not be overrun by the considerably larger nonwhite population but certainly there are other elements involved in the vigorous steps whites have taken to maintain domination. My purpose in the following sections of this chapter is therefore to outline, discuss, and explain the complex factors contributing to the emergence and accelerated growth of one of the most severe forms of racial oppression in human history.

The Emergence of Racism and Racial Stratification in South Africa

Continuous interaction between racial groups in South Africa began in 1652, when the Dutch East India Company established a refueling station on the Cape for Dutch ships sailing to and from the East Indies. Because the indigenous African tribes (Hottentot pastoralists and Bushmen hunters) resisted European efforts to use them as servile laborers, slaves were imported from the West Coast of Africa, the East Indies, Madagascar, and East Africa.[3] Within a few years after the initial white settlement, a system of racial stratification was firmly established in the Cape with slaves and a few Hottentots reduced to servile status performing virtually all of the manual labor. By 1805, the Cape settlement population included 29,545 slaves, roughly 28,000 Hottentots, and 25,757 whites.[4] Slavery in the Cape, according to van den Berghe, approximated a paternalistic form of race relations. "Spatial segregation was minimal and what there was of it was dictated by the dominant group's convenience and desire for privacy, rather than as a mechanism of social control. Unequal status was symbolized and maintained through an elaborate etiquette of race relations and through sumptuary regulations, in short through mechanisms of *social* distance."[5]

Available evidence on racial attitudes during the early years of the Cape settlement suggests that the white group's rationale for racial subordination represented a selective form of cultural racism—blacks were viewed as uncivilized heathens who had to be controlled and supervised by white Christians.[6] For instance, I. D. MacCrone states: "The line of distinction between the groups was less affected by differences of race or colour than by differences of religion"[7] and that "a non-European at the Cape, once he had been baptized, was immediately accepted as a member of the Christian community and, as such, was entitled to his freedom, if a slave."[8] As the slave population grew and the use of slave labor increased, racial attitudes changed near the end of the seventeenth century, and all non-Europeans were categorically subjugated. As MacCrone puts it, "What may be described as the 'human status' and the 'natural rights' of the slave steadily declined as vested interests, such as those represented by property in slaves, increased."[9] By 1685, marriage was forbidden between whites and "full-blooded" freed slaves.[10] Whereas slaves were formerly granted freedom on becoming Christians, by 1700 it had become increasingly difficult for individuals to emerge from slave status. The view that slavery was altogether proper for the black race was asserted and became popular.[11] Moreover, as rationales for retaining blacks in permanent servitude began to rely less on cultural or religious distinctions and more on racial or biological distinctions, all blacks—those in servitude and those who were free—were relegated to a status below that of the dominant white group. Although the full-blown philosophy of biological racism unfolded subsequent to this period, by the end of the eighteenth century biological racist norms—developed to reinforce racial stratification after many blacks became acculturated and religious and other cultural criteria no longer sharply differentiated white and nonwhite groups[12]—had become intertwined with traditional cultural racist norms.[13]

While racial attitudes were taking shape in the Cape Province, they were being molded in an even more intense fashion on the frontier. Here the Boers (the early Dutch settlers searching for land and cattle to steal or trade for from African tribes) pushed further away from the Cape region deeper into the Eastern interior. As first contacts were made with small wandering bands of Bushmen hunters and Hottentot pastoralists, the Boer cattle raids and encroachment on land previously solely occupied by Africans produced an "endless series of frontier wars and counterraids by the aborigines."[14] The Boers, with superior resources (guns, wagons, and horses), virtually exterminated the Bushmen who fought to retain their hunting grounds and eventually reduced the Hottentot tribes to the status of serfs after capturing their land and cattle.

Gradually expanding their settlement, the Boers reached the Great Fish River in the 1770s and confronted the Bantu migrating from Central Africa. Unlike the Bushmen and Hottentots, the Bantu were a large and highly cohesive group organized into complex nations. The two groups clashed in a series of "Kaffir" wars that virtually halted migration on either side and produced an uneasy symmetry until the Boers overcame the power of the Bantu during the Great Trek of the middle nineteenth century and successfully broke the equilibrium.[15]

The Great Trek deserves brief review, if only because it represented a significant turning point in South African history. After the Napoleonic Wars, South Africa became a British colony, and by 1820 five thousand Britons were settled in the Eastern Cape. Contact between the Boers and the Britons quickly produced tensions. Aside from language and cultural differences, the two groups could be distinguished in terms of their attitudes toward the non-Europeans. Influenced by the London Missionary Society, the British government initiated a series of reforms in the Cape Colony: in 1828, an ordinance was passed abolishing the vagrancy laws, which had "served as a pretext to reduce Hottentots to serfdom,"[16] and the Cape government granted free people of color, primarily Hottentots, the same legal status as whites;[17] in 1833, the British government abolished slavery throughout the Empire; and in 1853, franchise was granted to nonwhites in the Cape. These acts not only improved the status of non-Europeans but also weakened the postion of the Boers. In fact, as van den Berghe suggests, granting nonwhites voting privileges "was probably motivated in part by an attempt to attract the non-White elite into the British camp in order to offset the strength of the Dutch."[18]

The actions of the British threatened the economic existence of the Boers, who were frustrated in their repeated attempts to use non-Europeans as servile laborers.[19] Becoming more and more resentful of the British policies, the Boers accelerated their exodus from the Colony during the latter two thirds of the nineteenth century in what historians have called the Great Trek. Their expansion carried them into the North and East, and, after clashing with the British and the Zulus in what is now known as the Province of Natal (an area annexed by the British in 1843), they withdrew into the interior and established the Boer Republics of the Orange Free State and Trans-vaal. The African or Bantu nations (primarily the Ndebele, Sotho, and Zulu) resisting Boer invasion in these areas were defeated and eliminated as a military force after a series of frontier wars that lasted until 1880.[20] White domination in South Africa became firmly established.

Some African historians maintain that the intense racist feel-ings of present-day Afrikaners (descendants of the Boers) can be traced to the earlier period of frontier violence that domi-nated so much of their life. Although it is true that in the nineteenth century biological racism emerged as the dominant ideology of race exploitation among Boers when their eco-nomic status was jeopardized by British efforts to make the law color-blind,[21] it crystallized when their very existence was threatened by the Bantu in the endless series of "Kaffir" wars. Sheila Patterson, for instance, maintains that

> The attitudes which the frontier Boers developed during this period of turbulence have persisted almost unchanged to the present day. Perhaps the most important and potentially dangerous of these attitudes is that which sees the Africans as an enemy on the other side of a frontier, and not as a member of society at all. It is this attitude that enables the most kindly and humane people to feel satisfied with a sys-tem which imposes taxation without representation, moves whole townships arbitrarily from one place to another, re-stricts the movements of labour-seekers, and in general treats the majority of the population as unwelcome aliens, despite the fact that inseparable economic links have been forged between black and white.[22]

APARTHEID AND BIOLOGICAL RACISM

The discovery of diamonds around Kimberly in 1869 and of gold around Johannesburg in 1886 not only marked the begin-ning of South Africa's transformation from an agricultural and rural society to an urbanized and industrialized society but also led to the demise of the autonomous Boer Republics. As the British flooded into the Transvaal seeking their fortunes, tensions heightened and finally erupted into the Anglo–Boer War of 1899–1902. The Boer Republics were defeated in this conflict and incorporated as British colonies in 1902. Together with the British provinces of the Cape and Natal, the Transvaal and Orange Free State formed the Union of South Africa in 1910.[23]

Neither the Africans nor the Coloureds nor the Asians[24] took part in the formation of what van den Berghe has called a racist "Herrenvolk democracy," i.e., a country in which non-whites, who constituted roughly 80 per cent of the population, are ruled by a relatively small but powerful white population.[25] Despite British and Afrikaner tensions following the Anglo–Boer War, both were in agreement concerning the necessity of maintaining white supremacy.[26] The insertion of the color bar into the Constitution of 1909 and the passage of the Native Land Act (which apportioned the farmland into black and white tracts leaving the African majority roughly one tenth of the available land) were clear indications of a united white front against blacks. However, the two white groups did differ with respect to the intensity of their feelings regarding white domination and the programs of racial subordination they advocated and openly supported.

Afrikaners are the most fanatical supporters of white supremacy in twentieth-century South Africa. To some extent, as already indicated, this is a carry-over from the attitudes developed during the preindustrial days in the skirmishes and power struggles on the frontier against the Africans, whereas in other ways it stems from the economic disaster averted in the early twentieth century by the development of an almost impenetrable system of segregation and a fervent sense of group nationalism.

As the British rapidly transformed South Africa into an industrial society, many Afrikaner farmers, faced with a series of problems (droughts, antiquated agrarian methods, floods, hailstorms, plant diseases, and impoverished land conditions), were forced to migrate to urban areas and take positions as unskilled wage-earners.[27] This situation created "what was proportionally the world's worst 'poor white' problem."[28] On the one hand, the jobs Afrikaners were qualified for were in most cases being performed by Africans thrust into competitive relations with whites by the onslaught of industrialization,[29] whereas on the other hand "the managerial positions to which they would have liked to aspire were in the hands of the long urbanized, more prosperous English South Africans."[30] Gwendolyn Carter has commented on the after-effect of Afrikaners' economic experiences in the 1920s:

> Though today there are relatively few poor whites in the country, few Afrikaners forget that as late as the 1920's almost 60 per cent of their people were in or close to so degrading a status. Thus they support, with a vehemence often incomprehensible from outside, the means to which they attribute their rescue: the extended color bar in industry and commerce which protects white labor from the competition of Africans, Indians, and even Coloureds through laws or the action of white trade unions; the Government-sponsored industries like the Iron and Steel Corporation (Iscor) with its numerous jobs at European pay scales for relatively unskilled Europeans; their entrenched position in the administration and the police; and Nationalist political power.[31]

Although space will not permit a full description of the means by which Afrikaners extended the color bar to protect their group interests, preserve their sense of group position, and force competitive race relations into an increasingly restrictive pattern, a few points should be discussed in this regard.

Probably the most significant factor in the formation of a rigid color bar in industry was the political alliance between the English-speaking trade unions and the emerging Afrikaner nationalistic movement in the early 1920s. "This alliance," states Sheila Van der Horst, "was precipitated by a very serious strike on the coal and gold mines which culminated in a general strike on the Witwatersrand leading to the organisation of commandos by the strikers, the calling in of troops, the declaration of martial law, and a considerable number of casualties."[32] The strike erupted when white miners sensed that their competitive position was threatened as mine owners attempted to reduce rising costs by permitting nonwhites to substitute for whites in a limited number of semiskilled positions.[33] The strike represented the joint effort of Afrikaner laborers and English-speaking labor groups, "who marched together under the slogan 'Workers of the World unite to defend a White South Africa' "[34] and not only received white laborers' commitment to protect their privileged position but also discouraged management from directly challenging the color bar in the mining industry. More significantly, however, the industrial alliance of the Afrikaner nationalists and the English-speaking Labour Party was effectively transferred to the political arena in the 1924 elections as they combined to gain a majority of the seats in Parliament and establish J. B. M. Hertzog as the first Afrikaner nationalist Prime Minister. The nationalist–Labour coalition promptly passed a series of legislative acts that preserved white privileges in industries, essentially eliminated black competition in semiskilled and skilled positions, and firmly set the direction for a system of institutionalized racism that eventually expanded to incorporate basically every phase of black–white contact.[35]

Although in the beginning labor legislation was ostensibly concerned with upholding a "civilized labour policy" for white workers by ensuring that "employers would not take advantage of the willingness of non-whites to accept a wage lower than that which was considered necessary to maintain the 'civilized standard,' "[36] in actuality biological racist feelings helped to shift the focus from a *white survival line* to a *white supremacy line* that provided greater security against black encroachment in the more skilled occupations.[37]

In addition to establishing a firm color bar in industries, the Hertzog government further protected white interests by effectively nullifying the nonwhite vote during the 1930s: the Women Enfranchise Act reduced the relative weight of the nonwhite vote by granting voting rights solely to white women; the Franchise Laws Amendment Act waived the educational, property, and income qualifications for whites only;

the Native Representation Act removed Africans from the common voting roll in the Cape,[38] established a policy whereby Africans, from a separate roll, would elect three white representatives to Parliament,[39] and created a Natives' Representative Council (consisting of four nominated Africans, twelve elected Africans, and five nominated whites) whose powers were solely advisory.[40]

The expansion of institutional racism in South Africa, not only in industries and electoral franchise, but in other areas of life as well coincided with the political ascendancy of the Afrikaner Nationalist Party. Culminating decades of struggle in the rise of Afrikaner nationalism, which involved overcoming internal disputes and factions within the ranks of Afrikanerdom (leading to the recasting of their group into a single party named Die Herenigde Nasionale of Volksparty—the Reunited National Party, commonly called the HNP) and external opposition from non-nationals, including the more moderate, but nonetheless conservative, English-speaking United Party,[41] the Nationalist Party gained virtual control of the government in 1948 and established a cabinet consisting exclusively of Afrikaners. The Nationalists won the 1948 election by the successful exploitation of post World War II racial fears and by the call for stringent racial segregation (apartheid). World War II had accelerated industrialization in South Africa, generated a labor shortage, and thereby increased the migration of Africans from the Reserves to urban areas in order to work in expanding industries. The acute labor shortage enabled some Africans to move into semiskilled positions, thus reviving fears of African encroachment in areas where whites had prior claim. Overcrowding, increased crime rates, and demoralization resulted because urban housing facilities did not keep pace with the growing black urban population.[42] Finally, rising African militancy and rising expectations[43] that paralleled the growth of the black urban population increased racial tensions and produced cries among whites that blacks were "getting out of place." For all these reasons, racial tensions were heightened prior to the 1948 election. As Carter has observed,

The attitude toward non-Europeans became the major political issue in the elections of 1948. Jan Hofmeyer enunciated a program for the United Party which, though denying the essential equality of Europeans and non-Europeans, yet asserted the necessity of giving every group in South Africa the chance for free development in terms of its potentialities. His words were torn from their context and translated into flammatory phrases suggesting miscegenation. Even the liberal wing of the United Party was vaguely disturbed, and made little effort to fight back, while its most conservative group was antagonized. The H.N.P., in contrast, preached apartheid (racial segregation) without going into details about how it would be achieved. . . . The H.N.P. succeeded, to everyone's surprise, in gaining political power.[44]

Now in their greatest power position, the Nationalists began to expand, formalize, and more rigidly enforce the pattern of racial segregation that had already restricted black–white contact during the first half of the twentieth century. The Nationalist program of racial oppression consisted, first of all, of the enactment of apartheid legislation (including the Mixed Marriages and Immorality Act, Population Registration Act, Separate Amenities Act, Group Areas Act, Bantu Education Act and Industrial Conciliation Act) that firmly established what van den Berghe has called three levels of racial segregation—microsegregation in the separation of private and public facilities located in zones of interracial contact such as industries, mesosegregation in the separation of residential areas within urban areas, and macrosegregation in the separation of racial groups in formally defined territorial regions, e.g., the "Native Reserves" (or "Bantustans") of South Africa.[45]

"Apartheid as a policy," states Edward A. Tiryakian, "is nothing new in South Africa. What is new is that the implementation of this policy of separate development has taken place only since the Nationalists came to power in 1948. For the first time a South African government has a sufficient majority to enact the necessary legislation."[46] In order to enforce this program and to overcome opposition and resistance to apartheid, especially from Africans, the Nationalists passed a series of legislative measures that all but abolished civil liberties and the rule of the law. In the following section, I will discuss both the content of these legislative measures and the extent to which they successfully suppressed African and liberal opposition, but first let us briefly examine the ideological foundations of apartheid.

Rationalization for racial subordination in South Africa gradually moved from a dominant ideology of cultural racism in the seventeenth century to a dominant philosophy of biological racism in the nineteenth century and first half of the twentieth century. After the Nationalists assumed power in 1948, official justification for apartheid relied heavily on biological racist beliefs. However, according to Heribert Adam, a change has taken place in official apartheid ideology since 1958, when Hendrik Verwoerd (since assassinated) became South Africa's Prime Minister. Specifically, in an effort to impose greater "rationality" on the official ideology of racial subordination, arguments asserting the biological inferiority of blacks are now "officially regarded as outdated, though latently still assumed."[47] Emphasis is placed on the traditional social and cultural differences between blacks and whites.[48] The fact that Nationalist leaders are invoking "inherent" cultural differences as justification for racial separatism indicates,[49] in my frame of reference, that cultural racism is currently playing a major role in black subordination even though there is some evidence that biological racist attitudes linger on.[50]

AFRICAN RESISTANCE TO APARTHEID

Although black resistance against racial dominantion can be analyzed as a response to the escalation of racial oppression in South Africa, the form and content of such resistance are most appropriately explained in terms of the dialectical relationship between African and white power resources.[51] This entails a consideration of both the actual or potential resources each group possesses and each group's assessment of the other's (1) strengths and (2) motivation or willingness to mobilize its resources to protect or promote its vested interests. Related to such group perceptions are patterns of social thought. Whereas the prevailing philosophy among white South Africans, particularly Afrikaners, has increasingly crystallized around racial separation or apartheid, African social thought has gradually moved away from a philosophy of interracialism to support for racial solidarity and institutional nationalism.

Although some segments of the African population always supported racial solidarity and institutional nationalism, prior to 1948 African thinking was dominated by interracialism— a philosophy based to some extent on optimism both in the efficacy of multiracial protests to overcome racial oppression and in the establishment of an interracial society wherein neither white nor black racialism would dominate in South African society. Black faith in multiracial cooperation to eliminate racist suppression developed late in the nineteenth century. African aspiration had been raised by the Cape Colony's liberal tradition, and when the Union officially sanctioned a color bar in 1909 and took other steps to impose racial separation, a group of African intellectuals created the Native National Congress, later named the African National Congress (ANC), to voice their protest. However, members of the ANC were fully cognizant of their limited resources to effect change, and thus their responses to increased racial segregation (e.g., the Native Land Act of 1913) in these early years were restricted mainly to cooperating with liberal whites in petitioning the South African government and appealing to national governments and international organizations, but all to no avail.

The inability of the ANC to fend off the tide of racial oppression in the early twentieth century and to come to grips with the severe problems of African economic dislocation following World War I led to the creation of the largest and most effective African working-class movement—the Industrial and Commercial Workers Union (ICU). Disillusioned with the soft pressures (speeches, resolutions, and petitions) applied by the ANC, the ICU escalated the level of protests to strikes and court suits. Effectively organizing strikes along the Cape Coast, the ICU raised African expectations about their ability to effect change and consequently was pressured to move beyond trade unionism affairs and directly confront racism in all areas of South African life. However, the increasing power of the ICU alarmed governmental officials, the Union was suppressed and destroyed by police, and its leaders were banished after they attempted to organize a boycott of municipal beer halls in 1929.

Resistance to racial oppression the decade following the collapse of the ICU was feeble: the ANC was too weak to mobilize African resistance against the efforts of the Hertzog government to eliminate the African franchise in the Cape; the South African Communist Party attempted to organize pass-burning demonstrations and boycotts of municipal beer halls but achieved no real success; the All African Convention (consisting of white leftists and nonwhites), founded in 1935 to resist the Hertzog franchise bills, quickly disintegrated with no concrete gains.

During and after World War II, a new militancy emerged among urban blacks partly because of disillusionment with the Natives' Representative Council, which had taken a conciliatory policy toward governmental repression, and partly because African expectations had been raised by the wartime promises of the Allied leaders incorporated in such declarations as the "Four Freedoms" and the Atlantic Charter. African leaders felt that black rights would be extended after the war, and their faith in the Atlantic Charter idealism was reflected in a statement of "Africans' Claims in South Africa" published by the ANC in 1945. This new militant spirit among Africans was exhibited in multiracial strikes, boycotts, and manifestos, and it was also reflected in the resurgence of the ANC and the emergence of a new militant and black nationalist-oriented wing of the ANC—the African National Congress Youth League (ANCYL). The emphasis of ANCYL was militant racial (African) solidarity. Youth League members had not only become disillusioned with the mild pressure resources applied by the larger ANC during the first half of the century to reverse the tide of increasing governmental repression, but they also felt that a united black African front was crucial before meaningful interracial cooperation could be achieved.[52]

Although the Youth League's philosophy of racial solidarity protests was not endorsed by the ANC as a whole, when the Afrikaner Nationalists assumed power in 1948 the larger ANC was persuaded to adopt the Youth League's program of boycotts, strikes, civil disobedience, and an end to cooperation with the government. In 1952, the ANC joined a multiracial campaign of passive resistance against racist apartheid laws—including the Suppression of Communism Act (which was so vaguely defined that any advocate of "passive disobedience" was vulnerable to arrest and conviction), the Group Areas Act (which abolished the Natives Representative Council and attempted to reestablish the authority of the Tribal Chiefs), the Population Registration Act (which provided for issuance of racial identity cards for all South Africans and thus helped to reinforce the caste system), and the Separate Representation of Voters Act (which was designed to remove the Cape Coloured from the common voting roll and thus achieve the total elimination of nonwhite voting power). More than eight thousand persons, mostly Africans but also a number of Coloureds and Indians, were jailed for deliberately violating apartheid laws. Rather than forcing the government to yield on apartheid laws, however, the campaign of passive resistance actually produced more government repression. In 1953, the Criminal Law Amendment Act, prescribing harsh penalties for "passive disobedience" and thus seriously increasing the personal risks involved in active resistance to apartheid, was passed. This widened the gap between African expectations and gratification and underlined what Kuper has called "a dialectical relationship between nonwhite and white political power."[53] He states:

> As more power was assumed by whites—through changes in the franchise, the creation of new structures of control, the introduction of further penal sanctions, and increases in

police and military strength—so the power of non-whites —in terms of parliamentary participation, freedom of political association, and the right to oppose state policies— correspondingly diminished.[54]

The gap between African expectations and gratifications increased support, not only for black separation and racial solidarity, but also for more aggressive forms of protest. Let me amplify this point by briefly describing the series of events that rocked South Africa after 1954.

In 1955, an alliance called the Congress Movement was formed among the ANC and organizations representing Indians, Coloureds, and leftist whites. This multiracial front drafted a Freedom Charter, which demanded both equal rights for all and public ownership of monopoly industry, mineral wealth, and banks. In 1956, 156 persons (including Albert Luthuli, president of the ANC, and other major officials of the Congress Movement) were arrested on the charge of high treason—a charge based particularly on the Freedom Charter and similar documents. These arrests culminated a series of steps taken by the government to suppress both nonwhite and leftist white opposition to apartheid following the defiance campaign of passive resistance.

In 1957, the split within the ANC between the younger Youth League Africanists and the Charterists (those committed to multiracial cooperation) widened. The Youth League felt that the ANC should drop interracialism and adopt a position of racial solidarity and militant Pan-Africanism. In 1959, Africans, including Youth League members, who opposed the multiracial Congress Movement, formed the Pan-Africanist Congress (PAC). The basic philosophy of the PAC, though committed to the United Nations Declaration of Human Rights, was that "the salvation of Africans must be the work of Africans themselves"[55] and that although nonviolent protest was to be preferred, Africans were not obliged to remain peaceful in all cases, because passive demonstrations had provoked violent responses from the government.

The initial PAC attempt at mass civil disobedience was a

nonviolent demonstration on March 24, 1960, in Sharpeville protesting the broadened restriction of African movement through use of the pass system. The demonstration ended the same day when nervous police opened fire on peaceful demonstrators, killing 67 and wounding 186. On March 28, Albert Luthuli called for a stay-at-home Day-of-Mourning and publicly burned his pass as a gesture of defiance. Following the Sharpeville incident, the Nationalist government passed the Unlawful Organizations Act of 1960 (which banned African political organizations such as the PAC and the ANC), arrested and indefinitely detained 1,900 political suspects—including white Communists and some members of the Liberal Party[56]—under the Public Safety Act of 1953 (which had empowered the Governor-General to declare a state of emergency and suspend all laws in areas where public safety was threatened), and detained over 18,000 other persons under various other regulations and laws.[57]

The suppression of the ANC and PAC and the mass arrests of demonstrators and political activists in the early 1960s convinced many Africans that the only successful way to deal with government repression was to resort to violent means. Driven underground, both the ANC and PAC authorized the creation of subordinate organizations whose purposes would range from sabotage to armed revolt. An organization called Umkonto we Sizwe (Spear of the Nation), affiliated but not synonymous with the ANC, launched a campaign of sabotage to destroy public utility equipment in 1962. Shortly thereafter, the PAC secret organization Poqo (which unlike Umkonto was a purely African organization) emerged and committed itself to terrorist activities, including the killing of individual whites. In 1964, a group consisting primarily of young left-wing white intellectuals organized the African Resistance Movement (RAM) and devoted itself to sabotage. However, all three groups were quickly suppressed by police, who devised an elaborate intelligence network that included widespread use of paid informants and mass infiltration of the organizations. During a three-year period ending in December 1965, almost two hundred political and sabotage trials were held and 1,300 persons were sentenced to prison for an average of seven years.[58] With the suppression of the terrorist organizations, organized resistance to apartheid in the late 1960s and early 1970s was a mere shadow of what it had been prior to 1960. There is, however, growing support for territorial separation (i.e., an autonomous and independent state or area under the full control of Africans) among many African leaders who have abandoned the struggle to achieve meaningful racial equality within the larger society.[59] With the government-sponsored "Bantustan" areas, the issue of territorial separatism has reached the realm of practicality.[60] However, as Adam has noted, "having pressed for independence, some African politicians are now holding back. They feel that formal independence would finalize the white-dictated distribution of land and the world would be unlikely to support claims for lost land after independence."[61]

Despite the active protest movements during the 1950s and early 1960s, appeals to militancy by African organizations received a relatively poor response.[62] The overwhelming majority of Africans were not awakened by organizational efforts to mobilize support against increasing white suppression. Moreover, as Adam has observed, "the restrictions imposed on the mobility and freedom of the urban worker have as yet had no visible political effects since the final prohibition of African political organization in 1961."[63] Both Feit and Adam partly attribute this situation to the expanding economy, which has thus far made it possible to meet rising material expectations and to prevent a wide discrepancy between expectations and gratifications.[64] The basic arguments of this hypothesis are that the average black worker in South Africa has over the past few years experienced increases in salary exceeding his expectations (e.g., instead of expecting and getting thirty-five cents an hour during a particular year he received forty cents); that his relatively low expectations are due both to the fact that the underprivileged in general tend to establish a low estimate of the future (those who have less wish for less) and to the reality of racial oppression in South Africa, where laws exist to maintain low African status in all areas of life; that African resistance movements therefore have experienced difficulties in mobilizing mass opposition against the South African regime, not only because of severe legal constraints placed on them, but also because economic advance has kept the frustration of African workers at manageable levels.

Although it may be true that African material or economic expectations have kept pace with economic gains, an analysis of comparative data on subordinate-group protests suggests that factors of a quite different nature may be operating to maintain the lack of overt mass protest against apartheid. For example, in my analysis of the escalation of black protest in America during the middle and late 1960s, I was careful to point out that the widening gap between expectations and frustrations was largely related to the increase of white violence directed against black protest and that the period of intense black frustration occurred at the very time that blacks had experienced significant economic progress. In other words, my analysis did not stress a widening gap between expectations and economic gratification but rather a widening gap between expectations and emotional gratification. It is true that emotional gratification is often a function of economic gratification, but it can also be derived from group perceptions of racial progress in areas not directly related to the satisfaction of economic needs, e.g., increased political rights.

The question before us, then, is why did increasing governmental repression, especially in areas outside the economic realm, give rise to an escalation of militancy among African leaders and members of organizations such as the ANC (who obviously experienced a widening gap in expectations and emotional gratification) but not among the urban African masses?[65] In answering this question, we should at least consider the fact that African masses in South Africa, unlike black masses in the United States, are unable to develop political awareness via electronic media. Television has yet to be introduced in South Africa, and when it finally does arrive there is every reason to believe that its content will be so regulated by government agencies that, far from politicizing the few Africans who could afford a set, it will merely be used as another means of social control.[66] Although "radio ownership among the urban Bantu had increased from 26 percent to 48 percent"[67] over a two-year period (1967–1968), white-controlled programs are designed to manipulate African thought. Finally, virtually no Afrikaner newspaper is read by the 70 per cent of urban Africans who are literate, and only a very small percentage read the English-language newspapers (13 per cent in 1967–1968).[68]

If media, particularly electronic media, are unavailable or not used to communicate information about subordinate-group thought (protest activity and/or events that bear directly on subordinate-group status), political protest will largely be confined to the most sophisticated and privileged members of the oppressed racial group.[69] Unlike the masses, the latter tend to be cognizant of the circumstances surrounding racial exploitation, of alternative life styles, of tactics to overcome racial oppression, and of allies both within and outside of the country willing to support efforts to achieve racial equality. Accordingly, whereas African leaders and middle classes developed heightened expectations as a result of, say, the Atlantic Charter, United Nations declarations against racial oppression in South Africa, the Pan-African Movement, and the emergence of newly independent African states,[70] these events remained largely remote to the African masses preoccupied with the day-to-day struggle for survival. "For many of the South African subject people" states Adam, "the idea of equality and dignity for all human beings still remains abstract."[71] Under these conditions, activists naturally find it difficult to mobilize mass resistance against racial oppression.

Perhaps even more important is the fact that the rigid police state and fantastic discrepancy in power resources between the white and black populations severely reduce the chances of a successful mobilization of resources. Authors such as Feit, Ngubane, and Adam have emphasized the blind and unrealistic faith of the ANC, PAC, and other protest organizations in the use of various constraint resources (e.g., nonviolent resistance) to effect change and their miscalculation of the government's ability and willingness to overcome internal resistance.[72] So tight is government security that thousands of Africans are arrested each day for purely technical violations of discriminatory laws, e.g., failure to have proper "pass" identification. "So fine is the net" states Ngubane, "that in a city like Durban plainclothes police search people in broad daylight on the streets, and there is hardly a corner in central Johannesburg where Africans are not stopped to have their passes checked."[73] Moreover, many Africans themselves have been co-opted—enlisted by government officials to infiltrate surviving underground organizations, to beef up police security, and to identify potential or actual challengers to government authority. For all these reasons, the prospects for successful resistance against apartheid in the near future seems dim indeed. Adam is probably correct when he asserts that

> As long as the clearly defined ruling group shows no sign of deterioration or schism, and as long as there is no necessity for interracial coalitions or programmatic concessions, a downfall of the existing power structure in such a society is hardly conceivable. It seems illusory to assume that this overthrow will occur in the form of a brief explosion in which the oppressed masses suddenly liberate themselves. . . . Considering only the internal factors, the subjective starting point for change of the fossilized structures seems, therefore, to lie more in developments and contradictions within the ruling group than in initiatives of the subordinates, even though the dialectic of both cannot be overlooked.[74]

SOCIAL CHANGE AND COMPETITIVE RACE RELATIONS

One inherent contradiction in South Africa's racial policy is that although the government and the overwhelming majority of the white population pursue a policy of racial separation and exclusion, industry and trade would virtually collapse without black labor. In fact, over the years the dependence on black labor has increasingly paralleled the rapidly expanding growth of the South African economy. The color bar, initially established to eliminate black competition in the more skilled trades, has produced a severe bottleneck and therefore has been inched higher and higher to allow blacks to move into vacancies created by the shortage of skilled white workers.[75] Despite laws designed to prevent African encroachment in areas where Europeans had exclusive claim, the pressures for greater economic progress have led to the admission of some Africans into skilled positions, not only in all phases of industry, but also in the government-owned railway systems. However, this does not mean that the restrictive competitive pattern of race relations is becoming more fluid or that the so-called rational imperative of industrialization is finally beginning to undermine the color bar. Indeed, although some Africans have been able to upgrade their occupations and increase their incomes, their relative position vis-à-vis whites has remained basically the same. Specifically, in order to secure union permission to allow blacks to fill jobs traditionally reserved for Europeans, white wages have been significantly increased, thus reinforcing the severe income gap between the racial groups. Moreover, blacks are not permitted to advance to administrative and supervisory positions that carry authority over whites. Although there has been some opposition from white workers who fear that black encroachment in skilled positions will eventually undermine the competitive advantage they enjoy, the increases in salary and, in some cases, the elevation of white workers to supervisory positions made possible by the entry of blacks into new occupations have softened the criticism.

Despite the fact that the white manpower shortage has not produced a dent in the racial alignment, the mere fact that the imperative of economic growth requires that blacks enter the skilled occupations could have significant ramifications for the future of South African race relations. Because both segments of the white population—the Afrikaners and the English—have a vested interest in preventing economic stagnation, it is not inconceivable that the government may relax restrictions to allow some Africans to attain the educational and industrial training required for skilled positions. Under such conditions, a viable and larger black middle class with greater political sophistication and awareness and greater economic resources could develop, and hence the potential for mass mobilization of resources against apartheid could be significantly increased.

NOTES

1. "Apartheid" literally means separation but is used to denote racial segregation and oppression in South Africa.
2. Africans constitute the largest racial group in South Africa, 15.1 million or 70 per cent of the population. There are also 2 million Coloureds and 0.6 million Asians. These figures are based on preliminary results of the 1970 census and were reported in Heribert Adam, *Modernizing Racial Domination: South Africa's Political Dynamics* (Berkeley: U. California, 1971), p. 3. Although all three racial groups have been victims of apartheid, the oppression of Africans has been most severe. Because of space limitation our major focus will be on African and white contact, although some attention will also be given to the Asians and Coloureds.
3. L. E. Neame, *The History of Apartheid: The Story of the Colour Bar in South Africa* (London: Pall Mall, 1962), p. 111.
4. Pierre van den Berghe, *Race and Racism: A Comparative Perspective* (New York: Wiley, 1967), p. 97. The white settlement consisted mostly of Dutch, but there were also a few German and French Huguenots (who arrived after the revocation of the Edict of Nantes). All three groups were amalgamated in politics, language, and religion by the middle of the eighteenth century.
5. Ibid.
6. I. D. MacCrone, *Race Relations in South Africa: Historical, Experimental, and Psychological Studies* (London: Oxford U.P., 1937), Part I. Also see Edward A. Tiryakian, "Apartheid and Religion," *Theology Today*, 14:385–400 (Oct. 1957); Arthur G. J. Crijns, *Race Relations and Race Attitudes in South Africa* (Nijmegen: Drukkerij Gebr. Janssen, 1959), pp. 40–41; Pierre van den Berghe, *South Africa: A Study in Conflict* (Berkeley: U. of California, 1965), p. 15, and *Race and Racism*, op. cit., p. 96; and Neame, op. cit.
7. MacCrone, op. cit., p. 41.
8. Ibid.
9. Ibid., p. 78.
10. Neame, op. cit., p. 13.
11. MacCrone, op. cit., p. 79. This view was held despite the fact that "it was not until the end of the century that the question whether baptized slaves, in private ownership, could lawfully be retained in slavery was explicitly raised and answered in the affirmative." Ibid.

12. Crijns, op. cit., pp. 39–40, and van den Berghe, *South Africa: A Study in Conflict,*op. cit., p. 15.

13. MacCrone, op. cit., p. 131.

14. van den Berghe, *South Africa: A Study in Conflict,* op. cit., p. 23.

15. Ibid., pp. 25–26.

16. Ibid., p. 27.

17. Gwendolen M. Carter, *The Politics of Inequality* (New York: Praeger, 1958), p. 18.

18. van den Berghe, *South Africa: A Study in Conflict,* op. cit., pp. 27–28.

19. Ibid., p. 29.

20. Ibid., pp. 30–31.

21. See Carter, op. cit., p. 18.

22. Sheila Patterson, *The Last Trek: A Study of the Boer People and the Afrikaner Nation* (London: Routledge & Keegan Paul, 1959), p. 11.

23. South Africa withdrew from the British Commonwealth in 1961 and became a republic.

24. The Coloureds are descendants of the early unions between the whites (both Dutch and English) and nonwhites (primarily Hottentots). The Asians, a large percentage of whom are Indians, came to South Africa as contract laborers in the nineteenth and early twentieth centuries.

25. van den Berghe, *Race and Racism,* op. cit., p. 101.

26. Alex Hepple, *South Africa: A Political and Economic History* (London: Pall Mall, 1966), p. 98.

27. George V. Doxey, *The Industrial Colour Bar in South Africa* (London: Oxford U.P., 1961), p. 77.

28. Carter, op. cit., p. 25.

29. Africans first entered as "mine boys" in the nineteenth century. See William Henry Vatcher, Jr., *White Laager: The Rise of Afrikaner Nationalism* (London: Pall Mall, 1965), p. 12.

30. Carter, op. cit., p. 25.

31. Ibid.

32. Sheila T. Van der Horst, "The Effects of Industrialisation on Race Relations in South Africa," in *Industrialisation and Race Relations: A Symposium,* ed. by Guy Hunter (London: Oxford U.P., 1965), pp. 117–118.

33. Ibid., p. 118.

34. Ibid.

35. For a more complete discussion of these legislative acts, see Carter, op. cit., pp. 30–31; Doxey, op. cit.; Van der Horst, op. cit., pp. 117–119; and Hector Mentieth Robertson, *South African Economic and Political Aspects* (Durham, N.C.: Duke U.P., 1957), pp. 27–29.

36. Doxey, op. cit., p. 113.

37. The white supremacy line had its basis in traditional white racist attitudes that, according to Doxey, "could not admit that the nonwhite

is cabable of advance, or would not admit it because it would inevitably introduce nonwhite advancement and competition" (Doxey, op. cit., p. 123). Doxey also states: "There can be no doubt that traditional prejudice did not allow any thinking which would ultimately lead to an acceptance of the non-European on a par with the European in any sphere, whether economic or social. To the upholders of the traditional way of thinking, therefore, the civilized living standard approach could possibly be regarded as the means of preventing nonwhite encroachment on white preserves.

"There was ample evidence at the time to show that this was in fact the case and as a result of the inability of 'civilized standards' alone to withstand encroachment, subsequent developments, in which a more definite legalistic racial biased approach has become necessary to divide the white and nonwhite spheres of the labour market, have borne out the contention that traditional prejudice has underlined the general attitude of whites towards labour problems in South Africa" Ibid., p. 113.

38. The Cape Coloured were not affected by this act, but they too lost their voting rights subsequently.

39. van den Berghe, *South Africa: A Study in Conflict*, op. cit., p. 126. I have already explained why the English-dominated Cape Government granted the franchise to nonwhites in 1853 (this policy was retained after the formation of the Union in 1909, even though Africans could not vote in the other provinces). However, a question could be raised about Natal, the other English-dominated province, why it, like the Transvaal and Orange Free State, supported a racial franchise after Union settlement. Van den Berghe supplies the answer: "Natal, a British colony with few Afrikaners, was even less liberal than the Cape. It never had more than purely nominal and insignificant voting rights for non-Whites. This fact is easily understood when one considers that, in Natal, the English did not need any non-White vote to offset an already very weak White Afrikaner vote. This interpretation is further confirmed by that fact that, on the franchise issue, the Natal delegation sided with the ex-Boer Republics, and not with the Cape as one might have expected. The end result was a retention of the existing franchise laws in each of the four provinces. The basic agreement on colour issues between most Afrikaners and English has been a constant fact of the South African political scene for over a century. With outstanding exceptions that no amount of cynicism can dismiss, the English, as a group, have only shown liberalism (carefully minimized at that) when it suited their interests as opposed to those of the Afrikaners." Ibid., p. 35.

40. Commenting on the Natives' Advisory Council, Feit states: "However sincere and dedicated the 'Natives' representatives might be, and they were both sincere and dedicated, the separate ballot was obviously a poor substitute for direct representation and was clearly perceived by thinking Africans as just another retrograde step." Edward

Feit, *Urban Revolt in South Africa 1960–1964: A Case Study* (Evanston: Northwestern U.P., 1971), p. 12.

41. Carter, op. cit., pp. 27–37.

42. Irving Kaplan et al., *Area Handbook for the Republic of South Africa* (Washington, D.C.: G.P.O., 1971), p. 85. Van der Horst comments on this situation: "After the war, South Africa, like other countries, faced a critical housing shortage, especially over housing for Africans. In many of the larger towns a third or less of the African population was living in the official locations and even in them many were living in miserable shacks, hovels, and huts made of bits of tin, hessian, or any other material they could acquire. The larger towns were surrounded by 'black spots,' squatter settlements of desperate squalor. The urgency of the housing needs of Africans and the size of the urban African population, which in most towns was at least equal to the white, together with the expansion of industry, brought home that this urban movement was no temporary phenomenon and that many Africans had come to town permanently." Van der Horst, op. cit., p. 135.

43. African militancy and rising expectations are discussed in the next section.

44. Carter, op. cit., p. 36.

45. Pierre van den Berghe, "Racial Segregation in South Africa: Degrees and Kind," in *South Africa: Sociological Perspectives*, ed. by Heribert Adam (London: Oxford U.P., 1971), p. 37.

46. Edward A. Tiryakian, "Apartheid and Politics in South Africa," *Journal of Politics*, 22:682–687 (Nov. 1960).

47. Adam, op. cit., Also see Heribert Adam, "The South African Power Elite: A Survey of Ideological Commitment," in *South Africa: Sociological Perspectives*, op. cit., pp. 73–102.

48. Adam, *Modernizing Racial Domination*, op. cit., p. 71, and "The South African Power Elite," op. cit., p. 79.

49. Adam maintains that apartheid "no longer requires traditional ideological rationalization," i.e., biological racism (Adam, *Modernizing Racial Domination*, op. cit., p. 79). Because forced separatism has in effect accentuated cultural and social differences between blacks and whites, it has strengthened cultural racist arguments in support of segregation.

50. For an empirical analysis of racist attitudes among the South African power elite, see Adam, "The South African Power Elite," op. cit. Adam points out: "It is so common in South Africa to view social conditions in biological categories that socio-economic and historical–cultural circumstances are hardly conceived as possible reasons for different patterns of behavior. As such, sociological explanations are categorically rejected." Ibid., p. 79.

51. In much of the following discussion, I am heavily indebted to

185

Thomas Karis, "South Africa," in *Five African States*, ed. by Gwendolyn M. Carter (Ithaca, N.Y.: Cornell U.P., 1963), pp. 488–494; Leo Kuper, "The Political Situation of Non-Whites in South Africa," in *Southern Africa and the United States*, ed. by William A. Hance (New York: Columbia U.P., 1968), pp. 92–98, *Passive Resistance in South Africa* (New Haven: Yale U.P., 1960), and *An African Bourgeoisie: Race, Class, and Politics in South Africa* New Haven: Yale U.P., 1956); Jordan K. Ngubane, *An African Explains Apartheid* (New York: Praeger, 1963), pp. 69–147; Feit, *Urban Revolt in South Africa*, op. cit., pp. 3–64, *African Opposition in South Africa: The Failure of Passive Resistance* (Stanford, Calif.: The Hoover Institute, 1967), pp. 34–51; and Gwendolen M. Carter, "African Concepts of Nationalism in South Africa," in *South Africa: Sociological Perspectives*, op. cit.

52. As Ngubane puts it, the League felt that "The African was the poorest, largest, most backward, and most oppressed member of the community. These factors made it necessary for him to put his own house in order before attempting to collaborate with the better-placed members. If he reached to work with them before he had prepared himself for this task, he would never deal with them on the basis of real equality. The League concentrated, therefore, on working only among Africans." Ngubane, op. cit., pp. 96–97.

53. Kuper, "The Political Situation of Non-Whites in South Africa," op. cit., p. 87.

54. Ibid.

55. Kaplan et al., op. cit., p. 92.

56. The Liberal Party, founded by Alan Paton in May 1953, advocated social equality.

57. van den Berghe, *South Africa: A Study in Conflict*, op. cit., p. 138.

58. As A. S. Mathews points out, "The 'Sabotage Act' defines the offense of sabotage so widely that many comparatively innocuous political activities (such as disruption of traffic caused by a protest march) became a capital offense punishable by death." A. S. Mathews, "Security Laws and Social Change in the Republic of South Africa," in *South Africa: Sociological Perspectives*, op. cit., p. 235.

59. Gwendolyn M. Carter, "African Concepts of Nationalism in South Africa," op. cit., p. 119.

60. Ibid.

61. Adam, *Modernizing Racial Domination*, op. cit., p. 183.

62. See Feit, *African Opposition in South Africa*, op. cit.

63. Adam, *Modernizing Racial Domination*, op. cit., p. 102.

64. Edward Feit, "Conflict and Cohesion in South Africa: A Theoretical Analysis of the Policy of 'Separate Development' and Its Implication," *Economic Development and Cultural Change*, 16:484–496 (July 1966), and *African Opposition in South Africa*, op. cit., pp. 12–22; and Adam, *Modernizing Racial Domination*, op. cit., pp. 101–111.

65. In South Africa, as in other advanced nation states, the greatest opportunity for militancy and awareness occurs in urban areas.
66. Adam, *Modernizing Racial Domination*, op. cit., p. 108. As Adam notes, however, it is possible that television programs could indirectly "create appetites, difficult to satisfy for the rulers." Ibid.
67. Ibid., p. 106.
68. "The 'Bantu weeklies' and magazines which are mostly white-financed apolitical products, focusing on crime, sport, and other sensationalism have the highest readership." Ibid., p. 107.
69. For a discussion of this point, see Gerald A. McWorter, *Social Integration and the Legitimacy of Black Social Protest*, unpublished doctoral dissertation, University of Chicago (1971). Also see Marshall McLuhan, *Understanding Media: The Extension of Man* (New York: McGraw-Hill, 1964).
70. See, for example, E. A. Brett, *African Attitudes: A Study of Social, Racial, and Political Attitudes of Some Middle Class Africans* (Johannesburg: South African Institute of Race Relations, 1963), and Leo Kuper, *An African Bourgeoisie*, op. cit.
71. Adam, *Modernizing Racial Domination*, op. cit., p. 108.
72. Feit, *African Opposition in South Africa*, op. cit., pp. 190–193; Ngubane, op. cit.; and Adam, *Modernizing Racial Domination*, op. cit., pp. 111–118.
73. Ngubane, op. cit., p. 108.
74. Adam, *Modernizing Racial Domination*, op. cit., pp. 114–115.
75. Muriel Horrell, *South Africa's Workers: Their Organizations and the Patterns of Employment* (Johannesburg: South African Institute of Race Relations, 1969), pp. 88–126; Harold Wolpe, "Class, Race, and the Occupational Structure in South Africa," paper presented at the Seventh World Congress of Sociology, International Sociological Association, Varna, Bulgaria (Sept. 1970); Feit, "Conflict and Cohesion in South Africa," op. cit., p. 493; and Adam, *Modernizing Racial Domination*, op. cit., pp. 145–159.

CHAPTER NINE

Conclusion: A Theoretical Contrast of United States and South African Race Relations

DIFFERENTIAL power has been a significant feature in the interaction between the white and black races in both the United States and the Republic of South Africa, with the existing power discrepancies having their origins in the manner the races first established contact. In the United States, slave transfers put blacks under instant white domination; in South Africa, a combination of colonization and slave transfers characterized initial white control. Racial stratification in the United States initially developed because of attempts by the white landowning aristocracy to maximize material or economic rewards via imposed slavery, whereas in South Africa initial racial domination was prompted by attempts not only to exploit black labor for material gain but also to eliminate competition from Hottentot pastoralists and Bushmen hunters for land and cattle, especially as the white settlement expanded beyond the Cape region. These observations are consistent with one of my major theoretical propositions: that racial stratification is largely a function of dominant-group efforts to control scarce resources either by eliminating or neutralizing subordi-

189

nate racial members as competitors or by exploiting their labor.

Ideologies justifying forms of racial exploitation in both South Africa and the United States have shifted back and forth from cultural to biological racist arguments. In the seventeenth and eighteenth centuries in the United States, the "rationale" for racial domination was primarily belief in black cultural inferiority but was replaced by biological racist arguments in the nineteenth and early twentieth centuries. As the United States entered the latter third of the twentieth century, biological racism declined and was supplanted by cultural racism. By the same token, the "rationale" for racial domination in South Africa shifted from purely cultural racist arguments in the late seventeenth and early eighteenth centuries to an overwhelming emphasis on biological racism in the nineteenth and twentieth centuries. However, official ideology in South Africa now seems to be relying more heavily on cultural racist beliefs.

As I emphasized in my theoretical discussion, racism, be it cultural or biological in focus, is invoked as a line of defense when the system of racial stratification is threatened by either ideological attacks against racial domination or subordinate-group encroachment in areas where dominant members assume prior claim. I noted also that the greater the perceived threat to racial stratification, the more likely that biological racism as opposed to cultural racism will be used to justify or reinforce the superior position of dominant members. Biological racism displaced cultural racism after the latter proved ineffectual in the face of abolitionists' attacks against slavery in the United States and as a weapon against the increasing acculturation of nonwhites in early South Africa. It is the case, however, that the philosophy of racial exploitation invoked to reinforce racial stratification at a particular point in time is related to the prevailing currents of social, religious, philosophical, and scientific thought, that, say, biological racism can more easily be developed and sustained during one period than during another. Accordingly, because of twentieth-century changes in scientific and informed opinion, the premises of biological racism have been severely challenged, and consequently, apologists of racial stratification in both the United States and South Africa are relying more heavily on cultural racist ideology. Although blacks in the United States have penetrated many racist barriers, as reflected in the rapidly increasing black college population and the growth of skilled, professional, and managerial positions among middle-class blacks, the fact that lower segments of the black population are falling behind in relative economic stagnation enables cultural racists to continue to argue that black cultural and social inferiority justifies continued racial stratification.

However, racism in South Africa in both its cultural and biological forms continues to be more virulent than racism in the United States; it is, in other words, more frequently and passionately used to remind the races that they should be separated and that no equality should exist between them. I indicated in my theoretical discussion that the more dominant-group members internalize racist beliefs and norms, the greater is their support for a structure that denies the minority group access to positions of power and prestige, and the more likely they are to resist efforts toward a racial realignment. Obviously, the demographic fact that whites constitute only 17.5 per cent of the total population in South Africa heightens their fears of being overrun by the considerably larger nonwhite population. Racism therefore remains a very important weapon to help preserve advantages.

Although racial stratification is still quite prevalent in the United States, racism as a line of defense against black encroachment is not nearly as heavily relied on as it was in the late nineteenth and early twentieth centuries. It is true that despite the effective undermining of biological racist beliefs by informed opinion, many forms of institutional discrimination originally based on such beliefs continue to linger on with only minimal reduction. Moreover, it is important to remember that the rapid economic growth of the United States' economy during the latter half of the twentieth century that allowed blacks to make some breakthroughs in the occupational structure also enabled whites to further advance their positions. Under such conditions, whites are less aware of and less concerned about black upward mobility. Although racism loses its thrust in such situations, it could easily be revived if the United States' economy experiences sudden setbacks, creating an economic squeeze and making whites in marginal economic positions receptive to a mobilization of demagogic racism. Black advancement in such situations is more easily and quickly judged to be threatening.

By examining race relations in the United States and the Republic of South Africa in historical context, I was able to incorporate the proposition that "basic aspects of the social structure exert a considerable degree of determinism on the prevailing type of race relations."[1] In both countries, paternalistic patterns of race relations emerged during preindustrial periods of agricultural and handicraft production. Racial interaction was characterized by a very unequal symbiosis and a high degree of white exploitation of blacks. In the United States, the stability of the paternalistic regimes was virtually assured by the fantastic discrepancy in black and white power resources created by the slave transfer situation. Slave insurrections were attempted but tended to be infrequent and sporadic. In fact, the very nature of the slave system in the United States necessitated that acts of defiance be subtle and indirect, frequently individual rather than group endeavors. In South Africa, the major form of early conflict, aside from periodic slave revolts, was frontier skirmishes between the Boers and indigenous African tribes. To the extent the Boers were able to overcome resistance from Hottentot pastoralists and Bushmen hunters, the system of paternalistic race relations was expanded beyond the Cape settlement.

As industrialization replaced agricultural and handicraft production, paternalistic race relations were undermined and competitive relations became dominant in both South Africa and the United States. However, the system of competitive relations in each country has been variable. The variability of competitive race relations in South Africa can best be described in terms of degrees of restriction. As a consequence of apartheid laws and greater Nationalist repression, the most restrictive form of competitive race relations in South Africa emerged during the second half of the twentieth century. In contrast, race relations have reached their most fluid pattern in the United States during this same period.

The drift from restrictive to fluid competitive relations creates racial tension and hostility, particularly among the segments of the dominant group who must directly compete with subordinate-group members for scarce goods. I have already indicated that lower-status whites in the Southern part of the United States played a major role in pressing for Jim Crow legislation to reduce or eliminate the black competition that developed during the more fluid competitive period of Reconstruction. Likewise, the severe resistance of Southern whites to desegregation in the late 1950s and early 1960s has to be explained, in part, as an effort to shift the tide of increasing fluid competitive relations and preserve the white group's sense of superior position. However, regardless of whether the context is one of restrictive or fluid competitive relations, as subordinate racial members tend to increase proportionately to dominant members, the former are viewed as a greater competitive force, and dominant-group tensions develop and racial oppression increases. Indeed, the proliferation of race riots in the United States in 1919 was a direct result of the increasing urbanization of blacks and white fears of greater black competition for housing and for jobs, especially after the economic sag following World War I.

The very conditions that heightened racial tensions in the United States in the early twentieth century were also operative in South Africa. Because industrialization had thrown blacks into competition with whites, and black migration from the reserves to urban industrialized areas had increased, white workers made every effort to preserve their advantages. The crippling strike in the Witwatersrand was a reaction to management's effort to reduce rising costs by allowing blacks to enter some semiskilled or skilled positions. So severe was white worker resistance to black encroachment that industrialists never again took unilateral action to change the status of black workers without consulting white unions.

In this connection, Blumer's observation that the forces of

industrialization adapt to rather than significantly undermine the racial order can be supported by developments in both the United States and South Africa. Free blacks before the Civil War in the Northern United States were relegated to the most menial positions in the emerging industries, with this pattern continuing throughout the late nineteenth and early twentieth centuries in industries across the nation. In many cases, the ready supply of cheap immigrant labor caused industrialists to ignore blacks altogether. It was not until the acute labor shortage of the World War I period, caused by the drastic curtailment of European immigration and the drafting of thousands of white workers and potential workers into the armed services, that industrialists, faced with war production demands, openly recruited blacks and facilitated their mass migration from the South to the North. However, after the war blacks were systematically excluded from many industries, especially in the South, and it was only when the federal government established the Fair Employment Practices Commission in 1941 that blacks were able to hold jobs in significant numbers in the nation's industries. In recent years, the gradual breakdown of racial alignment in Southern industries has largely stemmed from the pressures of the desegregation movement and not from the inner imperatives of industrialization.[2]

In South Africa, the conditions hostile to black advancement have been more severe throughout the twentieth century, although the white supremacy line restricting black entry into semiskilled and skilled positions is now beginning to bend because of a significant white labor shortage in the skilled positions Accordingly, the pressures for greater economic growth have permitted the admission of some Africans into skilled positions. Nonetheless, the color bar in industry has not been significantly undermined, and the position of blacks with regard to whites remains basically the same. A shift in the racial order is occurring, but in a lateral direction. The income gap is as severe as ever, and although more whites are moving into supervisory positions (made possible by the entry of nonwhites into some skilled jobs), blacks are restricted from such positions.

However, as indicated in my theoretical discussion, although industrialization may not directly contribute to a realignment of the racial order, it can do so indirectly, because the growth of urbanization is associated with the growth of industrialization and because as expanding industry lures subordinate racial members into urban areas they find themselves in a better position to accumulate power resources—educational opportunities are greater, the chances of developing viable political, economic, and social organizations are greater, and political awareness and social cohesion may more easily develop. Industrialization, in short, can indirectly produce the political and social pressures ultimately necessary to bring about changes in the racial order both in industries and in the larger society.

In the United States, the urbanization of black citizens increased the significance of the black vote, facilitated the growth of a politically aware black middle class, provided the basis for the emergence of a black political machine, and increased the potential power of organized black protest. In South Africa, on the other hand, despite the possibilities urbanization affords for greater political protest (i.e., resources are much more easily mobilized, and the physical proximity of large numbers of Africans increases communication, group identity, the development of ideology, and collective action), it has had far less impact on racial stratification. Urbanization has created new resources (e.g., higher income, more jobs, and greater mobility) for South African blacks, but these resources have been offset by new restrictions introduced by the controlling white group, in particular the levels of segregation directed by apartheid legislation. In short, urbanization in South Africa has provided the *potential* for blacks to partake in a major assault against the racial order (this will become increasingly so if a larger black middle class develops as the result of increasing entry into skilled positions), but dominant-group controls severely reduce the probability of an *actual* assault against racial injustice.

The degree and extent of dominant-group controls have affected the character of black protest in the United States and South Africa. In my theoretical discussion of the factors associated with racial protests, I was careful to note that subordinate-group rebellions against inequality are least likely to occur in a rigidly stratified society, where the dominant group has the greatest control over the lives of racial subordinates. Given that proposition alone, it could be argued that racial protests are likely to be less frequent in South Africa. But the factors associated with emergence of such protest are of course much more complex than a mere consideration of the power gap between the dominant and subordinate racial groups.

It is true, as seen in both South Africa and the United States, that as subordinate-group status improves, expectations increase and dissatisfaction with continued racial inequality intensifies. The rise of the black middle class in America is directly associated with the sustained, disciplined protests during the middle 1950s and early 1960s. In fact, with a few notable exceptions such as the Marcus Garvey movement of the 1920s and the ghetto revolts of the 1960s, it has been the black middle class and black intelligentsia who have most frequently been associated with black protest throughout the period of competitive race relations in America. Likewise, it has been the middle-class segments and the black intelligentsia in South Africa who have been in the forefront of protest there.

One must be careful, however, in postulating a direct association between rising subordinate-group status and the outbreak of racial protests. In Chapter Four, I stressed the point that the power gap between the dominant and subordinate groups may be so great or perceived to be so great that the latter's desires for change are supplanted by strong feelings that any efforts to produce change will be abortive, and despite increased motivation among subordinate members to overcome oppressive conditions, interracial behavior may continue to achieve a state of normative integration. In the final analysis, a group's beliefs regarding its ability or inability to effect change are based on perceptions of both its own resources and the magnitude of the problem to be solved. Implicit throughout the previous theoretical discussion of racial conflict is the view that a subordinate group's assessment of its resources to effect change is not unrelated to the power differential between the racial groups. My analysis furthermore suggests that the more restrictive the competitive system of race relations is, the less frequent are subordinate-group protests. It is true that black protests did occur during the late nineteenth and early twentieth centuries in the United States—the heyday of restrictive competitive relations—but they were relatively infrequent and tended to be conservative by contemporary standards. Indeed, it was not until the United States moved into the relatively fluid competitive pattern of race relations in the second half of the twentieth century that blacks felt they had sufficient power resources to challenge the racial order in a militant fashion.

In South Africa, however, the association of the actual power discrepancy between the racial groups and African beliefs about their ability to challenge the racial order is less clear-cut. Examination of the conditions surrounding black protest in South Africa clearly reinforces the view that it is not enough for racial analysts to focus only on the degree of racial domination or on the actual racial power differential in order to predict and explain the emergence of subordinate group protests. It is true that prior to World War II black protest groups such as the African National Congress had little optimism about their ability to confront the system of racial domination. Aside from the vigorous efforts of the Industrial and Commercial Workers Union during the 1920s, African protest most frequently assumed the form of petitioning the government, holding political conventions, and issuing statements denouncing racial oppression. But the series of protests that occurred during the 1950s and early 1960s was not related to any relaxation of pressure or to any reduction in the power discrepancy between the racial groups; on the contrary, with the ascendency of Afrikaner nationalism in 1948, competitive race relations actually became more restrictive. What is crucial in this regard is the African leaders' belief that they actually had the resources to aggressively attack apartheid. It was not until the early 1960s that African leaders realized that they had seriously miscalculated both their own resources and the suppressive powers of the government. Racial protests in South Africa since 1964 have been a mere shadow of what they were between 1955 and 1964.

It is true, of course, that the mobilizations of black resources in these two countries differ because they occur in quite different contexts. In the United States the Bill of Rights and the ideal values of the American creed fostered and, in some instances, protected black programs for equality. In my theoretical discussion of subordinate-group demands and the government's response, I noted that demands are more likely to be satisfied if they are consistent with the values the government is pledged to uphold. Indeed, the success of the civil rights movement in the United States during the early 1960s was, in part, due to the presentation of specific demands consistent with prevailing values of freedom and democracy. However, it was also the case that the United States government, parading as the leader of the "free world" and therefore attempting to perpetuate an image of the preserver of freedom for all groups, was especially vulnerable to black protest during the last two decades. It was not until black demands more explicitly and forcefully called for a redistribution of resources in the late 1960s that the government's posture (and that of the American public) became more rigid.

In South Africa, on the other hand, far from defending black civil rights, the government has taken the lead in increasingly restricting black freedom. Informal norms as well as formal norms (e.g., the South African Constitution and apartheid legislation) consistently uphold the principles of a "Herrenvolk democracy," i.e., a democracy only for the dominant racial caste.[3] Accordingly, neither freedom of speech and behavior nor equality as an ideal value are institutionalized for South African blacks. Therefore, the government is much more likely to respond to black protests or demands with repressive action.

The escalation of subordinate-group protest in a particular society often leading to open rebellion or revolution was explained in my theoretical discussion by two propositions: that it is associated with (1) an extended period of increasing expectations and gratifications followed by a brief period in which the gulf between expectations and gratification suddenly expands and becomes intolerable and (2) beliefs that desired changes can only be successfully accomplished by intensifying and accelerating the protests.

Conclusion: U.S. and South African Race Relations

In the United States, the dramatic shift from nonviolent resistance to various manifestations of violent protests during the latter half of the 1960s can be directly traced to the sudden gap between expectations and emotional gratification caused by mounting white violence—an intolerable gap preceded by several years of rising expectations and rising gratifications associated with improving black competitive and pressure resources. Equally as important, however, was a very persistent view among black activists that the larger society had a high tolerance for belligerent protest during this period, hence the belief that in the face of white violence blacks could achieve real success *only* by intensifying and accelerating the protest even to violent levels. This belief, as I have attempted to show, underwent some change with the coming of the Nixon administration and the "law and order" atmosphere of repression in the late 1960s and early 1970s.

The rising expectations and emotional gratification among blacks that extended from World War II to the late 1950s in South Africa was caused not so much by internal as by external developments such as the wartime promises of the Allied leaders, the rise of the new African states, the Pan-African Movement, the denunciations of the South African regimes by the United Nations, and the proposed economic boycott of South African products by worldwide opponents of apartheid. There existed, in other words, a prevailing view among African leaders that in the face of external pressures the South African government could not continue its program of apartheid. Black expectations were intensely frustrated, however, when the Nationalist government ignored external pressures and began its campaign of severe repression in the 1950s, and the widening gap between expectations and emotional gratification increased support for the stepped-up campaign of passive disobedience, which was vigorously quashed, and the following period of terrorist activity, which was also put down.

Associated with various forms of protest activity are patterns of social thought. I emphasized in my theoretical discussion that in a society where the subordinate racial group and the dominant racial group share the same social order, i.e., where an interdependent relationship exists between the racial groups, nationalistic sentiment among subordinate members will tend to be high during times when struggles against racial inequality appear hopeless or when subordinate members have experienced intense disillusionment and frustration after a period of heightened expectations. The periods of despair, frustration, and disillusionment that have followed intervals of high expectation have all produced a greater sentiment for institutional and cultural nationalism. I specifically have in mind the disheartening decade of the 1850s in the United States, when nationalistic sentiment among free blacks in the North reached its peak before the Civil War; the violent period of Jim Crow segregation and biological racism in the late nineteenth and early twentieth centuries, when the movements of Booker T. Washington, Bishop Turner, Marcus Garvey, and the Harlem Renaissance emerged; and the "law and order" late 1960s and early 1970s, when the Black Power Movement crystallized, cultural nationalism flourished, and racial solidarity as a theme reached unprecedented heights. By the same token, sentiments for integration and interracialism tend to emerge when the struggle against racial inequality appears hopeful. Such periods have included the three decades following the emancipation of slaves in the North in the early nineteenth century, the Reconstruction era, the New Deal era, and the era of successful nonviolent resistance movements during the late 1950s and early 1960s.

In South Africa, the strongest support for nationalistic or separatist movements has also occurred during times of black frustration and despair. Heightened black separatism corresponds with the era of formal apartheid, especially after the black protest movement received its deathblow in the early 1960s. With little hope of seriously challenging the system of apartheid, African leaders, who prior to the 1950s widely supported a philosophy of interracialism, have increasingly emphasized territorial separation as the only way to preserve African integrity.

Finally, racism has had a pervading influence on black and white behavior in both the United States and South Africa. As indicated previously, racism, depending on the situation, can either heighten or diminish conflict. Racism, especially biological racism, has most certainly had some negative psychic effects on blacks in both the United States and South Africa, but its degree of influence can only be inferred from historical data, especially in cases where blacks attempt to imitate white standards of beauty and patterns of culture while rejecting black skin color and cultural traditions.

In the United States, the movement for black liberation, particularly since the emergence of the Black Power Movement, is marked by an avowed attempt, not only to reject racism and racist beliefs, but also to overcome the effects of a racist society via cultural revitalization (i.e., strong emphasis on black standards of beauty and black cultural heritage). So pervasive is the cultural revitalization or cultural nationalist movement that all segments of the black population of the United States have been awakened by it. There is, in short, very keen awareness of the effects of racism. In South Africa, the movement to reject racism that gained some momentum during the 1950s has been temporarily arrested by drastic government action. However, at no point in South African history has a movement of cultural revitalization transcended class lines, as has the current cultural nationalist movement in the United States, a movement based on a sense of real power, helping to sustain and increase race pride and cultural identity among all segments of the black population and creating an intense impatience with various forms of racism. And, to repeat a point emphasized earlier, racial conflict is most likely to emerge when subordinate-group members experience some improvements in their condition or sense the possibility of further improvements. It is then that the continued existence of racism in society becomes more of a catalyst for subordinate-group rebellion and less of a mechanism for dominant-group social control.

Notes

1. Pierre van den Berghe, *Race and Racism: A Comparative Perspective* (New York: Wiley, 1967), p. 26.

2. Herbert Blumer, "Industrialisation and Race Relations," in *Industrialisation and Race Relations*, ed. by Guy Hunter (London: Oxford U.P., 1965), p. 247.

3. van den Berghe, op. cit., p. 109.

Bibliography

Adam, Heribert. *Modernizing Racial Domination: South Africa's Political Dynamics.* Berkeley: University of California Press, 1971.

————. "The South African Power Elite: A Survey of Ideological Commitment," *South Africa: Sociological Perspectives,* ed. by Heribert Adam. London: Oxford University Press, 1971.

Allport, Gordon W. *The Nature of Prejudice.* New York: Addison-Wesley Publishing Co., Inc., 1954.

Aptheker, Herbert. *American Negro Slave Revolts.* New York: Columbia University Press, 1943.

————. "Slave Resistance in the United States," *Key Issues in the Afro-American Experience,* ed. by Nathan I. Huggins, Martin Kilson, and Daniel M. Fox. New York: Harcourt Brace Jovanovich, Inc., 1971.

Barth, Ernest A. T., and Donald L. Noel. "Conceptual Frameworks for the Analysis of Race Relations: An Evaluation," *Social Forces,* 50 (March 1972), 333–348.

Bauer, Alice and Raymond. "Day to Day Resistance to Slavery," *Journal of Negro History,* 27, No. 4 (October 1942), 388–419.

Bergman, Peter M. *The Chronological History of the Negro in America.* New York: Harper & Row, Publishers, 1969.

Bettelheim, Bruno, and Morris Janowitz. *Social Change and Prejudice.* New York: The Free Press, 1964.

Birch, David L. *The Economic Future of City and Suburbs.* New York: Committee for Economic Development, 1970.

Blackwell, James, and Marie R. Haug. "Black Bosses, Black Workers: Or Are Black Bosses Beautiful?" Paper read at the Annual Meeting of the American Sociological Association, Denver, Colorado (September 1971).

Blalock, H. M., Jr. *Toward a Theory of Minority-Group Relations.* New York: John Wiley & Sons, Inc., 1967.

Blauner, Robert. "Black Culture: Myth or Reality?" *Americans from Africa: Old Memories, New Moods,* ed. by Peter I. Rose. New York: Atherton Press, Inc., 1970.

————. "Internal Colonialism and Ghetto Revolt," *Social Problems,* 16 (Spring 1968), 395–408.

Bloch, Herman D. *The Circle of Discrimination: An Economic and Social Study of the Black Man in New York.* New York: New York University Press, 1969.

Blumer, Herbert. "Industrialisation and Race Relations," *Industrialisation and Race Relations: A Symposium,* ed. by Guy Hunter. London: Oxford University Press, 1965.

———. "Race Prejudice as a Sense of Group Position," *Pacific Sociological Review,* 1 (Spring 1958), 3–7.

Bone, Robert A. "The Negro Novel in America," *America's Black Past,* ed. by Eric Foner. New York: Harper & Row, Publishers, 1970.

Boskin, Joseph. "Race Relations in Seventeenth Century America: The Problem of the Origins of Negro Slavery," *Sociology and Social Research,* 49 (July 1965), 446–455.

Bracey, John H., August Meier, and Elliot Rudwick, eds. *Black Nationalism in America.* Indianapolis: Bobbs-Merrill Co., Inc., 1970.

Braithwaite, Lloyd. "Social Stratification and Cultural Pluralism," *Social and Cultural Pluralism in the Caribbean,* ed. by Vera Rubin. *Annals of the New York Academy of Science,* 83 (1960), art. 5. 816–831.

Brett, E. A. *African Attitudes: A Study of Social, Racial, and Political Attitudes of Some Middle Class Africans.* Johannesburg: South African Institute of Race Relations, 1963.

Brimmer, Andrew. "The Black Revolution and the Economic Future of Negroes in the United States," *The American Scholar* (Autumn 1969), 629–643.

———. "Economic Progress of Negroes in the United States: The Deepening Schism." Paper read at the Founder's Day Convocation, Tuskegee, Alabama (March 22, 1970).

Brink, William, and Louis Harris. *Black and White: A Study of U.S. Racial Attitudes Today.* New York: Simon & Schuster, Inc., 1966.

Broom, Leonard, and Norval D. Glenn. "The Occupations and Income of Black Americans," *Blacks in the United States,* ed. by Norval D. Glenn and Charles M. Bonjean. San Francisco: Chandler Publishing Co., 1969.

Brotz, Howard, ed. *Negro Social and Political Thought, 1850–1920.* New York: Basic Books, 1966.

Bryce-Le Porte, R. S. "The American Slave Plantation and Our Heritage of Communal Deprivation," *American Behavior Scientist* (March–April 1969), 2–8.

Bibliography

Bullock, Henry Allen. "Urbanism and Race Relations," *The Urban South*, ed. by Rupert B. Vance and Nicholas J. Demerath. Chapel Hill: University of North Carolina Press, 1954.

Burgess, M. Elaine. "Race Relations and Social Change," *The South in Continuity and Change*, ed. by John E. McKinney and Edgar T. Thompson. Durham, N. C.: Duke University Press, 1965.

Campbell, Angus, and Howard Schuman. "Racial Attitudes in Fifteen American Cities," *The National Advisory Commission on Civil Disorders, Supplemental Studies*. Washington, D.C.: Government Printing Office, 1968.

Cantor, Milton. "The Image of the Negro in Colonial Literature," *New England Quarterly* 36 (1963), 452-477.

Cantrell, H. *The Pattern of Human Concerns*. New Brunswick, N.J.: Rutgers University Press, 1965.

Caplan, Nathan S., and Jeffrey Paige. "A Study of Ghetto Rioters," *Scientific American*, 219 (August 1968), 15-21.

Carter, Gwendolen M. "African Concepts of Nationalism in South Africa," *South Africa; Sociological Perspectives*, ed. by Heribert Adam. London: Oxford University Press, 1971.

———. *The Politics of Inequality*. New York: Praeger Publishers, Inc., 1958.

Caulfield, Mina Davis. "Slavery and the Origins of Black Culture: Elkins Revisited," *Slavery and Its Aftermath*, ed. by Peter I. Rose. New York: Atherton Press, Inc., 1970.

Chicago Commission on Race Relations. *The Negro in Chicago, A Study of Race Relations and a Race Riot*. Chicago: University of Chicago Press, 1922.

Clark, Kenneth B. *Dark Ghetto: Dilemmas of Power*. New York: Harper & Row, Publishers, 1965.

Coleman, James S. *Equality of Educational Opportunity*. Washington, D.C.: Government Printing Office, 1966.

Cox, Oliver Cromwell. *Caste, Class, and Race: A Study in Social Dynamics*. Garden City, N.Y.: Doubleday & Co., Inc., 1948.

Craven, W. F. *Southern Colonies in the Seventeenth Century, 1607-1689*. Baton Rouge: Louisiana State University Press, 1949.

Crijns, Arthur G. J. *Race Relations and Race Attitudes in South Africa*. Nijmegen: Orukkerij Gebr. Janssen, 1959.

Cruse, Harold. *The Crisis of the Negro Intellectual*. New York: William Morrow & Co., Inc., 1967.

Cruse, Harold. *Rebellion or Revolution*. New York: Apollo Editions, 1968.

———. "Revolutionary Nationalism and the Afro-American," *Studies on the Left*, 2 (1962), 12–25.

Curtin, Philip D. "The Slave Trade and the Atlantic Basin," *Key Issues in the Afro-American Experience*, ed. by Nathan I. Huggins, Martin Kilson, and Daniel M. Fox. New York: Harcourt Brace Jovanovich, Inc., 1971.

Daniels, Roger, and Harry H. L. Kitano. *American Racism: Exploration of the Nature of Prejudice*. Englewood Cliffs, N.J.: Prentice-Hall, Inc., 1970.

Davies, James C. "The J-Curve of Rising and Declining Satisfactions as a Cause of Some Great Revolutions and a Contained Rebellion," *Violence in America: Historical and Comparative Perspectives*, ed. by Hugh Davis Graham and Ted Robert Gurr. New York: Bantam Books, 1969.

———. "Toward a Theory of Revolution," *American Sociological Review*, 27 (February 1962), 5–19.

Davis, David Brion. *The Problem of Slavery in Western Culture*. Ithaca, N.Y.: Cornell University Press, 1966.

Degler, Carl N. *Neither Black Nor White*. New York: Macmillan Co., 1971.

———. *Out of Our Past*. New York: Harper & Row, Publishers, 1959.

———. "Slavery and the Genesis of American Race Prejudice," *Comparative Studies of Society and History*, 21 (October 1959), 49–66.

Deutsch, Martin. "Happenings on the Way Back to the Forum: Social Science, IQ, and Race Differences Revisited," *Harvard Educational Review*, 39 (Summer 1969), 523–557.

Dizard, Jan E. "Response to Aggression and the American Experience." Paper read at the Annual Meeting of the American Sociological Association, Denver, Colorado (September 1971).

Downes, Bryan T., and Stephen W. Burks. "The Historical Development of the Black Protest Movement," *Blacks in the United States*, ed. by Norval D. Glenn and Charles M. Bonjean. San Francisco: Chandler Publishing Co., 1969.

Doxey, George V. *The Industrial Colour Bar in South Africa*. London: Pall Mall Press, 1961.

Elkins, Stanley M. *Slavery: A Problem in American Institutional and Intellectual Life*. Chicago: University of Chicago Press, 1959.

Bibliography

Ernst, Robert. *Immigrant Life in New York City, 1825–1863.* Port Washington, N.Y.: Kings Crown Press, 1949.

Essien-Udom, E. U. *Black Nationalism: A Search for an Identity in America.* New York: Dell Publishing Co., 1962.

Fanon, Frantz. *The Wretched of the Earth.* New York: Grove Press, Inc., 1963.

Farley, Reynolds. "The Changing Distribution of Negroes Within Metropolitan Areas: The Emergence of Black Suburbs," *American Journal of Sociology,* 75 (January 1970), 512–529.

———. *Growth of the Black Population: A Study of Demographic Trends.* Chicago: Markham Publishing Co., 1970.

Feit, Edward. *African Opposition in South Africa: The Failure of Passive Resistance.* Stanford, Calif.: Hoover Institute, 1967.

———. "Conflict and Cohesion in South Africa: A Theoretical Analysis of the Policy of 'Separate Development' and Its Implication," *Economic Development and Cultural Change,* 16 (July 1966), 484–496.

———. *Urban Revolt in South Africa 1960–1964: A Case Study.* Evanston, Ill.: Northwestern University Press, 1971.

Finley, M. I. "On David Brion Davis, *The Problem of Slavery in Western Culture,*" *American Negro Slavery,* ed. by Allen Weinstein and Frank Otto Gatell. New York: Oxford University Press, 1968.

Fishel, Leslie H., Jr., and Benjamin Quarles. *The Negro American: A Documentary History.* Glenview, Ill.: Scott, Foresman and Co., 1967.

Flax, Michael J. *Blacks and Whites: An Experiment in Racial Indicators.* Washington, D.C.: Urban Institute, 1971.

Foner, Eric. *America's Black Past.* New York: Harper & Row, Publishers, 1970.

Franklin, John Hope. *From Slavery to Freedom,* 3rd ed. New York: Alfred A. Knopf, Inc., 1967.

Frazier, E. Franklin. *Black Bourgeoisie.* New York: The Free Press, 1957.

———. *The Negro in the United States,* rev. ed. New York: Macmillan Co., 1957.

———. *Race and Culture Contacts in the Modern World.* New York: Alfred A. Knopf, Inc., 1957.

———. "Theoretical Structure of Sociology and Sociological Research," *British Journal of Sociology,* 4 (December 1953), 292–311.

Fredrickson, George M. "Toward a Social Interpretation of the

Development of American Racism," *Key Issues in the Afro-American Experience*, ed. by Nathan I. Huggins, Martin Kilson, and Daniel M. Fox. New York: Harcourt Brace Jovanovich, Inc., 1971.

Gamson, William. *Power and Discontent*. Homewood, Ill.: Dorsey Press, 1968.

Genovese, Eugene D. *The Political Economy of Slavery*. New York: Pantheon Books, Inc., 1965.

————. "The Roots of Black Nationalism," *Americans from Africa: Old Memories, New Moods*, ed. by Peter I. Rose. New York: Atherton Press, Inc., 1970.

————. *The World the Slaveholders Made*. New York: Random House, Inc., 1969.

Geschwender, James A. "Social Structure and the Negro Revolt: An Examination of Some Hypotheses," *Social Forces*, 43 (December 1964), 248–256.

Glenn, Norval D. "White Gains from Negro Subordination," *Blacks in the United States*, ed. by Norval D. Glenn and Charles M. Bonjean. San Francisco: Chandler Publishing Co., 1969.

Glick, Clarence E. "Collective Behavior in Race Relations," *American Sociological Review*, 13 (June 1947), 287–293.

Goldsby, Richard A. *Race and Races*. New York: Macmillan Co., 1971.

Gordon, Milton M. *Assimilation in American Life*. New York: Oxford University Press, 1964.

Gossett, Thomas F. *Race: The History of an Idea in America*. Dallas: Southern Methodist University Press, 1963.

Greeley, Andrew M., and Paul B. Sheatsley. "Attitudes Toward Racial Integration," *Scientific American*, 225 (December 1971), 13–19.

Grimshaw, Allen D. "Lawlessness and Violence in America and Their Special Manifestations in Changing Negro–White Relationships," *Journal of Negro History*, 64 (January 1959), 52–72.

Gutman, Herbert G. "Blacks and the Labor Movement: A Case Study," *America's Black Past*, ed. by Eric Foner. New York: Harper & Row, Publishers, 1970.

Handlin, Oscar and Mary F. "Origins of the Southern Labor System," *William and Mary Quarterly*, 3rd ser., 7 (April 1950), 199–222.

Bibliography

Harris, Marvin. *Patterns of Race in the Americas.* New York: Walker, 1964.

Hawley, Amos. "Dispersion Versus Segregation: Apropos of a Solution of Race Problems," *Papers of the Michigan Academy of Science, Arts, and Letters,* 30 (1944), 667–674.

Hempel, Carl G. *Aspects of Scientific Explanation.* New York: Free Press, 1965.

Hepple, Alex. *South Africa: A Political and Economic History.* London: Pall Mall Press, 1966.

Highan, John. *Strangers in the Land.* New Brunswick, N.J.: Rutgers University Press, 1955.

Horrell, Muriel. *South Africa's Workers: Their Organizations and the Patterns of Employment.* Johannesburg: South African Institute of Race Relations, 1969.

Janowitz, Morris. "Patterns of Collective Racial Violence," *Violence in America: Historical and Comparative Perspectives,* ed. by Hugh Davis Graham and Ted Robert Gurr. New York: Bantam Books, 1969.

Jensen, Arthur R. "How Much Can We Boost IQ and Scholastic Achievement?" *Harvard Educational Review,* 39 (Winter 1969), 1–123.

Jones, James M. *Prejudice and Racism.* Reading, Mass.: Addison-Wesley Publishing Co., Inc., 1972.

Jordan, Winthrop D. *White over Black: American Attitudes Toward the Negro 1550–1812.* Chapel Hill: University of North Carolina Press, 1968.

Kaplan, Irving, et al. *Area Handbook for the Republic of South Africa.* Washington, D.C.: Government Printing Office, 1971.

Karis, Thomas. "South Africa," *Five African States,* ed. by Gwendolyn M. Carter. Ithaca, N.Y.: Cornell University Press, 1963.

Keesing's Research Report. *Race Relations in the USA, 1954–68.* New York: Charles Scribner's Sons, 1970.

Killian, Lewis M. "The Adjustment of Southern White Migrants to Urban Norms," *Social Forces,* 32 (October 1953), 66–69.

———. "The Effects of Southern White Workers on Race Relations in Northern Plants," *American Sociological Review,* 17 (June 1952), 327–331.

———. *The Impossible Revolution?: Black Power and the American Dream.* New York: Random House, Inc., 1968.

———, James Fendrich, and Michael Pearson. "Alienation and

the Crisis in Black Leadership." Unpublished manuscript (1970).

Kilson, Martin. "Black Politicians: A New Power," *Dissent* (August 1971), 333–345.

Kuper, Leo. *An African Bourgeoisie: Race, Class, and Politics in South Africa.* New Haven: Yale University Press, 1956.

———. *Passive Resistance in South Africa.* New Haven: Yale University Press, 1960.

———. "The Political Situation of Non-Whites in South Africa," *Southern Africa and the United States,* ed. by William A. Hance. New York: Columbia University Press, 1968.

Laue, James H. "The Changing Character of Negro Protest," *Annals of the American Academy of Political and Social Science,* 357 (January 1965), 119–126.

Lenski, Gerhard. *Power and Privilege: A Theory of Social Stratification.* New York: McGraw-Hill Book Co., 1966.

Lewis, Hylan. "Innovations and Trends in the Contemporary Southern Negro Community," *Journal of Social Issues,* 10 (1954), 19–27.

Lieberson, Stanley. "A Societal Theory of Race and Ethnic Relations," *American Sociological Review,* 26 (December 1961), 902–910.

Litwack, Leon F. *North of Slavery: The Negro in the Free State, 1790–1860.* Chicago: University of Chicago Press, 1961.

Logan, Rayford W. *The Betrayal of the Negro.* New York: Macmillan Co., 1954.

Lomax, Louis. *The Negro Revolt.* New York: Signet Books, 1962.

MacCrone, I. D. *Race Relations in South Africa: Historical, Experimental, and Psychological Studies.* London: Oxford University Press, 1937.

McLuhan, Marshall. *Understanding Media: The Extension of Man.* New York: McGraw-Hill Book Co., 1964.

McWorter, Gerald A. *Social Integration and the Legitimacy of Black Social Protest.* Unpublished doctoral dissertation, University of Chicago, 1971.

Marshall, Ray. "Industrialisation and Race Relations in the Southern United States," *Industrialisation and Race Relations: A Symposium.* ed. by Guy Hunter. London: Oxford University Press, 1965.

———. *The Negro and Organized Labor.* New York: John Wiley & Sons, Inc., 1965.

Bibliography

Marshall, Ray. *The Negro Worker*. New York: Random House, Inc., 1967.

Marx, Gary T. *Protest and Prejudice: A Study of Belief in the Black Community*, rev. ed. New York: Harper & Row, Publishers, 1970.

———. "Two Cheers for the National Riot Commission," *Black America*, ed. by John F. Szwed. New York: Basic Books, 1970.

Mason, Philip. *Patterns of Domination*. London: Oxford University Press, 1970.

———. *Race Relations*. London: Oxford University Press, 1970.

Massotti, L. H., and D. R. Bowen, eds. *Riots and Rebellion: Racial Violence in the Urban Community*. Beverly Hills, Calif.: Sage Publications, 1968.

Mathews, A. S. "Security Laws and Social Change in the Republic of South Africa," *South Africa: Sociological Perspectives*, ed. by Heribert Adam. London: Oxford University Press, 1971.

Meier, August, *Negro Thought in America, 1880–1915: Racial Ideologies in the Age of Booker T. Washington*. Ann Arbor: University of Michigan Press, 1964.

Meier, August, and Elliot Rudwick. "The Boycott Against Jim Crow Streetcars in the South, 1900–1906," *Journal of American History*, 55 (March 1969), 756–759.

———. "Negro Boycotts of Jim Crow Schools in the North, 1897–1925," *Integrated Education*, 5, No. 4 (August–September 1967), 1–12.

———. *From Plantation to Ghetto: The Interpretative History of American Negroes*, rev. ed. New York: Hill and Wang, 1970.

———. "A Strange Chapter in the Career of 'Jim Crow,'" *The Making of Black America: Essays in Negro Life and History*, ed. by August Meier and Elliot Rudwick. New York: Atheneum Publishers, 1969.

Memmi, Albert. *The Colonizer and the Colonized*. Boston: Beacon Press, 1967.

Moon, Henry L. *Balance of Power: The Negro Vote*. Garden City, N.Y.: Doubleday & Co., Inc., 1948.

Moore, Wilbert E. *American Negro Slavery and Abolition: A Sociological Study*. New York: Third Press, 1971.

Morris, Marjorie M. "An Early Instance of Non-Violence: The Louisville Demonstrations of 1870–1871," *Journal of Southern History*, 25 (November 1966), 487–504.

Morris, Richard T., and Vincent Jeffries. *The White Reaction Study*. University of California, Los Angeles: Institute of Government and Public Affairs, 1967.

Mullin, Gerald W. "Gabriel's Insurrection," *Americans from Africa: Old Memories, New Moods*, ed. by Peter I. Rose. New York: Atherton Press, Inc., 1970.

Nash, Gary B. "Red, White, and Black: The Origins of Racism in Colonial America," *The Great Fear: Race in the Mind of America*, ed. by Gary B. Nash and Richard Weiss. New York: Holt, Rinehart & Winston, Inc., 1970.

Neame, L. E. *The History of Apartheid: The Story of the Colour Bar in South Africa*. London: Pall Mall Press, 1962.

Negro Convention Proceedings, reprint ed. New York: Arno Press, 1970.

Ngubane, Jordan K. *An African Explains Apartheid*. New York: Praeger Publishers, Inc., 1963.

Noel, Donald L. "Slavery and the Rise of Racism," *The Origins of American Slavery and Racism*, ed. by Donald L. Noel. Columbus, O.: Charles E. Merrill Publishers, 1972.

———. "A Theory of the Origin of Ethnic Stratification," *Social Problems*, 16 (Fall 1968), 157–172.

Opinion Research Corporation. *White and Negro Attitudes Towards Race Related Issues and Activities*. Research Park, Princeton, N.J., 1968.

Patterson, H. Orlando. *The Sociology of Slavery*. London: McGibbon & Kee, Ltd., 1967.

Patterson, Sheila. *The Last Trek: A Study of the Boer People and the Afrikaner Nation*. London: Routledge & Keegan Paul, Ltd., 1957.

Pease, William H. and Jane H. "The Negro Convention Movement," *Key Issues in the Afro-American Experience*, ed. by Nathan I. Huggins, Martin Kilson, and Daniel M. Fox. New York: Harcourt Brace Jovanovich, Inc., 1971.

Peterson, John. "Huey Newton," *The National Observer*, 7 (February 12, 1972), 1.

Pettigrew, Thomas F. *Racially Separate or Together?* New York: McGraw-Hill Book Co., 1971.

Quarles, Benjamin. *The Negro in the Making of America*. New York: Macmillan Co., 1964.

Raab, Earl, and Seymour Martin Lipset. "The Prejudiced So-

Bibliography

ciety," *American Race Relations Today: Studies of the Problems Beyond Desegregation*, ed. by Earl Raab. New York: Anchor Books, 1962.

Redkey, Edwin S. *Black Exodus: Black Nationalism and Back-to-Africa Movements, 1890–1910.* New Haven, Conn.: Yale University Press, 1969.

———. "The Flowering of Black Nationalism: Henry McNeal Turner and Marcus Garvey," *Key Issues in the Afro-American Experience*, ed. by Nathan I. Huggins, Martin Kilson, and Daniel M. Fox. New York: Harcourt Brace Jovanovich, Inc., 1971, Vol. II.

Report of the National Advisory Commission on Civil Disorders. New York: Bantam Press, 1968.

Robertson, Hector Menticth. *South African Economic and Political Aspects.* Durham, N.C.: Duke University Press, 1957.

Rogers, Mary. *The Concept of Power in Community Research.* Unpublished doctoral dissertation, University of Massachusetts, Amherst, Mass., 1971.

Rose, Arnold M. "Race and Ethnic Relations," *Contemporary Social Problems*, ed. by Robert K. Merton and Robert A. Nisbet. New York: Harcourt Brace Jovanovich, Inc., 1966.

Rose, Peter I. "Outsiders in Britain," *Trans-Action*, 4 (March 1967), 18–23.

———. *The Subject Is Race.* New York: Oxford University Press, 1968.

Rudner, Richard S. *Philosophy of Science.* Englewood Cliffs, N.J.: Prentice-Hall, Inc., 1966.

Rudwick, Elliot. *Race Riot at East St. Louis, July 2, 1917.* New York: World Publishing Co., 1966.

Schermerhorn, Richard. *Comparative Ethnic Relations: A Framework for Theory and Research.* New York: Random House, Inc., 1970.

———. "Toward a General Theory of Minority Groups," *Phylon*, 25 (1964), 238–246.

Shibutani, Tamotsu, and Kian M. Kwan. *Ethnic Stratification: A Comparative Approach.* New York: Macmillan Co., 1965.

Silberman, Charles. *Crisis in Black and White.* New York: Random House, Inc., 1964.

———. *Crisis in the Classroom.* New York: Random House, Inc., 1970.

Smith, M. G. *The Plural Society in the British West Indies.* Berkeley: University of California Press, 1965.

Spear, Allan. *Black Chicago: The Making of a Negro Ghetto.* Chicago: University of Chicago Press, 1967.

——. "The Origins of the Urban Ghetto, 1870–1915," *Key Issues in the Afro-American Experience,* ed. by Nathan I. Huggins, Martin Kilson, and Daniel M. Fox. New York: Harcourt Brace Jovanovich, Inc., 1971.

Scarr-Salapatek, Sandra. "Race, Social Class and IQ," *Science,* 174 (December 24, 1971), 1285–1295.

Spero, Sterling D., and Abram L. Harris. *The Black Worker.* New York: Columbia University Press, 1931.

Stampp, Kenneth. *The Peculiar Institution: Slavery in the Ante-Bellum South.* New York: Alfred A. Knopf, Inc., 1956.

Stincombe, Arthur L. "Environment: The Cumulation of Effects Is Yet to Be Understood," *Harvard Educational Review,* 39 (Summer 1969), 511–522.

Stuckey, Sterling. "Through the Prism of Folklore: The Black Ethos in Slavery," *The Massachusetts Review,* 9 (1968), 417–437.

Tabb, William K. "Race Relations Models and Social Change," *Social Problems,* 18 (Spring 1971), 431–444.

Taeuber, Karl E. and Alma F. "The Negro Population in the United States," *The American Negro Reference Book,* ed. by John P. Davis. Englewood Cliffs, N.J.: Prentice-Hall, Inc., 1966.

——. *Negroes in the Cities.* Chicago: Aldine Publishing Co., 1965.

Thompson, Edgar T. "The Plantation: The Physical Basis of Traditional Race Relations," *Race Relations and the Race Problem,* ed. by Edgar T. Thompson. Durham, N.C.: Duke University Press, 1939.

Thorpe, Earle E. "Chattel Slavery and Concentration Camps," *Slavery and Its Aftermath,* ed. by Peter I. Rose. New York: Atherton Press, Inc., 1970.

Tiryakian, Edward A. "Apartheid and Politics in South Africa," *Journal of Politics,* 22 (November 1960), 682–687.

——. "Apartheid and Religion," *Theology Today,* 14 (October 1957), 385–400.

Tocqueville, Alexis de. *Democracy in America,* ed. by J. P. Mayer. Garden City, N.Y.: Doubleday & Co., Inc. 1969.

U.S. Bureau of the Census. "Differences Between Incomes of

White and Negro Families by Work Experience and Region," *Current Population Reports*, ser. P-23, No. 39. Washington, D.C.: Government Printing Office, 1971.

————. "Social and Economic Characteristics of the Population in Metropolitan and Nonmetropolitan Areas: 1970 and 1960," *Current Population Reports*, ser. P-23, No. 37. Washington, D.C.: Government Printing Office, 1971.

————. "The Social and Economic Status of Negroes in the United States, 1970," *Current Population Reports*, ser. P-23, No. 38. Washington, D.C.: Government Printing Office, 1971.

————. "24 Million Americans—Poverty in the United States: 1969," *Current Population Reports*, ser. P-60, No. 76. Washington, D.C.: Government Printing Office, 1970.

————. "The Social and Economic Status of Negroes," *Current Population Reports*, ser. P-23, No. 38. Washington, D.C.: Government Printing Office, 1970.

————. "The Social and Economic Status of Negroes in the United States, 1970," *Current Population Reports*, ser. P-23, No. 39. Washington, D.C.: Government Printing Office, 1971.

van den Berghe, Pierre. *Race and Racism: A Comparative Perspective*. New York: John Wiley & Sons, Inc., 1967.

————. "Racial Segregation in South Africa: Degrees and Kind," *South Africa: Sociological Perspectives*, ed. by Heribert Adam. London: Oxford University Press, 1971.

————. *South Africa: A Study in Conflict*. Berkeley: University of California Press, 1965.

Van der Horst, Shelia T. "The Effects of Industrialisation on Race Relations in South Africa," *Industrialisation and Race Relations: A Symposium*, ed. by Guy Hunter. London: Oxford University Press, 1965.

Vander Zanden, James W. *Race Relations in Transition: The Segregation Crisis in the South*. New York: Random House, Inc., 1965.

Vatcher, William Henry, Jr. *White Laager: The Rise of Afrikaner Nationalism*. London: Pall Mall Press, 1965.

Wade, Richard C. *Slavery in the Cities: The South 1820–1860*. New York: Oxford University Press, 1964.

Wagley, Charles, and Marvin Harris. *Minorities in the New World*. New York: Columbia University Press, 1958.

Waskow, Arthur I. *From Race Riot to Sit-In*. Garden City, N.Y.: Doubleday & Co., Inc., 1966.

Wesley, Charles H. *Negro Labor in the United States, 1850–1925: A Study in American Economic History*. New York: Vanguard Press, Inc., 1951.

Westie, Frank R. "Race and Ethnic Relations," *Handbook of Modern Sociology*, ed. by Robert E. L. Faris. Chicago: Rand McNally & Co., 1963.

Williams, Eric. *Capitalism and Slavery*. Chapel Hill: University of North Carolina Press, 1944.

Williams, Robin M., Jr. "The Reduction of Intergroup Tensions," *Social Science Research Council Bulletin 57* (1947).

———. *Strangers Next Door*. Englewood Cliffs, N.J.: Prentice-Hall, Inc., 1964.

Williamson, Joel R. *After Slavery: The Negro in South Carolina During Reconstruction, 1861–1877*. Chapel Hill: University of North Carolina Press, 1965.

———. "Black Self-Assertion Before and After Emancipation," *Key Issues in the Afro-American Experience*, ed. by Nathan I. Huggins, Martin Kilson, and Daniel M. Fox. New York: Harcourt Brace Jovanovich, Inc., 1971.

Wilson, William J. "The Quest for a Meaningful Black Experience on White Campuses," *The Massachusetts Review*, 10 (Autumn 1969), 737–746.

———. "Race Relations Models and Ghetto Behavior," *Nation of Nations: The Ethnic Experience and the Racial Crisis*, ed. by Peter I. Rose. New York: Random House, Inc., 1972.

Wolpe, Harold. "Class, Race, and the Occupational Structure in South Africa." Paper presented at the Seventh World Congress of Sociology, International Sociological Association, Varna, Bulgaria (September 1970).

Woodward, C. Van. *Origins of the New South, 1877–1913*. Baton Rouge: Louisiana State University Press, 1951.

———. *The Strange Career of Jim Crow*. New York: Oxford University Press, 1966.

X, Malcolm. *The Autobiography of Malcolm X*. New York: Grove Press, Inc., 1964.

INDEX

Abolitionist movement, 97
Adam, Heribert, 171, 177, 179, 180, 182n, 185n, 186n, 187n
African National Congress (ANC), 172–80, 197
African National Congress Youth League (ANCYL), 173–75
African Resistance Movement, 176
African states, 126
Africans, 166, 182n: absence of protest among masses, 178–80; attitudes of, 172, 197, 199; economic conditions of, 169, 181; militancy of, 169, 172, 174–75, 197; resistance to apartheid, 171–80; rising expectations of, 169
Afrikaners, 168, 169: attitudes of, 165; newspapers, 179; policies of, 167, 170, 171, 181, 199. See also Boers
Allport, Gordon W., 45n
AFL (American Federation of Labor). See Labor unions
Anglo–Boer War, 166
Apartheid, 161: definition of, 182n; legislation, 168–71, 174, 176, 192

Aptheker, Herbert, 66n, 84, 91n, 92n
Asians, 166, 182n: militancy of, 174, 175
Atkins, Thomas, 160n

Bantu, 163, 164
Barth, Ernest A. T., 10, 13n
Bauer, Alice, 9, 13n, 91n
Bauer, Raymond, 9, 13n, 91n
Bergman, Peter M., 115n, 153n
Bettelheim, Bruno, 45n
Birch, David, 157n
Black Codes, 99
Black Panther Party, 149
Black Power Movement. See Nationalist movements
Blackwell, James, 14n
Blalock, Hubert, 7, 8, 13n, 28n, 65n
Blauner, Robert, 13n, 139, 156n
Bloch, Herman D., 96, 115n
Blumer, Herbert, 7, 12n, 13n, 27n, 28n, 35, 36, 37, 38, 39, 45n, 46n, 62, 63, 68n, 193, 202n
Boer Republics, 165–66
Boers, 163–65: English and, 164;

Boers [*cont.*]
non-Europeans and, 164. *See also*
Afrikaners
Bond, Julian, 160*n*
Bone, Robert A., 119*n*, 156*n*
Bonjean, Charles M., 90*n*, 118*n*,
152*n*, 157*n*
Boskin, Joseph, 88*n*
Bowen, D. R., 153*n*
Bracey, John H., 154*n*, 155*n*, 160*n*
Braithwaite, Lloyd, 13*n*
Brett, E. A., 187*n*
Brimmer, Andrew, 148, 158*n*, 159*n*
Brink, William, 154*n*, 155*n*
Britain: influence in South Africa,
164, 165
Broom, Leonard, 126, 128, 152*n*
Brotz, Howard, 116*n*
Bryce-Le Porte, R. S., 91*n*
Bullock, Henry Allen, 68*n*
Burgess, M. Elaine, 68*n*, 154*n*
Burks, Stephen W., 90*n*, 118*n*,
119*n*
Bushmen, 163, 189

Calhoun, William P., 104
Campbell, Angus, 155*n*, 156*n*, 158*n*
Cantor, Milton, 78, 89*n*
Cantrell, H., 154*n*
Cape: province of, 163–66, 184*n*
Caplan, Nathan S., 154*n*, 156*n*
Carroll, Charles, 104
Carter, Gwendolen M., 183*n*, 185*n*,
186*n*
Caulfield, Mina Davis, 91*n*
Chicago Commission on Race Re-
lations, 118*n*
Chisholm, Shirley, 160*n*
Clark, Kenneth B., 142, 143, 144,
157*n*, 158*n*
Coleman, James S., 157*n*
Colonization, 19–20, 189
Coloureds, 166, 182*n*: militancy,
174–75
Communist Party: in South
Africa, 173

Competition: intergroup, 23–24;
interindividual, 23–24
Competitive race relations, 52–64,
192: fluid, 56–59, 121, 145, 193,
197; restrictive, 56–58, 99, 104,
114, 192–93, 197; social change
in South Africa and, 180–82, 192
CIO (Congress of Industrial Or-
ganization). *See* Labor unions
CORE (Congress of Racial Equal-
ity), 134, 137, 149
Congress Movement, 175
Cox, Oliver Cromwell, 7, 12*n*, 13*n*
Craven, W. F., 87*n*
Crijns, Arthur G. J., 182*n*, 183*n*
Cruse, Harold, 4, 12*n*, 119*n*, 138,
154*n*, 155*n*
Cultural deprivation, 143
Cultural nationalism. *See* National-
ist movements
Curtin, Philip D., 83, 90*n*

Daniels, Roger, 45*n*
Davies, James C., 47, 49, 65*n*, 132,
148, 152*n*, 153*n*
Davis, David Brion, 79, 89*n*, 90*n*
Davis, John P., 157*n*
Degler, Carl, 87*n*, 88*n*, 90*n*
Delany, Martin R., 97
Demerath, Nicholas J., 68*n*
Deutsch, Martin, 156*n*
Dialectical relationship, 8–9
Discrimination, 34: institutional,
43, 142–44, 191
Dizard, Jan, 141, 157*n*
Dominant group: definition of,
12*n*
Douglas, Frederick, 97, 116*n*
Downes, Bryan T., 90*n*, 118*n*, 119*n*
Doxey, George V., 183*n*, 184*n*

Economic schism: among blacks
in United States, 145–48
Elkins, Stanley M., 66*n*, 85, 91*n*,
92*n*

English, South African: attitudes of, 166, 181; Boers, 164; and non-Europeans and, 164
Ernst, Robert, 115*n*
Essien-Udom, E., 119*n*
Ethnic groups: definition of, 6; variable meanings of, 6–7
Ethnocentrism, 30–33, 77: autonomy of racial groups and, 40–41; cultural, 31–33; defined, 31; physical, 31–32
Exploited racial labor, 24

Fair Employment Practices Committee (FEPC), 125, 194
Fanon, Frantz, 27*n*
Faris, Robert E. L., 156*n*
Farley, Reynolds, 118*n*, 157*n*
Feit, Edward, 117, 179, 184–85*n*, 186*n*, 187*n*
Fendrich, James, 67*n*
Finley, M. I., 89*n*
Fishel, Leslie H., Jr., 151*n*
Flax, Michael J., 150, 160*n*
Foner, Eric, 88*n*, 117*n*, 118*n*, 156*n*
Fox, Daniel M., 89*n*, 115*n*
Franklin, John Hope, 90*n*, 117*n*, 118*n*, 151*n*, 152*n*
Frazier, E. Franklin, 7, 11, 12*n*, 13*n*, 14*n*, 45*n*, 110, 116*n*
Fredrickson, George M., 89*n*, 90*n*, 95, 115*n*

Gamson, William, 26*n*, 58, 67*n*
Garvey, Marcus, 56, 113–14, 196, 200
Gattel, Frank Otto, 89*n*
Genovese, Eugene D., 82–83, 88*n*, 90*n*, 91*n*
Geschwender, James A., 65*n*, 153*n*
Ghetto revolts, 135–36. *See also* Protest movements
Gibson, Kenneth, 160*n*
Glenn, Norval D., 90*n*, 118*n*, 126, 128, 141, 152*n*, 157*n*

Glick, Clarence E., 153*n*
Goldsby, Richard A., 156*n*
Gordon, Milton M., 156*n*
Gossett, Thomas, 78, 89*n*, 116*n*, 117*n*
Graham, Hugh Davis, 65*n*, 118*n*, 152*n*
Great Fish River, 163
Great Trek, 164
Greeley, Andrew M., 156*n*
Grimshaw, Allen D., 119*n*
Group interests, 22–25, 42
Gurr, Ted Robert, 65*n*, 118*n*, 152*n*
Gutman, Herbert B., 118*n*

Hall, T. Arnold, 124
Hance, William A., 186*n*
Handlin, Mary F., 71, 87*n*, 88*n*
Handlin, Oscar, 71, 87*n*, 88*n*
Harlem Renaissance, 113, 139, 200
Harris, Abram L., 118*n*
Harris, Louis, 154*n*, 156*n*
Harris, Marvin, 12*n*, 73, 88*n*
Hatcher, Richard, 160*n*
Haug, Marie R., 14*n*
Hawley, Amos, 23, 27*n*
Hempel, Carl G., 13*n*
Hepple, Alex, 183*n*
"Herrenvolk democracy," 166
Herrnstein, Richard, 156*n*
Hertzog, J. B. M., 168, 173
Highan, John, 118*n*
Hofmeyer, Jan, 170
Horrell, Muriel, 187*n*
Hottentots, 162, 163, 164, 189
Huggins, Nathan I., 89*n*, 115*n*
Hunter, Huy, 12*n*, 27*n*, 68*n*, 116*n*, 183*n*

Immigrants, European: effect on blacks in the United States, 95–96, 103–104, 106–107
Indentured servants, 71–74
Industrial and Commercial Workers Union (ICU), 172–73, 197

Industrialization: blacks in the United States and, 105–107, 192; race in South Africa and, 167–68, 192–95; race relations and, 61–64

Institutional nationalism. *See* Nationalist movements

Integration: normative, 8, 10–11, 48, 196; support from Africans, 172, 200; support from blacks in the United States, 97, 100–101, 109–110, 200

Interracialism. *See* Integration

"J-Curve" theory, 49, 132, 148, 153*n*, 198–99
James, Lord, 90*n*
Janowitz, Morris, 45*n*, 118*n*
Jeffries, Vincent, 156*n*
Jensen, Arthur R., 156*n*
Jim Crow segregation. *See* Segregation
Johannesburg, 165
Johnson, Lyndon B., 152*n*
Jones, James M., 44*n*
Jordon, Winthrop D., 26*n*, 32, 44*n*, 71, 72, 77, 78, 84, 87*n*, 88*n*, 89*n*, 91*n*

Kaffir Wars, 164–65
Kaplan, Irving, 185*n*, 186*n*
Karis, Thomas, 186*n*
Keesing's Research Report, 153*n*, 160*n*
Kennedy, John F., 152*n*
Killian, Lewis M., 45*n*, 67*n*, 130, 137, 153*n*, 154*n*
Kilson, Martin, 89*n*, 115*n*, 160*n*
Kimberly, 165
King, Martin Luther, Jr., 135, 136, 154*n*
Kitano, Harry H. L., 45*n*
Ku Klux Klan, 128, 130, 134
Kuper, Leo, 186*n*, 187*n*
Kwan, Kian M., 13*n*, 67*n*

Labor unions: relationship with blacks, 107, 124
Labour Party, 168
Laue, James H., 153*n*
Lenski, Gerhard, 20, 23, 27*n*
Lewis, Hylan, 68*n*
Liberal Party, 186*n*
Lieberson, Stanley, 12*n*, 18, 19, 26*n*, 27*n*
Lipset, Seymour Martin, 89*n*
Litwack, Leon F., 93, 115*n*
Logan, Rayford W., 117*n*
Lomax, Louis, 153*n*
Long, Edward, 90*n*
L'Ouverture, Toussaint, 80
Lucy, Autherine, 128
Luthuli, Albert, 175, 176

MacCrone, I. D., 162, 182*n*, 183*n*
McKinney, John E., 68*n*
McLuhan, Marshall, 187*n*
McWorter, Gerald A., 187*n*
Majority group. *See* Dominant group
Malcolm X, 134, 138, 155*n*
Marshall, Ray, 68*n*, 100, 116*n*, 117*n*, 118*n*, 152*n*
Marx, Gary T., 29, 44*n*, 47, 65*n*, 156*n*
Mason, Philip, 66*n*
Massotti, L. H., 153*n*
Mathews, A. S., 186*n*
Meier, August, 91*n*, 111, 116*n*, 119*n*, 124, 131, 152*n*, 153*n*, 154*n*, 155*n*, 160*n*
Memmi, Albert, 27*n*
Merton, Robert K., 156*n*
Migration of blacks in the United States, 105–107
Minority group. *See* Subordinate groups
Moon, Henry L., 152*n*
Moore, Wilbert E., 89*n*, 90*n*, 115*n*
Morris, Marjorie M., 119*n*
Morris, Richard T., 156*n*
Muhammad, Elijah, 138

Mullins, Gerald W., 92*n*

Nash, Gary B., 26*n*
Natal: province of, 164, 166, 184*n*
Nation of Islam, 134, 138
NAACP (National Association for the Advancement of Colored People), 17, 112, 129, 130, 132
National Urban League, 112, 129
Nationalist movements: Afrikaner, 169, 197; among Africans, 172–77, 200–201; among blacks in the United States, 97, 110–13, 136–40, 149–50, 200–201; emergence of, 50, 199–200; success of, 51
Nationalist Party. *See* Afrikaners
Native Land Act, 166
Natives' Advisory Council, 184*n*
Natives' Representative Council, 169, 173
Ndebele, 165
Neame, L. E., 182*n*
Negro Convention Movement, 97
New Deal, 122–23
Newton, Huey, P., 160*n*
Ngubane, Jordan K., 179, 186*n*, 187*n*
Nisbet, Robert A., 156*n*
Nixon, Richard M., 149, 152*n*
Noel, Donald L., 10, 12*n*, 13*n*, 26*n*, 27*n*, 28*n*, 30–31, 32, 33, 40, 44*n*, 45*n*, 46*n*, 72, 88*n*, 115*n*
Nonracial ethnics. *See* Ethnic groups
Nonviolent resistance. *See* Protest movements

Opinion Research Corporation, 156*n*
Orange Free State: province of, 165, 166, 184*n*

Paige, Jeffrey, 154*n*, 156*n*
Pan-African Congress (PAC), 175–76, 179

Paternalistic race relations, 52–55, 60–64, 82, 85: effect on black slaves, 86, 192; south Africa and, 162, 192
Paton, Alan, 186*n*
Patterson, H. Orlando, 90*n*
Patterson, Sheila, 165, 183*n*
Pearson, Michael, 67*n*
Pease, Jane H., 115*n*
Pease, William H., 115*n*
Peterson, John, 160*n*
Pettigrew, Thomas, 149, 153*n*, 159*n*, 160*n*
Populist Movement, 102–103
Poqo, 176
Power, 5–7: ability and, 15–17; active, 15–17; changing character of black protest and, 129; competitive race relations and, 55–59; definition of, 15–16; differential and protest, 47–50, 196–97; origins of racial stratification and, 17–25, 41; paternalistic race relations and, 54–55; racial conflict in the ante-bellum United States and, 81–87; racial stratification in America and, 72–76; relations in South Africa, 161; struggle for scarce goods and, 22–25, 41–42
Power resources: applied against governmental authorities, 57–59; applied in South Africa, 171–72; competitive, 16, 122–29; constraint (or pressure), 16, 54, 56–59, 129, 131; definition of, 16; inducement, 16, 56–59; mobilization of, 48–49; perception of, 48–50; persuasion, 16, 56–59. *See also* Power
Prejudice: compared to racism, 38–39; definition of, 38; dominant group feelings, 36
Prosser, Gabriel, 80
Protest movements: among whites in the United States, 133–35;

Protest movements [*cont.*]
during Reconstruction, 109;
early twentieth century United
States, 111–12; in 1960s in
United States, 131–40; in South
Africa, 171–80

Quarles, Benjamin, 87*n*, 151*n*

Raab, Earl, 89*n*
Race relations: approaches to, 3–4
Race riots, 113: precipitants of,
108–109, 152*n*, 193
Racial groups: definition of, 6
Racial stratification: emergence of
in South Africa, 162–65; origins
of, 17–25, 189; role of ruling
classes and, 24–25
Racism, 5–7: effect on antebellum
whites, 86–87; biological, 33–34,
42–43, 76, 79, 93, 98, 101, 105,
121, 140–44, 161, 163, 165, 168,
171, 190–91, 200; challenge to
racial domination and, 35, 42,
191; collective, 34, 43, 59; cultural, 33–34, 42–43, 76, 79, 121,
143–44, 161, 163, 171, 190–91; defined, 32; economic decline and,
141–42, 150, 192; emergence of,
35–43, 190; emergence of in
South Africa, 162–65; emergence
of racial stratification and, 40–
41; individual, 34, 43, 59; institutional, 34, 43, 59, 142, 169;
institutionalization of black slavery and, 76–81; Jim Crow segregation and, 98–109; maximal, 30–
31; minimal, 30–31; oppression
of free blacks and, 95–98; racial
conflict and, 59–60, 201; variable
meanings of, 29–34
Randolph, A. Philip, 67*n*, 124, 125
Reconstruction Period, 99–101, 109–
110, 193
Redkey, Edwin S., 119*n*

Report of the National Advisory
Commission on Civil Disorders,
29, 44*n*, 154*n*, 156*n*
Revolutionary nationalism. See Na-
tionalist movements
Robertson, Hector Mentieth, 183*n*
Rogers, Mary, 25*n*, 26*n*
Roosevelt, Franklin D., 67*n*, 124,
125
Rose, Arnold M., 156*n*
Rose, Peter I., 12*n*, 13*n*, 27*n*, 46*n*,
90*n*, 91*n*, 156*n*
Rubin, Vera, 13*n*
Rudner, Richard S., 12*n*
Rudwick, Elliot, 91*n*, 111, 116*n*,
124, 131, 152*n*, 153*n*, 154*n*, 155*n*,
160*n*
Ruling classes, 24–25

Scarr-Salapatek, Sandra, 156*n*
Schermerhorn, Richard, 8, 12*n*,
13*n*, 26*n*, 27*n*, 30–31, 32, 33, 44*n*,
48, 65*n*, 68*n*
Schockley, William, 156*n*
Schuman, Howard, 155*n*, 156*n*,
158*n*
Segregation, 193: Jim Crow, 98–
109, 200; levels of in South
Africa, 170
Sense of group position, 35–42,
128: among dominants, 36–38;
among South African whites,
161, 167; among subordinates,
39–40; factors that contribute to,
36, 41
Separatism. See Nationalist movements
Sheatsley, Paul B., 156*n*
Shibutani, Tamotsu, 13*n*, 67*n*
Shufeldt, Robert W., 104
Silberman, Charles, 136, 142, 154*n*,
157*n*, 158*n*
Slave: codes, 82; day-to-day resistance, 84; insurrection, 80, 84;
insurrection in Latin America,

Slave [*cont.*]
   82–84; insurrection in the United
   States, 84–85, 192; transfers, 19–
   20, 75, 189, 192
Slavery: effects on blacks, 85–87;
   American Indians and, 20, 74–
   76; control of scarce resources
   and, 73; in South Africa, 162–
   63; in the United States, 71–87,
   93–95; racism and, 86; replace-
   ment of indentured servitude
   and, 72
Smith, M. G., 10, 13n
Smith, William B., 104
Social change: in South Africa,
   180–82; types of race relations
   and, 60–65
Social structure: effect on race
   relations, 52, 192
Sotho, 165
SCLC (Southern Christian Leadership Conference), 137
Spear, Allan, 104, 106, 117n, 118n
Spero, Sterling D., 118n
Stampp, Kenneth, 74, 87n, 88n,
   90n, 92n
Strincombe, Arthur L., 156n
Stratified society and racial protest, 47, 196
Strikebreakers: use of blacks as,
   107–108
Stuckey, Sterling, 92n
SNCC (Student Nonviolent Coordinating Committee), 132, 134,
   137, 149
Subordinate groups: definition of,
   12n; demands aimed at governmental authorities, 57, 132, 198;
   escalation of protest, 48–49, 198;
   perceptions of the efficacy of
   protest, 47–50, 196, 199; rising
   status and changing attitudes of,
   47–50, 196
Supreme Court: decision of 126–
   29, 131
Szwed, J., 44n

Tabb, William K., 44n
Taeuber, Alma F., 142, 157n, 158n
Taeuber, Karl E., 142, 157n, 158n
Thompson, Edgar T., 20, 26n,
   68n, 88n
Thorpe, Earle E., 46n, 85, 91n,
   92n
Tiryakian, Edward A., 170, 182n,
   185n
Tocqueville, Alexis de, 98, 116n
Transvaal: province of, 165, 166,
   184n
Turner, Henry McNeal, 56, 112,
   200
Turner, Nat, 80

Umkonto we Sizwe, 176
United Party, 170
U.S. Bureau of the Census, 157n,
   158n, 159n
Urbanization: effect on race relations and, 64, 113, 123, 126, 169,
   195

Value consensus, 11. *See also* Integration
van den Berghe, Pierre, 12n, 13n,
   45n, 52, 66n, 90n, 118n, 162, 182n,
   183n, 184n, 185n, 186n, 201n,
   202n
Van der Horst, Sheila T., 167,
   183n, 185n
Vance, Rupert B., 68n
Vander Zanden, James W., 126,
   153n
Vatcher, William Henry, Jr., 183n
Verwoerd, Hendrik, 171
Vesey, Denmark, 80
Voluntary migration, 19–21: as
   contract labor, 21

Wade, Richard C., 91n
Wagley, Charles, 12n
Washington, Booker T., 107, 110,
   111, 137, 138, 200

Waskow, Arthur I., 118n
Weinstein, Allen, 89n
Weiss, Richard, 26n
Wesley, Charles H., 118n
Westie, Frank R., 156n
White, Charles, 90n
White, Walter, 124
White Citizens Councils, 128, 130
Williams, Eric, 89n

Williams, Robin M., Jr., 13n, 27n, 68n
Williamson, Joel R., 90n, 119n
Wilson, William J., 12n, 158n
Witwatersrand, 167, 193
Wolpe, Harold, 187n
Woodward, C. van, 103, 117n

Zulus, 164, 165